TAXATION IN FRANCE

A FOREIGN PERSPECTIVE

Virginie Deflassieux

COMPLIMENTARY COPY

PKF (Guernsey) Limited

Taxation in France
A foreign perspective

2008 Edition

ISBN 0-9543490-4-0

A CIP catalogue record for this book is available from the British Library

PKF (Guernsey) Limited
PO Box 296, St Peter Port, Guernsey GY1 4NA
Telephone: +44 1481 727927. Facsimile: +44 1481 710511
email: french.tax@pkfguernsey.com
www.pkfguernsey.com

Typeset and design by PKF (Guernsey) Ltd
and Roger Williamson, Bath

Cover: Lavender field - Vaucluse

© Basse Dieter / Coll C.D.T. Vaucluse

Disclaimer

The information contained in this book is offered as a basis for further consideration only and is not to be acted upon without independent advice from suitably qualified professionals based on the actual circumstances of the taxpayer.

Neither the publisher nor the author can accept any responsibility for any loss occasioned to any person no matter howsoever caused or arising as a result of or in consequence of action taken or refrained from in reliance on the contents of this book.

This book has been printed using paper from sustainable forests.

About this Publication

This publication is based on Charles Parkinson's original work and is an update of the last available edition known as Taxation in France 2004. Mr Parkinson retired from PKF (Guernsey) Limited in 2004.

Virginie Deflassieux runs the French tax department of PKF (Guernsey) Limited where she has been advising clients on the French tax implications of their move to France or French property purchases for the last 15 years. She handles the preparation and submission of French tax returns and offers advice on areas such as exposure to the main French taxes and tax planning. Virginie was born and educated in France. She obtained a degree in business studies (which included French and international taxation modules) from IPAG (Paris), a French business school, in 1993.

Every care has been taken in updating this book and ensuring, insofar as possible, the accuracy of the contents. However, the application of French tax rules may vary considerably depending on the specific circumstances of individual taxpayers.

PKF (Guernsey) Limited produce a French tax bulletin containing up to date French tax rates and details of any major changes to the French tax system. For more information, visit www.pkfguernsey.com

PKF (Guernsey) Ltd
PO Box 296
St Peter Port
Guernsey
GY1 4NA
Telephone: +44 (0) 1481 727927
Facsimile: +44 (0) 1481 710511
E-mail: french.tax@pkfguernsey.com

INTRODUCTION

The aim of this book is to explain the main features of the French tax system. It is addressed to readers who are foreign to the system in France and therefore adopts the perspective of an outsider 'looking in'. To the French tax adviser this perspective might well appear distorted, because emphasis is given to matters which a foreigner needs to know (such as the French tax on the real estate holdings of certain companies) which are not, in the total picture of French taxation, very important topics. Equally, the computational details of the various French taxes are described only in broad terms, to ensure that the main principles are not lost from view.

The fundamental elements of an exposure to a foreign tax are a taxing jurisdiction, a taxable person (as defined by that jurisdiction) and a connection between the two. This relationship can be illustrated diagrammatically:

Of these, the key element is the connecting factor, which determines not only the taxes to which the taxable person may be subject, but also the basis on which his liability may be computed. For example US citizenship exposes an individual to the full range of US taxes, but French nationality does not have significant tax consequences. The ownership of a French source of income does expose the owner to French taxation, but, if that is his only connection with France, the basis on which his liability to French income tax will be computed is restricted to the amount of his French source income.

However even the other two elements are more complex than may at first appear. The definition of the territory of a taxing jurisdiction may contain surprises, and it may in effect vary according to the taxable person under consideration. Many foreigners would not be aware that 'France' includes Guadeloupe, Guyana, Martinique and Reunion. And although for most people Monaco is a separate taxing jurisdiction, for a French national it is in effect part of France (as it is for VAT purposes). A specific area of complexity with which this book is not concerned is the definition of territorial sea, and the rights of a country to tax exploration and exploitation activity in adjacent sea areas. This is a topic that will be mainly of interest to those involved in oil and gas production.

The concept of a taxable person is of interest not only in relation to the taxation status of minor children and incapacitated individuals, but also with regard to the recognition of legal forms of personality. Several French legal forms of association which look to a foreigner like a company are treated as fiscally transparent in France. Therefore tax based on the activities of the company is imposed on the shareholders and not the company. To an individual from a 'common law' jurisdiction (eg the USA, the UK, Australia, Canada, India etc) the difficulty which the French have in determining the tax status of trusts may also be significant.

The taxable person may not be the person who pays the tax. The tax system may give the tax administration the right to recover tax from someone else – for example someone who has received property from the taxpayer. The French tax system includes a true "inheritance tax", as opposed to an estate tax, in that it is the recipient of a taxable gift or legacy who pays the tax. Liability to tax depends in general on the residence of the donor or deceased individual (or the situs of his assets), but the donee, who may have no direct connections with France at all, pays the tax. An alternative way of looking at this would be to say that the recipient is indirectly connected to France by virtue of the gift or legacy from a French resident or out of the French estate of a non-French resident.

There is also a temporal dimension to the exposure to a foreign tax. Normally it is fairly easy to predict when the exposure will begin and end, but the rules of some countries contain traps for the unwary. For example an individual who arrives in the UK to take up permanent residence for the first time on 1 September in any year is technically resident in the UK from the previous 6 April. Fortunately the French tax system is relatively free of such pitfalls. However there have been examples of extended exposure in French taxation, and it is not beyond the bounds of possibility that there will be problems in this area in the future.

Having established that a potential exposure to one or more taxes in the foreign country exists, eg because the person concerned has an asset in that country, it is necessary to consider whether the tax concerned is a tax on status, or whether a liability to the tax will only arise on the occurrence of some defined event. For example an individual with a valuable villa in France may be exposed to French wealth tax each year, merely because of the value of his French situated assets; he will not be subject to French capital gains tax unless and until he sells the villa.

In cases where the liability to tax is triggered by something which the taxpayer does, or which happens to the taxpayer, it is clearly important to define carefully the event which causes the tax charge to crystallize. The French call this event the *'fait générateur'*. For example, if the owner of the villa cited above makes a gift of the property, instead of selling it, he will not suffer French capital gains tax. In several countries a gift is treated as a disposal at market value.

Even where all the other elements of a tax charge are present, the foreign taxpayer may yet escape liability if he is protected by a double tax treaty between France and the country of which he is a resident or a national. The terms of a double tax treaty prevail over French domestic law – unlike the rule in the USA where domestic law prevails if enacted since the treaty was signed.

Proceeding from this analysis, this book is divided into three parts. In the first part the basic elements of French taxation as described above, and some of the tax terms which are unavoidably used in the remainder of the text, are explained. The reader who finds that he needs to know more about any particular French tax may then turn to the second part of the book, where the computation of liabilities in respect of each French tax is described in more detail. The level of detail given is intended to highlight the main features, and is not sufficient to enable the reader to produce tax computations that will be accurate to the last euro. The French tax code contains as much fine print as any other tax system.

The final part is a collection of reviews, on a topical basis, of the tax considerations involved in several forms of connection with or activity in France. This is intended to pull together the specific areas of the first two parts that need to be considered in the case in question.

The law is stated as at 1 January 2008. The rates of corporation tax cited are those relating to accounting periods ending after 1 January 2008. Since French income tax (and capital gains tax as it relates to individuals) is assessed each year in the name of the previous year (ie the tax paid in 2008 is the assessment for 2007) the rates of income tax, amounts of expenditure qualifying for income tax relief etc cited in this edition are mainly the rates, amounts etc applying to 2007 income and expenditure. Where taxes are based on data relating to another period or point in time, this is stated in the text. For example wealth tax is based on the wealth of the taxpayer as at 1 January in the tax year. The amounts, rates and rules stated throughout this edition of Taxation in France are those available at the time of going to print. Some tax limits or rules may be amended afterwards.

CONTENTS

PART 1

General Information and Basic Concepts

1. GENERAL INFORMATION

1.1. The French Economy

a) France has the third largest economy in Europe, after Germany and the UK, with a Gross Domestic Product ('GDP') in 2006 of €1,792 billion. Metropolitan France, including Corsica, is also the second largest country in Europe, after Russia, with an area of 551,000 square kilometres (213,000 square miles). The population is approximately 63 million.

b) However France is one of the most heavily taxed of the larger industrial nations, and in 2006 the total of taxes and compulsory social insurance contributions amounted to €737 billion.

c) A significant problem for France is its persistently high rate of unemployment 8.8% average in 2006 (compared with 5.5% in the UK and 4.6% in the USA at that time).

1.2. The Public Revenue

a) The French government is heavily dependent on indirect taxes, local taxes and social insurance contributions for finance. The total raised for public funds in 2006 can be analysed approximately as follows:

	€
Social security contributions	284
VAT	127
Local taxes	101
CSG, CRDS, PS and other contributions	84
Income tax	58
Corporation tax	49
Petrol tax and other direct levies (TIPP)	20
Other levies	14
Total	737

Source: Ministère des Finances et de l'Industrie

b) This dependence on social insurance contributions and VAT is unusual, and many foreigners dealing with France ignore these topics, assuming that direct taxation is the real issue which should concern them. The burden of the state is heavy in France, and tends to be skewed away from income tax and corporation tax, towards social security contributions and VAT. It is beyond the scope of this book to examine the French social security or VAT systems in any depth, but readers should be aware that direct taxes may be the least of their problems, when planning an investment in, or migration to, France.

1.3.   Tax Law

a) The basic tax law in France is the *Code Général des Impôts (CGI)* which dates originally from 1948. The *CGI* is subject to frequent amendment, both by specific *lois fiscales* and the annual finance law, the *loi de finances*, which is passed at the end of December each year relating to the government's revenue for the forthcoming year. For example, the 2008 *loi de finances* was passed at the end of December 2007. Once the government's tax and spending plans have been approved, any departure from the Budget deficit level may need to be made good by further fiscal measures in the form of a *loi de finances rectificative*. Such laws are frequently introduced in the summer months of the year to which they relate. Certain administrative matters are dealt with in the *Livre des Procédures Fiscales (LPF)*. The French tax administration produces internal manuals called *documentation administrative de base* which do not have the force of law but which can provide a useful insight into their approach to a problem.

b) The French legal system is a 'civil law' system, that is to say a member of the family of legal systems which are derived from Roman law as opposed to the 'common law' systems (ie the family of legal systems which are derived from English law). In civil law systems the concept of 'precedence' as applied in common law countries is unknown. This means that decisions of a court in interpreting the law are not binding on subsequent courts of the same or junior rank, as they would be in a common law country. It is therefore possible for the tax administration to maintain its position on an interpretation of the law, even after a court has ruled against it. Previous court decisions are however of influential value, and are therefore studied carefully.

c) The *CGI*, like the other great codes of French law, contains provisions expressed in general terms. The Articles of the *CGI* are generally short, and the wording of the law is of sweeping generality. The Administration comments on the law in the form of *'Instructions'*, to explain its interpretation of the legislative language and to fill in the practical details.

1.4.   The Tax Year

The tax year in France is the year to 31 December.

1.5.   French Direct Taxes

The principal direct taxes imposed in France are:-

a) income tax (*impôt sur le revenu*), including the *CSG*, *CRDS* and *PS* (see 1.6.2)

b) corporation tax (*impôt sur les sociétés*)

c) inheritance tax and gifts tax (*droits de succession et de donation*)

d) capital gains tax (*régime des plus-values*)

e) tax on the market value of real estate owned by certain companies (*taxe sur les immeubles détenus en France par certaines personnes morales*)

f) wealth tax (*impôt de solidarité sur la fortune*).

1.6.   Social Security Charges

1.6.1   General

a) As we have already seen in a global sense the French state is heavily dependent on social security charges as a source of revenue. But contributors do not simply pay regular contributions to a single government agency. The provision of social services is organised by various bodies, to each of which French residents are required to make contributions. Examples of these are the *Caisse nationale d'assurance maladie des travailleurs salariés ('CNAMTS')*, which deals with health insurance, and the *Caisse nationale d'assurance vieillesse des travailleurs salariés ('CNAVTS')*, which deals with the basic state pensions. Those in work are required to contribute to 'complementary' pension arrangements. Employees contribute to the scheme appropriate to their industry, organised by the *Association des régimes de retraites complémentaires ('ARRCO')*, and management personnel pay contributions to *ARRCO* and additional contributions to a member of the *Association générale des institutions de retraites des cadres ('AGIRC')*. Insurance against unemployment is provided by the *Union nationale interprofessionnelle pour l'emploi dans l'industrie et le commerce ('UNEDIC')* and contributions are collected by various *Associations pour l'emploi dans l'industrie et le commerce ('ASSEDIC')*. Some of these agencies are nominally private sector organisations, but they are all controlled by the government and financed by state-imposed levies.

b) To slightly simplify the operation of this system, contributions for health, family allowances and the basic state pension are collected by one organisation, called the *Unions de recouvrement des cotisations de sécurité sociale et d'allocations familiales ('URSSAF')*. The *URSSAF* also collects the *CSG* and *CRDS* (see 1.6.2. below). Therefore in terms of contributions to the system, most French residents deal primarily with the *URSSAF* in the department of France where they live, the organisation which deals with their occupational pension under *ARRCO* and their local *ASSEDIC* for insurance against unemployment. Management also deal with a member organisation of the *AGIRC* for their additional pension obligations.

c) In addition to contributions for health insurance, pension benefits etc. there are several 'social contributions' which are effectively supplementary income taxes. These are collected by direct assessment or by withholding, alongside income tax liabilities, and are described below under 1.6.2.

d) In general, only French residents pay French social security contributions. Foreigners employed in France on a short term basis may be able to elect to continue to contribute to their domestic social security systems, rather than the French system, under reciprocal social insurance or 'totalisation' agreements between their home country and France.

e) The retirement age is 60 for both men and women.

1.6.2   The 'Social Contributions'

a) Most forms of income are subject to a general social contribution *(contribution sociale généralisée* or *'CSG')* and a contribution to the deficit of the social security system *(contribution au remboursement de la dette sociale* or *'CRDS')*. There are a few exceptions, notably interest on specific savings account. In general it is the gross amount of the income received which is assessable, but the taxpayer can deduct 3% from his earned income in respect of expenses, before calculating the amounts due. Generally speaking, the *URSSAF* recovers the social surcharges on earned income and pensions. The social surcharges applicable to investment income, property income and self-employed income in respect of activities which are not registered at the *Registre du Commerce et des Sociétés* are normally recovered by the local tax collector's office.

b) The imposition of the *CSG* and the *CRDS* on earnings derived from other EU countries has been opposed by the European Commission, because the employed and self-employed are required under EU law to contribute only to the social security system of the country in which they work. The European Court of Justice confirmed on 15 February 2000, that the application of the *CSG* and *CRDS* to foreign source earned income or pensions received by French residents, who are not registered under the French social security system, is contrary to the Council Regulation. The ECJ considered that the *CSG* and *CRDS* were created to fund the French social security system and therefore could not be regarded as separate taxes on income. In response to the ECJ, the French authorities issued a *Communiqué* on 2 March 2000 analysing the decision of the court and extending it to the whole of the European Economic Area. The *Communiqué* stipulates that the *CSG* and *CRDS* can no longer apply to foreign earnings received by French residents carrying on an independent professional activities in another European country, if they are registered under and effectively paying contributions to that country's social security system. This was followed by an *ordonnance* clarifying their position on the above. As a result anyone who is French resident for tax purposes, and affiliated to one of the compulsory French social security regimes, is liable to the *CSG* and *CRDS* on his foreign earnings or pension. Individuals in this situation have to declare spontaneously their foreign earnings or pensions to their local *URSSAF* office.

c) On the contrary, any foreign national living in France and covered for health under another country's social security system, is not exposed to the social charges on their foreign pensions or earnings. Typically, UK nationals living in France and who are covered for health under one of the DSS's reciprocal regimes (Form E121, E106, etc.) would not suffer these social charges on their UK source pensions or earnings (but see (j) below).

d) Up until 23 November 2007, individuals who were not eligible for health under a national social security system, were obliged to contribute to the *Couverture Maladie Universelle* (*CMU*). This brought their foreign earning or pensions under the scope of the *CSG* and *CRDS* as they did not fulfil the two criteria outlined above in b). Nevertheless since 23 November 2007 eligibility to the *CMU* was restricted as a result of an EU directive. This is explained in greater detail under the next heading 1.6.3.

e) The *CSG* is applied at the rate of 8.2% to most types of income, but at the reduced rate of 6.6% to pension income, unemployment benefits and social security benefits. If the taxpayer's liability to income tax on his previous year's income was less than €61, the rate of *CSG* applicable to pension income, unemployment benefits and social security benefits can be reduced to 3.8%, depending on a complicated formula. Of the total charge, part is deductible from the income to which it relates for the purposes of calculating income tax when the income is assessed on the income tax scale (many forms of income are subject to fixed withholding tax rates at source, and therefore do not benefit from this relief). Where the full 8.2% rate of *CSG* is paid, 5.8% is deductible from the income for income tax purposes, and where the 6.6% rate is applied, 3.8% is deductible.

f) The *CRDS* rate is 0.5% on the same basis as for the *CSG*. Theoretically the *CRDS* is a temporary tax, which was introduced for a period of 13 years commencing on 1 February 1996. However in the 1998 Finance Law the duration of the tax was extended by a further 5 years, following a pattern familiar to France's 'temporary' taxes.

g) Investment income and the profits of property development bear further 'social contributions' (*prélèvement social*) totalling 2.3%.

h) The effect of the above is that almost all forms of income bear a minimum level of tax of 8% or 11% (in the case of investment income).

i) So far the *CSG, CRDS* and *PS* have allowed the Government to by-pass the problems of reforming income tax. The latter contains too many well-entrenched tax breaks which are fiercely defended by special interest groups and which deprive the tax of much of its force. Instead the "social contributions" act as an additional tax on income and now produce more revenue than the income tax does.

j) There is growing pressure to have the *CSG* and *CRDS* categorised as proper income tax charges rather than social contributions. After all, these levies do not entitle the contributors to any social benefits. If this re-categorisation does go ahead, the ECJ decision referred to in (b) will logically be void. The upshot could be a full exposure of foreign earnings and pensions to these charges, regardless of the type of health cover (French or foreign).

k) At a glance, the current *CSG, CRDS* and *PS* charges have the following impact:

Type of Revenue	CSG*	CRDS	PS	Total
Investment and rental income property and investment gains	8.20%	0.5%	2.3%	11%
Salaries and unemployment benefits *(on 97% of the gross amounts received)*	7.50%	0.5%	0%	8%
Retirement or Disability Pensions	6.60%	0.5%	0%	7.1%

*Notes: * Part of the CSG (currently 4.2% on pensions, 5.1% on salaries and 5.8% for other income) is deductible from the following year's taxable income.*
Foreign pensions may be exempt from the CSG and CRDS if the pensioner is eligible to continued health cover under one of the DSS forms (E121, E106) or another form of health cover provided by his country of origin. Foreign investment income (interest, dividend and annuitiess) and gains are not exempt from these charges.

1.6.3 Social Insurance

a) Social insurance contributions were exclusively levied on earned income until the creation of the *Couverture Maladie Universelle ('CMU')* with effect from 1 January 2000 (see below (e)). The total amount paid consists of a multitude of contributions to separate agencies, as explained in 1.6.1 above. As a result it is beyond the scope of this book to set out the contributions that will be payable by any particular individual. These will depend on a number of factors, including the industry in which he works, the number of employees in the business, whether he is employed or self-employed, and if he is an employee, whether he is a manager or a just a member of the staff.

b) The table below shows the 2008 contributions typically paid (by both employer and employees) in respect of employees in a business employing more than 9 people, when the employer is not exempt from any contributions. The employer might be exempt, eg because it is established in a 'revitalisation zone' or because it is a qualifying 'new enterprise' or because the employee was recently a young unemployed person. These are calculated as a percentage of the employee's salary, but for some elements of the total contribution the amount of salary taken into account is subject to bands or a ceiling.

c) It will be seen that the employers' contributions can easily amount to 50% of the employees salary, and the employee will often suffer deductions of the order of 18% – 20%.

Rates of Social Contributions on 2008 Salaries

	Monthly Salary Limits €	Total %	Employer %	Employee %
Payable to URSSAF				
Health	Whole Salary	13.85	13.10	0.75
Family allowances, basic state pension, etc.		7.50	7.40	0.10
Occupational pension, etc.	2,773	15.05	8.40	6.65
Payable to ASSEDIC Unemployment Insurance +AGS	11,092	6.55	4.15	2.40
Payable to ARRCO/APEC/AGFF Executives				
	First 2,773	11	7.20	3.80
	between 2,773 and 11,092	22.56	13.936	8.624
	between 11,092 and 22,184	20.30	optional division	
CET	22,184	0.35	0.22	0.13
Other employees				
	Up to 2,773	9.50	5.70	3.80
	between 2,773 and 8,319	22.20	13.30	8.90

Notes:

i) The 'complementary pension contributions' listed in the table are compulsory. In addition many firms operate voluntary supplementary schemes to cover expenses which are not fully covered by the national schemes. For example these may provide full reimbursement of medical costs, and insurance against disability suffered before the age of 60.

ii) In addition to the amounts shown, the employer pays work injury insurance on the total salary of the employee, at rates which vary according to the nature of the business.

iii) There are several other charges which can be made, including in Paris and some other towns a transport levy of 0.2% to 2.5% (depending on area) paid by employers who have more than 9 employees. Employees in Alsace-Moselle pay an extra health insurance contribution.

iv) In addition to these amounts, it should be noted that there are a number of other taxes on salaries (see 1.8).

v) CET: Contribution Exceptionnelle et Temporaire.

vi) The CSG and CRDS charges described in 1.6.2. apply to salaries in addition to the above contributions.

d) Most self-employed individuals pay social security contributions based on their business profits. The annual rates outside the agricultural sector are typically as follows:

2008 Social Contributions for Self Employed

Type of Activity	Artisanal	Commercial Industriel	Professions Libérales (non commerciales)
For family allowances Total net taxable profit		5.40%	
For health benefits Up to €33,276 Up to €166,380		0.60% 5.90%	
Indemnités journalières Up to €166,380	0.70%	0.70%	0%
For pension rights i) *Retraite de base* (basic) • First €33,276	16.65%	16.65%	–
• Up to €28,285, and Between €28,285 and €166,380	– –	– –	9.60 1.60
ii) *Retraite complémentaire* (pension top-up) • Up to €133,104 • Up to €99,828	 7.00% –	 – 6.50%	Limits and rates for the professions depend on the nature of the activity
For Disability – Death cover Total net taxable profit	2.00%	1.50%	–
Formation Professionnelle (Training) • Up to €33,276	–	0.15%	–

Notes:

i) There may be substantial variations depending on the exact nature of the non-commercial professional activity. The social surcharges (CSG and CRDS) must be added to the above.

ii) There is an exemption of family allowances contributions if the total professional income is below €4,489 (2008), This is revised every year.

iii) There are several regimes of compulsory complementary pension contributions. The amounts and rules vary depending on each type of profession.

e) The *CMU* was introduced to remedy the inequalities in the French social security system, as highlighted in surveys conducted by the *CREDES (Centre de Recherches, d'Etudes et de Documentation en Economie de la Santé)*. Its main objective is to allow the poorest people to access public healthcare. The *CMU* offers a free affiliation to the basic social security to applicants who:

   i)   are resident in France in a stable and regular manner, and

   ii) are not currently covered under any other state health insurance scheme, and

   iii) have a net taxable income for their fiscal household below €8,644 (by reference to 2006 net taxable income). This limit is updated every year to take inflation into account.

   Households with an annual taxable income exceeding €8,644, need to contribute to the *CMU* scheme at a level of 8%. This contribution is calculated by reference to the total net taxable income that is reflected on the household's income tax assessment. The 8% rate only applies to the income in excess of the above limit. The *CMU* annual contribution is calculated for the period from 1 October to 30 September and is divided into four instalments each payable at the end of each quarter.

   Individuals listed below are excluded from the *CMU*:

   i)   Diplomats and members of their families;

   ii) Families residing in France who can benefit from health cover under the French voluntary contribution scheme through the exercise of a professional activity abroad by one of its members;

   iii) People who come to France specifically to find medical treatment;

   iv) People retired from an international organisation, who do not have a French pension and who are deemed to be already covered under a health insurance scheme that they paid for whilst they were still working.

   People who qualify for the *CMU* need to register at their local *Caisse Primaire d'Assurance Maladie* and provide evidence that they fulfil criteria (e)(i)(ii). They also need to file a form showing their net taxable income used for the determination of the contribution level (if any).

f) Up until 2007, the qualifying criteria of the *CMU* inadvertently concerned people who were below retirement age, resided in France without working, and who were not covered under any public health insurance scheme (French or foreign).

The British government normally covers four groups of Britons in France:

i) Short-term visitors who need urgent care. Such individuals claim on a European Health Insurance Card (EHIC).

ii) Individuals seconded by their employers to work in France, generally for less than 12 months. They claim on form E106.

iii) Individuals living but not working in France may claim under Form E106 for up to 2 years. If eligible the UK Incapacity Benefit Form E106 may be valid for longer. There are various conditions for claiming under this form, including that the individual concerned has paid a certain amount in contributions in the previous 3 years.

iv) Individuals who have reached the UK statutory retirement age or who claim Long-Term Incapacity Benefit or Severe Disablement Allowance or Widow's Benefits. They claim on Form E121.

Prior to 23 November 2007, British expatriates who did not benefit from health cover under any of these categories had to make themselves known to the French social security department and register for the *CMU*. Private health cover was not accepted as an alternative and if their income exceeded the *CMU* limits they could face expensive contributions (see also 1.6.2(b)).

g) In fact, for most the *CMU* deal was good judging by the reaction of British expatriates affiliated to the *CMU* when it was announced that their cover was threatened. The threat came from a European Directive (29 April 2004) which took three years to be transcribed into the French social security system through the *décret 2007-371*. Although this was published on 21 March 2007, its full effects could not be measured by the people concerned until October 2007 when the Social Security offices dealt with the *CMU* renewals.

The decree was formulated in a circular issued in September 2007 instructing all local Social Security centres (*CPAM*) to, with effect from 31 March 2008, cancel the *CMU* rights for all EU and EEA nationals who were:

i) living in France and,

ii) who were neither retired nor professionally active and so did not qualify for continued health cover under the reciprocal agreement and by way of an "E" form.

For the reasons explained above in (f), this change was potentially affecting a considerable part of the British population living in France, who would have had no choice but to turn to private health cover from 1 April 2008.

This caused a real uproar and as a result of pressures put on the French health ministry the French officials decided to grant continued *CMU* eligibility to:

i) those who have been resident in France for at least 5 years;

ii) to anyone registered before 23 November 2007;

iii) those with pre-existing medical conditions (in precise circumstances).

iv) Finally, anyone living in France and covered under a Form E106 as at 23 November 2007 should be able to apply for *CMU* cover when their Form E106 runs out. However, people who have recently submitted an application on this ground have experienced difficulties.

Under the new law, newcomers to France (in the situation described in (g) above) will now have no choice but to prove that they are fully insured for health (even privately) prior to taking permanent residence in France.

h) A top-up cover *(CMU Complémentaire)* was also introduced at the same time as the *CMU*, for individuals with lower income. People with earnings below certain set limits are automatically affiliated to the complementary regime for free. Qualifying individuals are relieved from the obligation to pay the costs of their health care up front. The *CMU Complémentaire* is not compulsory and people registered under the basic *CMU* may opt for top-up cover offered by private insurance companies.

1.7. Value Added Tax

a) Value added tax *(taxe sur la valeur ajoutée, TVA)* applies to most goods and services supplied in France. The tax was invented by the French, who consider it the masterpiece of their tax system. The principle is that every business involved in a chain of commercial transactions accounts for tax on the value it has added to the goods or services, with the tax ultimately being paid by the end-consumer.

b) The basic principle that French *TVA* applies to transactions in France is complemented by specific rules for intra-EU transactions, international transport, leasing etc. In particular it should be noted that French *TVA* applies to any transactions in French real estate (including estate agency services relating to the sale of French real estate). Special rules apply in Corsica.

c) Certain activities are generally exempt from *TVA*, including the rental of residential accommodation (but not the provision of hotel-type services), the renting of agricultural land and medical services.

d) Special regimes apply to some areas of business, for example agriculture, travel agencies, newspapers, banking and property development. In the latter case, a developer who makes an undertaking to construct on a plot can acquire the plot without suffering *TVA* on the purchase cost, and will then account for *TVA* on the value he has added to the property – ie the difference between the sale price of the property and the cost of the plot. The exoneration from *TVA* on the purchase price of the plot will usually be revoked if the developer does not start work within 4 years.

e) The rates of *TVA* are as follows:

	%
i) Medicines paid for by the social security system *Redevance audiovisuelle (TV tax)*	2.1
ii) Food products, building works not amounting to construction or reconstruction on dwellings more than 2 years old, water, hotel accommodation, subscription to cable and satellite TV, non-refundable medicine etc.	5.5
iii) Normal rate	19.6

1.8. Minor and Indirect French Taxes

There are an enormous number of specific taxes and duties in France, and it is beyond the scope of this book to describe them all. The following list covers several of the taxes that the reader is most likely to encounter, and gives a flavour of French public policy towards taxation, as a tool to encourage certain forms of expenditure and to discourage others.

a) salary tax (*taxe sur les salaires*). Salary tax is payable by some companies which are resident in France or which possess a permanent centre of operations in France, and which are not subject to value added tax on at least 90% of their turnover. There are a number of exempt categories of company, which together with the exemption for value added tax paying companies mean that this tax is only payable by some state and public bodies, the members of certain professions, land-owners, co-operative organisations, banking and insurance companies and certain companies with 'civil objects' (eg *sociétés d'investissement* and *sociétés civiles immobilières*). The tax is based on the remuneration paid to each employee in the preceding year, and is levied at the following rates for 2008:

Total Salary	Rate %
Less than €7,250	4.25
€7,250 to €14,481	8.50
€14,481 upwards	13.60

b) apprenticeship tax (*taxe d'apprentissage*). Apprenticeship tax is payable, generally at the rate of 0.5% on the total remuneration paid to employees in the preceding year by companies and partnerships subject either to French corporation tax or subject to income tax on their commercial industrial or agricultural profits. Subject to the approval of its works council (*comité d'entreprise*), the employer may deduct from the tax payable any sums it has expended on the training of employees. Effectively the rules impose a minimum level of investment in training apprentices.

c) employers participation in vocational training (*participation des employeurs à la formation professionnelle continue*). Virtually all private sector employers who are resident or established in France are obliged to invest in the ongoing training of their employees. The way this works is that they are obliged to pay a tax from which they can deduct the expenses they incur in training. The tax is calculated on the company's payroll (as defined for this purpose) and varies between 0.55% and 1.60% depending on the number of employees.

d) construction participation (*participation des employeurs à l'effort de construction*). Employers, excluding state and public bodies, who have at least 10 employees must invest 0.45% of the total remuneration paid to their staff in the preceding year in the construction of dwellings. The investment can take the form of loans to employees to facilitate their purchase of a home, or of contributions by way of loan or subscription of share capital to housing associations, or, with the consent of the local authorities, the construction or renovation of housing. Failure to meet this obligation results in a charge to tax of 2% of the total payroll of the employer.

e) company car tax (*taxe sur les voitures de sociétés*). Companies pay a tax based on the number of cars registered in France, and less than 10 years old, which they own. Cars held for the purpose of resale, cars used for short term hire business and taxis are excluded. The annual tax charges depend on the rate of emission of carbon dioxyde or horsepower of the vehicles.

f) tax on insurance contracts (*taxe sur les conventions d'assurances*). A tax is imposed on many forms of insurance contract, based on the premiums paid. The rates vary according to the type of policy. Life assurance contracts are exempt, but the tax applies to fire insurance policies (30%), most health insurance policies (7%), motor insurance policies (18%), marine insurance policies for pleasure boats (19%) etc. Insurance activities are exempt from value added tax.

g) social solidarity contribution of companies (*contribution sociale de solidarité des sociétés et contribution additionelle*). This is a contribution to social security funds of 0.16% of turnover paid by certain types of company with a turnover exceeding €760,000. The companies concerned are most *SAs, SARLs, EURLs, sociétés en commandite, SNCs, GIEs, GEIEs, sociétés par actions simplifiées*, certain public companies, and foreign companies subject to French corporation tax.

h) land taxes (*taxes foncières*), residential tax (*taxe d'habitation*) and business tax (*taxe professionnelle*), are taxes levied by the state for the benefit of the local government subdivisions. These are described in the last chapter.

i) sundry taxes: Office space in the Ile-de-France region, alcoholic products, pornography, public spectacles, bowling alleys, juke boxes, sporting displays, petroleum products, tax on supermarkets and television advertisements are among a wide range of items each of which is subject to a special tax.

j) registration taxes: Conveyances of real estate, insurance documents, certain leases, and capital transactions in connection with companies attract tax at varying rates.

   i) Contributions of land, *fonds de commerce*, clientele and certain interests under leases to the capital of a company subject to French corporation tax by a person who is not subject to French corporation tax attract registration taxes at 5% over and above €23,000. There are specific rates and limits for goodwill and depending on the situation of the company.

   ii) Capitalisations of earnings in corporation tax paying companies in the form of a stock dividend or bonus issue of shares generally attract a registration tax of €375 or €500 depending on the level of share capital.

   iii) A verbal or written contract transferring an interest in a company which is not a real estate holding company (see (v)) attracts a registration tax of 1.1%, subject to a maximum of €4,000. However transactions in quoted shares escape this charge.

   iv) A transfer of shares in an unquoted company which holds real estate interests constituting the greater part of its assets is taxed at 5%.

   v) On the liquidation of a corporation tax paying company, the distribution of its assets attracts a registration tax of 1.1%. If there are no assets to distribute, a registration tax of €375 or €500 if the share capital is above €225,000 is payable.

   vi) A transfer of a new building is likely to be subject to VAT, and will then benefit from a reduced rate of registration taxes of 0.6%.

   vii) A transfer of 'second hand' movable property if spontaneously declared attracts a fixed registration duty of €125.

k) The *Contribution sur les Revenus Locatifs* (*CRL*) is a tax on leases which applies to the rental income received from properties which are over 15 years of age. This tax only applies to companies liable to corporation tax. It is calculated as 2.5% of the rents.

1.9. Exchange Controls

1.9.1 Outward Payments

French residents are generally not subject to French exchange controls in respect of outbound payments, but they are required to declare certain payments abroad and their foreign bank accounts (see 6.13.).

1.9.2 Non-resident Investment in France

a) Inbound investments are generally free of French exchange controls, except that certain investments in sensitive sectors, such as investments involving public order, public health and the manufacture of munitions, require prior authorisation.

b) A post-transaction declaration is required for the following transactions:

i) the creation of a company or branch when the investment is more than €1,525,000;

ii) the acquisition of agricultural land for wine production;

iii) the liquidation of a direct investment in France.

1.10. The Euro

1.10.1 The Euro has been in circulation since 1 January 2002 in France, Germany, Austria, Belgium, Spain, Finland, Greece, Italy, Ireland, Portugal, Netherlands and Luxembourg. The legacy currencies are no longer legal tender in these countries. Slovenia joined the euro on 1 January 2007, less than three years after joining the EU on 1 May 2004.

1.10.2 The rates between the former national currencies and the Euro were fixed as follows:

Currency	Value of the Euro	Currency	Value of the Euro
FRF	6.55957	NLG	2.20371
DEM	1.95583	BEF	40.33990
ITL	1,936.27	FIM	5.94573
ESP	166.386	GRD	340.750
PTE	200.482	LUF	40.3399
ATS	13.76030	SIT	239.640
IEP	0.787564		

1.10.3 Taxpayers have to prepare their tax returns in Euros even if they have received income in other currencies. When converting into Euros the amount must be rounded up or down depending on whether the third digit after the comma is above or below five.

1.11. Non-Fiscal Investment Incentives

1.11.1 EU Funds

Regional aid may be available from the EU. Information on the availability of such assistance can be obtained in the first instance from the relevant office of the IFN (see 1.11.2 below).

1.11.2 *DATAR*

a) The French government provides regional development grants through *DATAR ('Délégation à l'Aménagement du Territoire et à l'Action Régionale')*. *DATAR* and the regional authorities form an association called the Invest in France Network ('IFN'), and *DATAR*'s offices outside France are called 'Invest in France Agencies' ('IFAs'). There are IFAs in most western European countries, the USA, Hong Kong, Japan and Taiwan.

    i)   The head office of the Invest in France Network is situated at:

         77bd Saint-Jacques, 75680 Paris Cedex 14
         Tel: (33) 1 44 87 17 17 Fax: (33) 1 44 74 73 27
         email: info@investinfrance.org

    ii) The London office of the Invest in France Agency can be contacted at:
         21 Grosvenor Place SW1X 7HU
         Tel: (44) 207 823 0900 Fax: (44) 207 235 8453 www.investinfrance.org

b) The *DATAR* grant is called a *Prime d'Aménagement du Territoire* (or *'PAT'*). Such grants are available for:

    i)   industrial projects, and

    ii) research businesses, and enterprises engaged in leasing of buildings or equipment to industrial companies ('tertiary activities').

c) To qualify, the investment must be in one of the designated zones.

d) The amount of the grant is calculated as a percentage of the total investment, varying depending on the size and activity of the business.

1.11.3 *Regional and Local Grants*

a) There is a grant available from regional authorities for setting up new businesses.

b) There is also a regional grant for the creation of jobs (the *'Prime Régionale à l'Emploi'*).

c) Most French municipalities and chambers of commerce administer business centres or industrial zones, providing land at cheap prices. They may also subsidise up to 25% of the cost of new buildings or of redeveloping existing buildings. Even the cost of development of hotels and *gîtes* can qualify for grants in certain areas. Enquiries should be directed in the first instance to the local town hall (the *'Mairie'*).

d) Soft loans are available in some areas from large industrial companies which have retrenched in those areas. Again, the best source of information will be the local *Mairie*.

e) Export credit insurance is available through the French foreign trade organisation *COFACE*, the main shareholder in which is AGF, the French insurance company.

1.12. The Machinery of Taxation

1.12.1 Parliament

a) The legislative arm of government is the Parliament (*Parlement*) which consists of two chambers, the *Assemblée Nationale* (the Chamber of Deputies) and the *Sénat* (Senate). The 577 deputies of the *Assemblée Nationale* are elected for a five year term by direct universal suffrage. The minimum age for a deputy is 23. The 321 senators in the *Sénat* are elected for nine year terms by indirect suffrage, that is to say by the deputies and the representatives of the local collectives. The minimum age for a candidate for election to the senate is 35, and elections are held every three years for one-third of the chamber, in rotation.

b) Parliament enacts each year a *loi de finances* which covers, in its first part, the government's sources of finance, including borrowing as well as taxation. In the second part the law sets out the government's spending programme, by department, and allocates resources to any proposed new operations. The legislative programme of the government in the remainder of the year cannot commit the government to spending which has not been authorised. To raise additional revenues during the course of the year, the government has to pass a *loi de finances rectificative*.

c) The finance bill (*projet de loi de finances*) for the following year is prepared by the Ministry of Finance and presented to the senior members of the government (the *Conseil des Ministres*) in September each year, before the bill is placed before the *Assemblée Nationale* for debate at the end of September. When it has passed through its first reading in the *Assemblée Nationale* the bill is debated by the *Sénat*. It is then sent back to the *Assemblée Nationale* for a second reading during which many of the amendments made by the *Sénat* are struck out. After its second reading in the *Assemblée Nationale* it is deemed to have been adopted by Parliament. After Parliament has considered the law, it is then submitted to the *Conseil Constitutionnel* who check that the law does not infringe the constitution. Finally it is promulgated by the President of the Republic, and published in the *Journal Officiel*, all before the end of December.

1.12.2 The Ministry of Finance

The Minister of Finance (*Ministre de l'Économie et des Finances*) is the head of the government's finance ministry. This ministry is responsible for planning tax law changes and it also controls the administration of tax.

1.12.3 The Administration

a) The French civil service is referred to simply as the administration, and the agents of government responsible for collecting taxes are not a distinct service in terms of nomenclature. However they are known colloquially as *'le fisc'*.

b) The head of the tax administration is the *Directeur Général des Impôts*. He is assisted by a *Directeur Général Adjoint*, and a cabinet of senior officers. He is ultimately in charge of more than 82,000 tax agents.

c) The central organs of the administration comprise four large services, *le Service du Personnel et du Budget*, *le Service de l'Organisation et de l'Informatique*, *le Service des Opérations Fiscales et Foncières*, and *le Service du Contentieux*.

d) The task of collecting taxes falls on exterior services, which form a heirarchy comprising the *Directions à Compétence Nationale*, the *Directions Régionales*, the *Directions Départementales* and the *Services de Bas*. Because of its size and importance the Ile-de-France region (which includes Paris) has its own organisation. There are 21 regional directorates and 102 departmental directorates in metropolitan France. The French resident taxpayer will normally be dealing with one of more than 800 *Centres des Impôts*, appropriate to the place where he lives. Non-residents will normally be dealing with the *Centre des Impôts des Non-Résidents* at 10, rue du centre, 93160 Noisy-le-Grand.

1.12.4 The Court System

a) The courts in France are divided into two groups, the Administrative Courts and the Ordinary Courts. In general, matters in which the French government is a party are heard in the Administrative Courts. Cases involving direct taxes or taxes on turnover (including VAT) go through the Administrative Courts, starting in a *Tribunal Administratif*. Cases concerning registration taxes, stamp duties and other indirect taxes are dealt with by the Ordinary Courts, starting in a *Tribunal de Grande Instance*.

b) For our purposes the structure of the two court systems can be illustrated as follows:

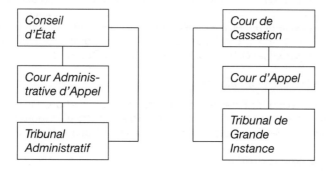

c) The *Conseil d'État* is the highest administrative court of appeal. The court has a role as adviser to the government on legislation, and particularly on the constitutional propriety of proposed legislation. Its advice is private. One of its specialised sections advises on finance laws. It can hear appeals either directly from the administrative tribunals, in which case it can review the findings of both fact and law in the lower court, or, more usually from the *Cour Administrative d'Appel*, in which case its jurisdiction is confined to appeals on points of law.

d) The administrative court of appeal (*Cour Administrative d'Appel*) is a layer of appeal courts which was created in January 1989 to relieve the backlog of appeal cases awaiting a hearing before the *Conseil d'État*. There are five courts, situated in Paris, Bordeaux, Lyon, Nantes and Nancy. Cases are normally heard by five judges, of whom the president is a member of the *Conseil d'État*.

e) There are twenty-six *Tribunaux Administratifs* in metropolitan France, and these are the courts which normally hear a first appeal from a decision by the administration on direct tax matters.

f) The highest Ordinary Court is the *Cour de Cassation*, which has both a civil and a criminal division. The *Cour de Cassation* judges only questions of law. It is rare for the parties to a case to appear before the court, as all the pleadings are written.

g) The next highest Ordinary Courts are the 25 courts of appeal (*Cours d'Appel*), situated in main cities and each serving several departments of France. These courts have the power to review the facts of the case as well as making judgements of law.

h) Below the courts of appeal there are two lower types of court, the *Tribunal d'Instance*, and above that the *Tribunal de Grande Instance*. We are only concerned with the latter, which is where appeals from administrative decisions on indirect taxes start. There is in theory one *Tribunal de Grande Instance* for each department, but in practice there may be several in the most heavily populated departments. The *Tribunal* is comprised of 3 judges (*magistrats*) who hear the more important civil and criminal cases at first instance.

1.12.5 Tax Returns

a) Although the French direct tax system is not based on self-assessment, the taxpayer is required to play an active role in the process of tax collection. The onus is on the taxpayer to complete and submit the returns which the law obliges him to make. There are penalties for failure to comply with these obligations and the tax due will be increased by a minimum of 10%.

b) The basic income tax declaration is form 2042 (there are various versions of this form). This is a declaration of total income, and where relevant it is supported by other returns for particular categories of income, for example:

i) the blue annex (form 2044) relates to income from real estate;

ii) the pink annex (form 2047) relates to foreign source income;

iii) the green annex (form 2049) relates to capital gains other than those on financial investments;

iv) form 2074 relates to capital gains on financial investments.

1.13. Taxpayer Morality

a) A report of the *Conseil des Impôts* published in 1990 estimated that one non-salaried taxpayer in three underdeclares a substantial portion of his income.

b) The non-resident investor in France is likely to encounter the black economy at an early stage in the development of his relationships with local businesses. He may be asked to pay part of the purchase price of any real estate 'under the table' (*sous la table*), and this places his advisors in a particularly difficult situation because the consequences of the discovery of such transactions can be severe for both the purchaser and seller (see 18.1.5).

1.14. General Definitions

1.14.1 Income

a) France adopts an economic definition of business income, taking profit to be the difference between net assets at the start of the period and at the end of the period, increased by withdrawals of capital and reduced by additions of capital. Unrealised gains are generally excluded from taxable income.

b) In the taxation of business income, the starting point is the accounting profit of the business for the year. Accounting treatment is far more standardised in France than it is in most other countries. There is a national accounting plan (*Plan Comptable Général*) which lays down the accounts and their code numbers which are to be used for bookkeeping in all businesses. The plan also specifies the double entry bookkeeping for many kinds of transaction. Some sectors of the economy (for example construction) have specialised accounting plans, again laid down by the national authority (the *Conseil National de la Comptabilité*). The accounting plans go further, and specify the format of reported accounts. It may also be mentioned in passing that the code of commercial law, the *Code de Commerce*, contains a number of laws relating to accounting matters, prescribing the books of account to be maintained by every business – daybooks in which all of the transactions are to be recorded chronologically, a *grand livre* ('great book') to which the entries from the daybooks are to be transferred and a balance book (*livre d'inventaire*) into which the accounting totals are transferred each year.

c) Accounting principles are broadly similar to those adopted in other countries, but there are some differences. The *Code de Commerce* lays down six mandatory principles:

 i) the going concern concept;

 ii) prudence;

 iii) consistency;

 iv) the historic cost basis of valuation;

 v) independence of accounting periods;

 vi) the netting off of accounts is prohibited (so that a provision for bad debts is shown as a separate figure from the total of debtors, for example).

d) The most obvious difference between this list and any list of accounting principles used in the Anglo-Saxon world is that the accruals principle is not expressly mandatory, although it is to some extent implicit in the notion of independence of accounting periods. The result is that provisions have in the past been used to smooth reported income figures from one year to another and for tax deferral purposes as much as to allocate expenses to the periods to which they relate. This has changed as a result of the EU Fourth Directive. It is also noticable that the concept of materiality has no place in French accounting, so that quite trivial categories of income or expense are measured with striking precision.

e) Historically an auditor was required to certify that, respecting the requirement of prudence, the accounts were 'regular' and 'sincere'. By a law of 30 April 1983, the scope of his report was extended to certify that the accounts also gave a true and fair view (*image fidèle*) of the company's situation. However after due deliberation the *Compagnie Nationale des Commissaires aux Comptes* announced that the 'true and fair' concept was 'indissoluble' from the notions of regularity and sincerity. In effect, French accountancy is much more concerned with normalisation, ie compliance with the general accounting plan, than with forming judgements on subjective issues like truth and fairness.

f) Until 1965 the French tax administration enjoyed considerable success in narrowing the differences between financial profit and taxable income. By that point in time it was established in case law that any expense claimed for tax purposes had to be charged against accounting profits. Thus for example accelerated depreciation allowed for tax purposes had to be written off book values for accounts purposes. However this resulted in distortions of economic reality which made it difficult for French companies to compete with companies from Anglo-Saxon countries in capital markets. Large French companies took to publishing two versions of their accounts. Following the EU Fourth Directive, enacted into French law with effect from 1 January 1984, the depreciation charged against ordinary profits is purely economic depreciation. Any extra depreciation allowed for tax purposes is charged as an extraordinary item (the French do not recognise any distinction between extraordinary and exceptional items). The economic depreciation is deducted from the balance sheet asset value, but the additional accelerated depreciation is shown as a special 'provision required by regulations' in the shareholders' equity section.

g) The EU Seventh Directive on group accounts was enacted into French legislation with effect for accounting periods beginning from January 1986. Groups are not obliged to produce group accounts using the same principles that are employed in producing the accounts of their subsidiaries, but are free to produce accounts according to the requirements of the financial markets in which they operate. They can therefore use different depreciation policies in the group accounts, capitalise leases, use a Last In First Out basis for evaluating stocks of goods and materials or whatever is necessary to comply with local generally accepted accounting practice. This has still further divorced accounting profits from taxable income.

h) Nevertheless it remains true that there is a stronger linkage between the accounting profit of a French company (rather than a group) and its taxable income than is found in most other countries. Certain forms of income credited in the accounts may not be taxable, eg the profits of a foreign branch. But although some expenses borne in the accounts may not be deductible in computing taxable income, it is rare to find expenses that can be deducted for tax purposes but which do not have to be borne as a charge against accounting profit.

i) For the purposes of income tax:

   i) Income for individuals is the income of the family. For a married couple this means that the family tax return includes the income of both spouses and of all of the dependent members of the household. The return is signed by both spouses and they are jointly and severally liable for the tax due.

   ii) Income is 'disposable income', which means that the income must be at the disposal of the recipient. The exception to this is that industrial or commercial income is taxable on an accruals basis under normal accounting principles.

1.14.2 Distributions

Distributions include:

a) Dividends;

b) Excessive interest paid to shareholders;

c) Redemptions of share capital, unless the company is quoted and the repayment forms part of a profit sharing scheme or a scheme to regulate the value of the company's shares; and

d) Liquidation distributions.

1.14.3 Other Terms and Abbreviations Defined

Abattement ('abatement'): a deduction from the taxable base of a fixed amount or fixed percentage.

Base forfaitaire: a taxable base determined by estimation rather than computation.

Centre de Gestion Agrée (CGA): Approved management centre for tax audits.

DOM: the overseas territories that form, with the metropolitan departments, France.

EU: the European Union.

FrF: French franc, the former currency of France. The French franc has been a 'non-decimal subdivision' of the euro since 1 January 1999. The euro is worth 6.55957 francs.

Fonds de commerce: personal tangible and intangible property used in a business. Also used to describe the business of a sole trader.

Forfait: an amount of tax fixed by law or by the tax administration.

Non-commercial professions: the traditional professions which do not buy and sell goods, eg accountants, architects, doctors and lawyers.

Non-French resident: refers to a non-resident of France.

PACS: *Pacte Civil de Solidarité*, registration of unmarried heterosexual and homosexual couples as one fiscal household – see 3.1.

Plafonnement: upper limit, or ceiling – see 6.11.2.

Prélèvement forfaitaire: withholding tax.

Prélèvement forfaitaire libératoire: withholding tax which represents a final tax liability, so that no further tax need be paid.

Quotient familial: 'the family quota' – see 6.10.2.

Société à prépondérance immobilière: an unquoted property holding company of which more than 50% of its assets consists in real property which is not used by the company for its own agricultural, industrial or commercial activity.

Société mère: holding company (literally 'mother company').

TOM: the former French colonies, now known as *Collectivités d'Outre-Mer*.

2.   FRANCE DEFINED

2.1.   Land Area

a) France consists of mainland France and Corsica (together known as metropolitan France) and, subject to modified rates of taxation, the overseas departments (collectively known as the *départements d'outre-mer* or *DOM* for short) of Guadeloupe, Guyana, Martinique and Reunion. Of the small islands in French coastal waters, the only ones which do not belong to France are the Channel Islands, the Ecrehous and the Minquiers (which are all British). Andorra's status is somewhat ambiguous, but it clearly does not form part of France for fiscal purposes. Constitutionally its status is determined by an agreement signed in 1278 between the Bishop of Urgell and the Comte de Foix, who became the co-princes of the territory.

b) The former French colonies and possessions which exercise their own fiscal sovereignty were called *Territoires d'Outre-Mer* or *TOM* but are now known under the term *Collectivités d'Outre-Mer*. These are Mayotte (population 201,234), Wallis and Futuna Island (population 14,166), French Polynesia (population 274,578), St Pierre et Miquelon (population 7,000), St Martin and St Barthélemy. New Caledonia (population 232,258) has a specific status. French tax law does not apply to the *collectivés*, but some investment incentives are available to French residents who invest in the *collectivés*, for example in new dwellings.

c) For the purposes of French nationals, France also includes the Principality of Monaco, by agreement with the Monegasque authorities (Article 7 of the France – Monaco (Income) Tax Treaty of 18 May 1963).

2.2.   Territorial Seas and Continental Shelf

France lays claim to territorial seas in a band around the above territories 12 miles wide. Further she has, by agreement with her European neighbours, rights to exploit the seabed resources in areas of the European continental shelf in the Bay of Biscay and English Channel. Under many of her double tax treaties, such areas are recognised as forming part of France.

3.   TAXABLE PERSONS

3.1.   Individuals

a) An individual is any living human being.

b) The French system of taxation of individuals, including non-residents, centres on the household. The tax returns of married taxpayers are signed by both husband and wife, they both have power to deal with the tax affairs of the household and they are jointly liable for the tax assessed. The income of the household includes the income of any dependent children or any severely disabled person living in the home as a dependant, whether a blood relative or not (a severely disabled person is someone with a *carte d'invalidité* showing at least 80% disability). Because of the French system of the family quota (*quotient familial*) it is often in the taxpayer's interest to claim the maximum number of dependants.

c) Persons who are living together unmarried (in *concubinage*) constitute two separate households. If they have children, their children can be treated as part of the household of either parent, as the parents choose.

d) Heterosexual and homosexual couples registered under the *Pacte Civil de Solidarité (PACS)* are treated as one fiscal household from the date of the *PACS* registration. The *PACS* was introduced on 13 October 1999 and also has effects in terms of inheritance tax (see 10.4.).

e) A married couple are only taxed as separate households if:

  i)   they have separate estates and are no longer living under the same roof; or

  ii) being in the throes of a divorce or separation they have been authorised to live apart; or

  iii) one spouse having abandoned the matrimonial home, they have separate incomes.

f) As regards the quantification of the dependants of the household, the following should be noted:

  i)   Any child born alive in the year of computation whose birth is registered (even if he or she subsequently died in the year of computation) is included in the household;

  ii) Minor children (under 18) who are married, whether or not living under the same roof as the head of the household, can be included in the household with their consent;

iii) If they so request, and their parents agree, certain adult children can be 're-attached' to the household. Those who may be re-attached are those:

under 21, or
under 25 and pursuing their studies, or
performing their military service (whatever their age).

g) However in some cases the tax return for the household may exclude the income of some of its members, for part or all of the tax year:

i) The taxpayer may demand to have the tax attributable to the income of his children assessed separately;

ii) Subject to the elections described above, children who become 18 during the course of the year of computation are responsible for their own affairs from the date of their 18th birthday;

iii) The income of a wife in the year of marriage up to the date of marriage is separately assessed;

iv) In the year of a divorce or separation, the affairs of the parties to the marriage are treated separately from the date of the divorce or separation;

v) If one party to the marriage dies during the year of computation, tax for the year is assessed in two separate assessments. The period from 1 January until the date of death includes the income of both spouses (and their dependants), while the assessment for the remainder of the year includes only the income of the survivor (and his or her dependants). However, the survivor is taxed as a married person for both parts of the year since his or her status is assessed as at 1 January.

3.2. Companies

3.2.1 Taxable Companies

a) Corporation tax is imposed on the taxable income of 'capital companies' (sociétés de capitaux), a category comprising the following types of company:

i) sociétés anonymes (SAs) (public limited companies, or corporations). This form of company is suitable for larger concerns, and is the only type of company that can offer its shares to the public and obtain a quote on a Stock Exchange. The minimum capital is €37,000, of which one quarter must be paid up on formation, and the company must have a minimum of 7 shareholders;

ii) *sociétés par actions simplifiée (SAS)*. This is a simplified form of *SA* which may not offer its shares to the public. The minimum number of shareholders is 1 person (individual or company) and the minimum share capital is €37,000. There is greater flexibility in the management structure and internal constitution than there is in an *SA*;

iii) *sociétés à responsabilité limitée (SARLs)*. These are private limited companies with a minimum capital of €1. All the authorised or nominal capital of the company must be issued. The company must have at least two and not more than 100 shareholders. *SARLs* under family control can elect to be treated as fiscally transparent (see 3.2.2(d)(ii) below);

iv) *sociétés en commandite par actions* (limited partnerships with a share capital);

v) *sociétés coopératives* (co-operatives are subject to corporation tax, but with an exemption for the profits of trading with their members which are returned to the members).

b) The other forms of company are collectively called *sociétés de personnes*, and are generally not subject to corporation tax unless they elect to be so taxed (see 3.2.2(b) and 3.3.(b)). However *sociétés civiles* are subject to corporation tax, even in default of this election, if they undertake industrial or commercial business which accounts for more than 10% of their turnover.

c) The companies listed in (a) above are exempt from corporation tax, and taxed as fiscally transparent, if they are *sociétés immobilières de copropriété transparentes* (see 3.2.2(c) below).

3.2.2 Fiscally Transparent and Semi-Transparent Companies

a) The category of *sociétés de personnes* includes the French equivalents of partnerships (see 3.3.), but also a number of other legal entities, some of which have the benefit of limited liability.

b) Such companies are not generally 'transparent' in the Anglo-Saxon sense of the word because a French partnership type of entity has a separate legal and fiscal personality. Tax is calculated at the corporate level before being apportioned to the shareholders, whereas in an English partnership the income is attributed to the partners before the tax is calculated. For example, in France, if the business of a partnership is sold, a partner pays capital gains tax at the rate appropriate to a sale of shares in respect of the gain on his share of the business. He is not treated as if he had sold a proportion of each of the assets of the business (real estate etc) as he would be in the UK. This basis is sometimes described as 'semi-transparency' (the term which the French use is *translucide*, which means translucent).

c) The only exception to this principle of 'semi-transparency' is the tax status of a *société immobilière de copropriété transparente*. This is a French company (of any legal form – even an *SA* can qualify) which has for its sole purpose either the acquisition or construction of buildings for the purpose of dividing them into fractions to be attributed to the shareholders, or the management of the buildings, or for letting the buildings for the benefit of some or all of the shareholders. Such a company is deemed, for direct tax purposes only, to have no personality distinct from its members.

d) The types of company which are 'semi-transparent' are:

i) *sociétés civiles* (companies formed for purposes not classified as commercial – eg for property holding and professional activities). Further information on *sociétés civiles* in the context of property ownership is provided at 18.5.2;

ii) *sociétés à responsabilité limitée de caractère familial* (private limited liability companies with a commercial purpose but a 'family company' character are able to opt that their members be assessed under the income tax rules);

iii) *entreprises unipersonelles à responsabilité limitée (EURLs)* (one person limited liability companies);

iv) *exploitations agricoles à responsabilité limitée (EARLs)* (*sociétés civiles* formed for agricultural purposes and owned by one individual or the members of one family, or formed between a landowner and a farmer or their families);

v) *groupements d'intérêt économique ('GIE'), groupements d'intérêt public* (a group of persons formed to cooperate in the development of the economic activities of its members. This is the French original on which the European Economic Interest Grouping is based);

vi) *sociétés en participation* (joint ventures – for example financial syndicates);

vii) *indivisions* (joint ownerships);

viii) *sociétés de copropriétaires de navires* (co-owners of ships);

ix) *groupements forestiers, groupements agricoles* (groups formed for forestry or agricultural purposes);

x) *sociétés de fait* (companies which are deemed to exist because two or more persons contribute capital or labour towards a common object, share in the management and control, and participate in the profits).

e) *EURLs* whose shareholders are individuals and *EARLs* with single shareholders can elect to be subject to corporation tax. If the shareholder of an *EURL* is itself a capital company, the *EURL* is compulsorily subject to corporation tax. For an *EARL* with several shareholders, the position is complex. With regards to *sociétés en participation*, the shareholders who have unlimited liability are treated as receiving their shares of the income, but if any shareholders have limited liability, or their identities have not been disclosed to the administration, their shares are subject to corporation tax (which will be assessed on the managers). *Sociétés de fait* can also elect to be subject to corporation tax. Any *société civile* other than a professional firm may elect to pay corporation tax.

f) The European Economic Interest Group (in French the *Groupement Européen d'Intérêt Économique* or *GEIE*) is an association formed under an EU Regulation (number 2137/85) of 25 July 1985. It is formed by a contract between the members, who may be individuals, partnerships or companies formed or carrying on business in any EU state. The association has most, if not all, of the qualities of legal personality, but it is fiscally semi-transparent.

3.3. Partnerships

a) There are two forms of partnership:

   i) *sociétés en nom collectif* (partnerships);

   ii) *sociétés en commandite simple* (limited partnerships).

b) Either of these may elect to be subject to corporation tax.

c) If they do not elect to be subject to corporation tax, the basic principle is that the members pay tax on their shares of the profits: if the member is an individual he or she will pay income tax, but if the member is a company it will pay corporation tax on its share. Again, the basis of taxation is 'semi-transparency', with tax calculated at the corporate level and then apportioned to the partners.

d) In a *société en commandite simple* there are two classes of partners. The partners with unlimited liability for the debts of the firm are the *(associés) commandités* and the limited partners are the *commanditaires*. The profit shares of the latter partners are always subject to corporation tax.

3.4. Trusts

a) The *projet de loi* of a French form of "trust" called *fiducie* drafted in 1992 was finally enacted on 22 February 2007 after many alterations. It is strictly reserved to corporate entities.

The French *fiducie* enables a corporate settlor to dispose of all or part of the assets or rights which it owns for the benefit of other persons or objects. This is done by way of a contract recorded on a national register. The *fiducie* fund forms a corpus distinct from the settlor's or the trustees' assets and cannot be seized by creditors.

Practically speaking, the French version of "trust" in its current state can only be used in the following specific contexts by corporation tax paying entities:

i) *Fiducie sûreté:* This allows an arrangement whereby the trustees hold the funds in escrow for the benefit of one or more creditors (ie the beneficiaries) as debt collateral until the settlor company has settled the debt.

ii) *Fiducie gestion* (or management trust): this allows appointed trustees to manage funds for the benefit of designated beneficiaries in lieu of a simple revocable mandate.

b) The use of the above arrangements by individuals in the context of estate planning, in a similar way to trusts established on Common Law jurisdictions, is strictly forbidden. French *fiducie* arrangements suspected to have been registered for estate planning purposes will simply be declared null and void. Given the above, the introduction of the *fiducie* unfortunately does not provide any further guidance in interpreting the French tax treatment of Common Law trust arrangements.

c) French courts do tend to recognise the concept of such trusts as an original institution created by foreign law provided they do not conflict with the French concept of "public order". The requirements of the latter include the preservation of inheritance rights under French Law *(la réserve héréditaire)*. These rights are given to the members of the family of French residents and foreign residents in respect of their French estate, and to the French national children of non-residents. It is debatable whether a French resident has the capacity to constitute a common law trust over French property. However, there would seem to be no absolute bar to the creation of a trust by a French resident over property situated outside France. There is no provision in French law for the taxation of trustees as such, and there would be a risk that trustees resident in France (or foreign trustees with assets in France) would be taxed in respect of the trust property as if they were the absolute beneficial owners of the property. It is possible that the trustees would be taxed as a company given the wide range of entities classified as companies in France (see for example the *société de fait* referred to in 3.2.2(d)(x)).

d) The French civil code allows the creation of a 'usufruct' (*usufruit*) which is the right of a person to enjoy the use of property belonging to another as if he owned it, but subject to the condition that he conserves the substance of the property. If the assets subject to the usufruct are fungible (ie by their nature replaceable, such as cash) the obligation of the person with the usufruct (the *usufruitier*) is merely to deliver up to the residual owner (the *nu-propriétaire*) similar assets. However in other cases the *usufruitier* has to retain the property in its existing state. For example if the subject of the usufruct is a painting, the *usufruitier* must conserve the painting, for the benefit of the *nu-propriétaire*. Under a trust, the trustees are obliged to weigh up the different interests of the beneficiaries, and usually have the power to alter the trust property so as to balance those interests. Thus if a beneficiary with an interest in possession has a requirement for income, but the initial trust property is a painting, the trustee could sell the painting and reinvest the proceeds to produce income.

3.5. Recognition of Foreign Entities

a) France does not have clear rules for the recognition of foreign entities, and characterisation is effected by comparing the foreign entity with those recognised by French law. The criteria applied are not defined, but certainly include:

    i)   limited or unlimited liability;

    ii) the transferability of the shares in the entity; and

    iii) the amount of publicity accorded to the shareholders of the entity.

b) The Liechtenstein Anstalt and Stiftung are regarded as capital companies unless they can prove that they have charitable objects.

4.   CONNECTIONS

4.1.   Nationality

Nationality has very limited consequences for individuals in the French system of taxation. However the country in which a company is incorporated is often of importance.

4.2.   Domicile

a)   The French do not make a distinction between the place(s) where a person is resident for the time being (if anywhere) and his or her permanent home. In common law countries a person may be resident in one country but 'domiciled' in another (the country or state to which he or she ultimately intends to return). Indeed in the UK there is even a third level of residential connection, the concept of 'ordinary residence', and there are significant tax advantages attached to the statuses of 'resident but not domiciled' or 'resident but not ordinarily resident'. The word *domicile* in France means something akin to principal home, and the concept is the sole residential connection between an individual and France. The word is in this context something of a *faux ami* (a 'false friend'), because it leads people familiar with the common law concept of domicile to suppose that the French too make a distinction between residence and domicile. For this reason it is sometimes thought that the French permit temporary immigrants to pay French income tax on the basis of their French source income and remittances of income from abroad, as the UK system does. This is simply not the case.

b)   While there are many similarities between the meaning in French of *domicile* and the common law concept of the same name, for tax purposes it is better to treat the French word *domicile* as equivalent to 'residence'.

c)   However domicile has significance far outside the world of tax, and an individual's domicile governs many aspects of personal law, such as legitimacy, capacity to marry and succession law. As will be seen, the rules of French succession law are strikingly different from those which prevail in most common law states. Because this is a subject of great interest to many people who become resident in France or who acquire French real estate, and because of the impact that the rules governing the distribution of French estates has on the inheritance tax burden, the rules of French succession law are explained in some detail in this book. In this and other non-tax contexts, it is safe to think of the French term *domicile* as equivalent to the English word.

d)   One difference is that, in France, domicile is a concept of attachment to a specific place – largely for taxation purposes – whereas in common law countries it is a concept of attachment to a legal system (of a country or, in federal systems, a state). For example the French say that a company is domiciled at its registered office, whereas common lawyers would say it is domiciled in the state where it was incorporated. The comments in the following paragraphs describe the French concept of *domicile* for general purposes, excluding tax.

e) Where a person has his domicile is essentially a question of fact. For individuals the following factors are taken into account in determining domicile:

i) residence and length of stay;

ii) the exercise of a business activity;

iii) other factors, including the payment of taxes, inscription on the electoral roll, receipt of correspondence, declarations of the individual concerned, family attachments, business connections etc.

f) An individual has a domicile of origin which is derived from his parents at birth, and his domicile remains dependent on his parents while he is a minor. If the parents are separated, the child takes the domicile of the parent with whom he resides. This domicile persists unless the intention of adopting a new domicile is established with certainty. The domicile of dependence also persists while the individual does not earn any income and therefore cannot fend for himself.

g) The domiciles of a married man and his wife are determined independently of each other (NB this is very different from the position with regard to *domicile fiscal*, or tax residence).

h) A change of domicile results from the establishment of a real home in the new place, together with the intention to fix the individual's principal residence there. The intention to change a domicile can be evidenced expressly by a declaration made to the municipality which is being left, and a declaration to the municipality to which the domicile is being transferred. Failing such an express statement of intention, the proof of the intention of the individual is dependent on the facts. A citizen of another country may be said to have acquired a domicile in France if he has manifested his intention to fix his principal home there.

i) For certain purposes the French have regard to 'special domiciles', such as a commercial domicile and an electoral domicile. The 'special domicile' which concerns this text is the fiscal domicile, and this is described below.

4.3. Residence

4.3.1 Residence for Individuals

a) In practice, the question of where an individual is resident is very often determined under a double tax treaty. However under French domestic law, tax residence *(domicile fiscal)* for individuals is determined according to three criteria, the first of which is in reality two separate tests – the 'home' and the 'principal residence' tests. If any one of the tests is satisfied the individual is considered to be resident in France for the tax year.

   i) His home or principal residence is in France. The concept of home *(foyer fiscal)* embraces the notions of stability and permanence. It means, for example, that a person will be considered fiscally domiciled in France, even if he himself works abroad, if his wife and children live in France. A person's residence in France is his principal residence if he resides in France for more than 183 days in the tax year regardless of what accommodation he occupies. Even if he does not reside in France for more than 183 days, he may still have his principal residence in France if he has spent more time there than at any other home.

   ii) He carries on any occupation in France whether salaried or on his own account, unless he can prove that the occupation is ancillary to his main occupation elsewhere. Individuals sent abroad by French employers and French state employees on service abroad retain their French residence.

   iii) The centre of his economic interests is in France. This rule affects individuals whose income is largely derived from French sources. The criteria applied are:

   Location of main investments
   Main situs of business or businesses
   Location from which possessions are managed
   Centre of activities
   Source of main part of income

b) The 'home' test takes precedence over the 'principal residence' test, and if it is possible to determine the place where a family usually gather or live, the time-spent criterion can be ignored. The 183 day rule is only applied where a couple does not have a 'home' in this sense, and if the *foyer fiscal* is found to be outside France, the couple will only be considered to be resident in France if one of the other two tests is satisfied. The fact that they may have spent more than 183 days in the year in France is ignored. This principle clearly has more significance for married couples than for single individuals. However where a couple are married under a separation of estates regime (as most British and many American couples are) and they are living apart, it will not avail the spouse who is living in France to argue that he or she should not be treated as a resident of France because his or her spouse (and children if any) have their home outside France. Because of their matrimonial regime and the fact of their separation, the residence of each spouse will be determined independently of the other.

c) For new permanent residents of France the following rules apply for income tax and capital gains tax purposes in the year of arrival:

i) New permanent residents who were not taxable in France before their acquisition of French resident status become taxable in France on their worldwide income received or at their command after the date of their arrival.

ii) New permanent residents who owned a dwelling in France before becoming resident in France may be taxable on the *base forfaitaire* (see 6.6.2.(b)) prorata temporis for the period prior to the acquisition of French residence; for the period after the acquisition of French resident status until the end of the year they are taxable on their worldwide income.

iii) New permanent residents who had French source income prior to their arrival are taxable on the basis of their French source income up to the date of their arrival and their worldwide income thereafter.

d) For individuals transferring their residence out of France, the following rules apply for income tax and capital gains tax purposes in the year of departure:

i) Emigrants who cease to have any French source income are liable to French income tax on the income they have earned or received up to the date of their departure. Income assessed on a *base forfaitaire* is time apportioned, and industrial or commercial profits are subject to the same rules as if there had been a cessation of source.

ii) Emigrants who retain one or more dwellings in France are taxable on their worldwide income prior to departure and may be taxed on the *base forfaitaire* for the period after their departure (see 6.6.2(b)).

iii) Emigrants who retain other French sources of income are taxable on their worldwide income up to the date of their departure and on their French source income thereafter.

e) When one partner to a marriage is living in a home in France, but the other is living mainly elsewhere, the question of whether the partner living outside France is treated as a French resident depends:

i) on the application of any relevant double tax treaty and, failing that, on

ii) whether the couple are 'living together' (ie they have a *vie commune*).

f) If the couple are married under community property rules, it is likely that they will be regarded as living together, so that the absent spouse will be considered to have his or her 'household' in France within the meaning of 4.3.1(a)(i) above. However if the couple are married under a 'separate estates' regime (as most couples from common law countries are) and they are living under separate roofs, the rules set out in 4.3.1(b) apply and the couple may be taxed separately.

g) If one of the spouses is treated as a non-resident, the couple are exposed to French income tax on:

i) the worldwide income of the resident partner; and

ii) the French source income of the non-resident partner.

4.3.2 *Residence for Companies*

a) The residence of a company is not defined by the *CGI*, because for many purposes it is irrelevant.

b) The application of French corporation tax to business income is based on the territoriality principle, unlike either French income tax or the income and corporation taxes of most countries. A company (wherever it is incorporated) pays French corporation tax on the profits of any business carried on in France, but not on the profits of any business carried on outside France.

c) However, the French corporation tax system is not a purely territorial system, because French companies and French branches of foreign companies can be subject to French corporation tax on their foreign source investment income.

d) French companies are normally assessed to tax at their head office (*'établissement principal'*), but the tax administration can choose to assess a company at the place where its seat of effective management is located or at its registered office (*'siège social'*). Since every French company has a *siège social* in France, they are all by definition taxable in France. Bearing in mind that residence, to the French, is a concept of attachment to a place and not a concept of attachment to a legal system, the place where the liability is established may be said to be the place where the company is resident.

e) It follows that a foreign company will not be regarded as resident in France if neither its *établissement principal*, its seat of effective management or its *siège social* are in France.

4.4.   Individuals and Companies with Assets in France

a) The owners of real estate in France are treated as possessing a French source of income.

b) Certain companies are also subject to an annual tax on the value of their French real estate (see chapter 12).

c) Other assets considered to be situated in France include movable objects in France, French government stocks, debts owed by French residents and shares issued by companies which either:

    i)   are formed under French law; or

    ii)   have their registered office in France; or

    iii) have the seat of their effective management in France.

4.5.   Individuals and Companies with French Source Income

a) The taxable income of non-residents is defined by the *CGI*, in a listing which is considered to be exhaustive. If a non-resident has a source of income from France which is not on the list, it is probably not taxable in France. The following are considered to be French sources of income, wherever the payer of the sums involved may be resident:

    i)   income from immovable property (ie land or buildings) situated in France or from rights relating to such property;

    ii)   income from French securities and all forms of capital invested in France;

    iii) income from businesses situated in France;

    iv)   earned income, whether from salaried employment or self-employment, from activities carried on in France;

    v)   sums paid in respect of artistic or sporting services supplied or used in France.

b) The following are considered to be French sources of income if the payer is resident in France:

    i)   pensions and annuities;

    ii)   royalties received by inventors and authors or persons who develop certain new varieties of vegetables, and all income derived from intellectual property; and

iii) sums paid in respect of services of all kinds supplied or used in France.

c) Amounts paid to an individual, company or other legal entity outside France for services rendered by a resident of France are taxable in the name of the French resident if the French resident controls the foreign entity or is unable to prove that the foreign entity has a commercial or industrial activity other than the rendering of such services or, in any event, if the foreign entity is based in a tax haven.

4.6   Individuals and Companies with Capital Gains on French Assets

The following are considered to be French capital gains, regardless of where the vendor of the asset may be resident:

a) A gain from a sale of real estate situated in France;

b) A gain from a sale of shares in an unquoted company (other than a *SICOMI*) if the majority of its assets consist of real estate or rights relating to real estate situated in France including property which is simply rented out furnished or unfurnished (excluding any real estate used for the company's own industrial, commercial, agricultural or professional business);

c) A gain on a sale of shares in a French company if the vendor, his spouse, and their ancestors or descendants have at any time in the previous 5 years collectively held more than 25% of the profit shares in the company.

5. GENERAL DESCRIPTION OF THE MAIN FRENCH TAXES

5.1. Income Tax

5.1.1 Outline of the Tax

a) French income tax is a tax on the income of individuals.

b) Income is defined by reference to its source (eg income from real estate, industrial or commercial profits, income from investments etc), and separate rules of computation exist for each of the taxable sources. Indeed much of the complexity of the present system of income taxation can be traced to the fact that until the early part of the 20th century there was no overall income tax as such. In fact taxpayers paid separate taxes in respect of specific sources of income.

c) The system of income tax is declaratory, and the onus is on the individual to complete an annual return if he is taxable. He is also obliged to complete a tax return if he possesses one or more of the 'apparent signs of wealth' – see 6.16.

5.1.2 Taxable Persons

a) Income tax is paid by single individuals, married or *PACS* couples as explained in 3.1.

b) It should be noted that certain forms of company are fiscally transparent or semi-transparent, so that the members of the company pay the tax which is assessed in respect of the company's profits (see 3.2.2).

c) In the French tax system, companies themselves are never subject to income tax.

5.1.3 Connections

Individuals are subject to French income tax if either

a) they are resident in France, or

b) they have a French source of income.

5.1.4 Jurisdiction

France is defined in 2.

5.1.5 Events

a) The event which gives rise to liability is the receipt of income, or, if the taxpayer files his tax return on an accruals basis, the recognition of income.

b) An individual can be treated as having received income which he has not declared if his lifestyle is inconsistent with his declared income – see 6.16.

5.1.6 Period

a) Individuals who are resident in France are liable to French income tax while they are resident in France. Former French residents do not continue to be subject to French income tax after they have ceased to be resident (unless they are French nationals who have become resident in Monaco).

b) Individuals who are not resident in France are liable to French income tax in any tax year in which they receive income from France (including in some cases a notional income from real estate in France (see 6.6.2(b)).

5.1.7 Treaty Exemption

a) France is party to about 105 treaties covering income taxes.

b) Many of these double tax treaties provide that certain types of income are exempt from French taxation in the hands of non-French residents (see 14).

5.2. Corporation Tax

5.2.1 Outline of the Tax

French corporation tax is not a tax on French companies. It is a tax on the income of certain kinds of company carrying on business in France. Therefore it does not apply to French companies carrying on business outside France or to French companies which are not 'capital' companies. But it does apply to foreign 'capital' companies carrying on business in France. The tax developed from the income tax on commercial and industrial profits and many of the corporation tax rules of computation are common to this part of the income tax system.

5.2.2 Taxable Persons

a) The forms of company that are subject to French corporation tax are set out in 3.2.1.

b) However some companies which under general principles would be subject to corporation tax (because they are 'capital companies') can be exempt from the tax, and are then generally taxed like partnerships:

i) family controlled *SARLs* that elect not to pay corporation tax;

ii) certain real estate owning companies, including *sociétés immobilières de copropriété transparentes, sociétés immobilières de gestion, sociétés immobilières d'investissement* and *sociétés immobilières pour le commerce et l'industrie (SICOMIs)*;

iii) certain investment companies including *sociétés d'investissement à capital variable (SICAVs)*;

iv) public bodies;

v) venture capital companies, called *sociétés de capital-risque (SCRs)*.

5.2.3 Connections

Companies are subject to French corporation tax on the profits of any business carried on in France. This is a very different basis than that which applies for income tax, because a French resident company is not in general subject to French corporation tax on the profits of a business carried on overseas. There are three bases on which a company may be said to be carrying on a business in France:

a) It has a permanent establishment in France;

b) It has a dependent agent in France; and

c) It habitually carries out a complete commercial cycle in France (eg purchase and sale).

These concepts are explored in greater detail at 7.2.

5.2.4 Jurisdiction

France is defined in 2.

5.2.5 Events

The event which gives rise to liability is the making of a profit.

5.2.6 Period

Companies are exposed to French corporation tax in any year during which they conduct a business in France.

5.2.7 Treaty Exemption

a) France is party to about 105 treaties covering corporation tax.

b) Under many of these treaties, a company is exempt from French corporation tax in respect of the profits of a trade or business if it is a resident of the treaty partner country and does not trade in France through a permanent establishment.

c) Below is the list of double tax treaties containing a clause allowing France to effectively tax the profits of a permanent establishment situated in the other territory:

Albania	Estonia	Mexico	Switzerland
Algeria	Ghana	Mongolia	Trinidad &
Armenia	Guinea	Namibia	Tobago
Austria	Israel	Norway	Turkey
Azerbaijan	Italy	Oman	Ukraine
Bolivia	Jamaica	Pakistan	United Arab
Botswana	Japan	Qatar	Emirates
Cameroon	Kazakhstan	Quebec	USA
Canada	Kuwait	Russia	Uzbekistan
Chile	Latvia	South Africa	Venezuela
Croatia	Lithuania	Spain	Vietnam
Czech Rep.	Macedonia	St Pierre	
Ecuador	Madagascar	& Miquelon	
Egypt	Malta	Sweden	

5.3.   Capital Gains Tax

5.3.1   Outline of the Tax

The French capital gains tax is technically a part of the French income tax and corporation tax systems. However capital gains are generally taxed more favourably than income, with numerous categories of exempt gains and special tax rates, especially for gains realised on assets held in the long term.

5.3.2   Taxable Persons

Capital gains tax is suffered by both individuals and companies.

5.3.3   Connections

The connecting factors on which liability is based are

a)   residence in France, or

b)   the ownership of

    i)   land in France; or

    ii)   shares in most companies more than 50% of the assets of which consist of French real estate unrelated to a trade; or

    iii)   more than 25% of the shares in a French company subject to corporation tax.

5.3.4   Jurisdiction

France is defined in 2.

5.3.5 Events

a) The events which give rise to liability are:

   i) a sale of a capital asset;

   ii) the export of precious metal, jewellery, a work of art or an antique (unless the individual is taking up residence in another EU country); and

   iii) A charge to capital gains tax can arise in connection with the emigration of a taxpayer in two circumstances:

   - When the taxpayer has been resident in France during at least 6 of the previous 10 years and he owns (directly or indirectly, and together with his family) more than 25% of a company, he is deemed to have sold and reacquired his shareholding immediately prior to his departure. However, if he does not dispose of the shares within 5 years of his departure the tax due is forgiven.

   - When the taxpayer owns shares into which a capital gain has been rolled-over, the rolled-over gain becomes immediately chargeable.

     This has been successfully challenged in the case Hughes de Lasteyrie du saillant v Ministry of Finance as an impediment to the freedom of movement of capital. It was also condemned in March 2004 by the European Court of Justice.

b) Capital gains tax is **not** payable in respect of

   i) gifts of assets;

   ii) transfers of assets on death (but note that death constitutes a disposal for the purpose of operating the five-year rule described in (a)(iii) above); or

   iii) the event of taxpayers' becoming or ceasing to be resident in France (except in the case of certain assets, noted at (a)(ii) and (iii) above).

c) To become taxable the appreciation of an asset must be 'realised'. Except in the context of an emigration, there is generally no tax on unrealised gains.

5.3.6 Period

a) Taxable persons are exposed to French capital gains tax:

   i) while they are resident in France; or

   ii) while they hold French real estate or shares in a foreign company which mainly owns French real estate; or

iii) while they, with their families, hold more than 25% of the shares of a French company (or while they have done so in the previous 5 years).

b) Exposure to the tax generally commences when residence commences or the taxable assets are acquired by the non-resident, and ceases when residence ceases or the taxable assets are alienated. However a sale of shares from a 25%-plus shareholding within 5 years of emigration can result in a tax charge.

5.3.7 Treaty Exemption

French double tax treaties generally do not relieve the non-French resident taxpayer from any liability to French tax on capital gains arising on disposals of French real estate (or real estate owning companies), but often exempt residents of a treaty partner country from liability to French tax on capital gains arising on disposals of shareholdings exceeding 25%.

5.4. Gifts Tax

5.4.1 Outline of the Tax

a) French gifts tax and inheritance tax are in effect the same tax on capital transfers cumulated during life and on death.

b) However French gifts tax applies only to gifts which are required to be made by deed or with judicial recognition. A lifetime gift by manual transfer is not normally taxable (unless it is revealed to the tax administration), although such gifts are brought into account when inheritance tax is computed if the donee also figures among the legatees of the estate.

5.4.2 Taxable Persons

The donee of the gift suffers the tax.

5.4.3 Connections

a) The gift is taxable if the donor is resident in France.

b) A gift is also taxable if the recipient is resident in France and has been so resident for at least 6 of the 10 tax years prior to the year in which the gift is received.

c) A gift from one non-resident to another non-resident is taxable if the gift is made out of French assets. French assets include:

i) real estate situated in France;

ii) shares in French companies;

iii) shares in unquoted foreign companies to the extent that the value of the shares reflects the French real estate assets of the company;

iv) tangible movable assets situated in France;

v) debts owed by French residents;

vi) bank accounts at French banks.

d) As stated above, gifts tax does not normally apply to assets which are transferred without making a legal deed, so in practice the only items that are likely to result in a gifts tax liability if transferred inter vivos by one non-resident to another non-resident are real estate situated in France, assets of a business (*fonds de commerce*) in France or an interest in a French company which does not have a capital divided into shares.

5.4.4 Jurisdiction

France is defined in 2.

5.4.5 Events

The taxable event is the receipt of the gift.

5.4.6 Period

Since anyone could receive a gift of taxable assets at any time, the exposure to the tax is continuous for every person.

5.4.7 Treaty Exemption

a) Only 7 French double tax treaties relate specifically to gifts tax – the treaties with Austria, Guinea, Italy, New Caledonia, St Pierre & Miquelon, Sweden and the USA. These determine which of the contracting states has the primary right to tax gifts, generally in the same way as French inheritance tax treaties.

b) France unilaterally gives credit relief to French residents for foreign tax suffered on gifts made out of foreign assets.

5.5. Inheritance Tax

5.5.1 Outline of the Tax

a) French inheritance tax is paid by the heirs of a deceased individual in respect of their shares in his estate – including any assets received by gift during his lifetime.

b) Because it applies to the whole of the estate of the deceased, and not simply assets that must in law be transferred by a deed or under judicial process, French inheritance tax has a far greater scope than French gifts tax.

5.5.2 Taxable Persons

The inheritor suffers the tax.

5.5.3 Connections

a) The inheritance is taxable if the deceased was resident in France.

b) Subject to the terms of any relevant double estate duty treaty the inheritance may also be taxed if the heir is resident in France, and has been so resident for at least 6 of the 10 tax years prior to the year in which he inherits.

c) The inheritance is taxable if it is made out of assets situated in France. French assets are listed in 5.4.3(c).

5.5.4 Jurisdiction

France is defined in 2.

5.5.5 Events

The taxable event is the death of the individual from whose estate the inheritance derives.

5.5.6 Period

Since anyone could inherit taxable assets at any time, the exposure to the tax is continuous for every person.

5.5.7 Treaty Exemption

a) French inheritance and gifts tax treaties determine the rights of the contracting states to tax gifts and legacies where the donor/decedent is resident in one country but the assets subject to the gift or legacy are situated in the other. For example, under the France – UK treaty, each state is entitled to tax real estate and tangible movable property situated in that state, and shares in companies incorporated in that state. In contrast under the France – USA treaty tangible movable property which was used for the normal personal use of the decedent or his family is taxable only in the state where he was domiciled. Most other tangible movable property and all real estate is taxable in the state where it is situated. Shares in companies are taxable by one of the states only if the donor or decedent was domiciled in or a citizen of that state.

b) France has double tax treaties relating to inheritance tax with the following countries:

Algeria*	Congo	Mayotte*	Senegal*	United
Austria*	Finland*	Monaco	Spain*	Kingdom
Bahrain	Gabon*	Morocco	St Pierre &	USA*
Belgium*	Italy*	New	Miquelon	
Benin	Ivory	Caledonia	Sweden*	
Burkina	Coast*	Niger*	Switzerland*	
Faso*	Kuwait	Oman	Togo*	
Cameroon*	Lebanon*	Qatar	Tunisia*	
Cent. African	Mali	Saudi	United Arab	
Republic*	Mauritania*	Arabia*	Emirates	

c) The treaties with countries marked with an asterisk provide for exemption from French inheritance tax of assets situated in the other country. However the value of the exempt foreign assets is taken into account in determining the rate of French inheritance tax payable on the assets taxable in France. The other treaties provide relief by a credit for any foreign inheritance tax paid in respect of assets subject to French inheritance tax. This credit is provided for unilaterally in the *CGI*, and therefore extends to taxes levied by countries with which France has no double tax treaty.

5.6. Wealth Tax

5.6.1 Outline of the Tax

Individuals resident in France on 1 January in the tax year and non-residents with sufficiently large values of taxable assets in France are taxed on the basis of their assets as at 1 January in the tax year.

5.6.2 Taxable Persons

Wealth tax is payable by individuals. The assets of an individual, whether resident or not, include the assets of his spouse and minor children if the spouse or minor children were themselves resident in France on 1 January in the tax year. The assets of an unmarried couple openly living together are similarly aggregated.

5.6.3 Connections

a) Individuals who are resident in France and have net taxable assets worldwide exceeding €770,000 (as at 1 January 2008) in value are subject to French wealth tax.

b) Individuals who are not resident in France but who have net taxable assets in France (which in this case excludes portfolio investments) with a value exceeding €770,000 (as at 1 January 2008) are subject to French wealth tax. Assets situated in France include:

i)   real estate situated in France;

ii) shares in French companies (other than portfolio investments);

iii) shares in unquoted foreign companies, to the extent that the value of the shares reflects the French real estate assets of the company;

iv) tangible movable assets situated in France;

v)   debts owed by French residents (other than portfolio investments).

5.6.4   Jurisdiction

France is defined in 2.

5.6.5   Events

Wealth tax is a tax on status, not dependent on any event.

5.6.6   Period

Exposure to the tax exists while an individual is resident in France and has a sufficient value of net taxable assets or, being a non-French resident, has a sufficient value of net taxable assets (excluding portfolio investments) in France.

5.6.7   Treaty Exemption

a) Wealth tax is expressly covered by France's double tax treaties with:

Algeria	Germany	Macedonia	Spain
Armenia	Guinea	Malta	Sweden
Austria	India	Mongolia	Switzerland
Azerbaijan	Israel	Namibia	Ukraine
Bahrain	Italy	Norway	United Arab
Bolivia	Ivory Coast	Oman	Emirates
Canada	Kazakhstan	Qatar	USA
Chile	Kuwait	Russia	Uzbekistan
Czech Republic	Latvia	Saudi Arabia	Vietnam
Estonia	Lithuania	South Africa	Zimbabwe

typically residents of these countries are liable to French wealth tax only in respect of French real estate or real estate companies, and the assets of any business permanent establishment in France.

b) The other French treaties which contain agreements sufficient to determine the right to tax wealth are:

Argentina	Finland	Mauritius	Slovak Rep.
Cyprus	Hungary	Netherlands	
Denmark	Indonesia	Poland	
Egypt	Luxembourg	Romania	

c) The *Cour de Cassation* held in a decision dated 24 March 1992 that the wording of the treaty with Switzerland, as it then was, gave Switzerland an exclusive right to tax real property situated in Switzerland, even though this inference is not as unambiguous as it is under the Danish, Egyptian, German and Luxembourg treaties. The France-Switzerland double tax treaty has since been amended to make it clear that France can impose its wealth tax on French residents who own Swiss real estate, but the decision has wide implications, because in its previous form the French treaty with Switzerland was substantially identical in this respect to the treaties with Argentina, Cyprus, the Czech Republic, Finland, Hungary, Indonesia, Italy, Malta, Mauritius, the Netherlands, Poland, Romania, the Slovak Republic and Spain.

d) As a result of the above court case, the tax administration published a Bulletin on 23 September 1992 stating that French residents who own real estate in Argentina, Czech Republic, Finland, the Netherlands, Spain and Switzerland were no longer required to include such property in their taxable wealth. The amendment of the France-Switzerland Treaty, which became effective on 1 August 1998, has since removed Switzerland from the list of exempt countries. The basis of the selection in the Bulletin appears to be that these countries, among those listed above, impose their own wealth taxes. It is highly questionable whether the exemption can be limited to those countries which have a wealth tax.

e) The tax administration clarified the above situation in 1999 and confirmed the exemption of real estate situated in Denmark, Egypt and Luxembourg, as these countries have the exclusive right to tax assets situated there. It also considers that residents who own real estate in Argentina, Czech Republic, Finland and the Netherlands are no longer required to include these in their taxable wealth.

f) The effect of these treaties is not, of course, solely to define the types of foreign asset which are exempt from French wealth tax in the hands of a French resident. They also define classes of French asset which are exempt from French wealth tax in the hands of a resident of the treaty-partner country.

g) Movable property is taxable only in the state of residence of the taxpayer unless it is connected with a business permanent establishment, except that:

i)   under the treaties with Argentina and Egypt, movable assets situated in France are subject to French wealth tax;

ii)   under the treaties with Argentina, Austria, Bolivia, Canada, Cyprus, Czech Republic, Egypt, Finland, Germany, Hungary, India, Indonesia, Israel, Italy, Ivory Coast, Luxembourg, Malta, Mauritius, Mongolia, Namibia, the Netherlands, Norway, Poland, Romania, Russia, Slovak Republic, South Africa, Spain, Sweden, Switzerland, USA, Vietnam, Zimbabwe, movable assets forming part of a fixed base used for the purpose of performing independent personal services in the other states, may be taxed in the other state.

iii)   shares in transparent real estate owning companies (ie in terms of French taxation *sociétés immobilières de copropriété transparentes*) are generally treated like real estate itself, with the sole exception of the treaty with the Netherlands, under which they are treated as movable assets;

iv)   the shares of other real estate holding companies (eg in terms of French companies *sociétés civiles immobilières*) are treated as real estate in the treaties with Austria, Bahrain, Bolivia, Canada, Cyprus, Germany, Hungary, India, Israel, Italy, Ivory Coast, Kuwait, Mauritius, Mongolia, Namibia, Norway, Qatar, Russia, Saudi Arabia, South Africa, Sweden, Switzerland, United Arab Emirates, the USA, Vietnam and Zimbabwe. Under all the other treaties, the shares of a real estate owning company are treated as movable assets. In general the shares of a company which owns real estate are taxable in the country where the real estate is situated (see (j) below); and

v)   under the treaties with Bahrain, Israel, Ivory Coast, Namibia, Qatar, Saudi Arabia, South Africa, Spain, Sweden, United Arab Emirates, USA, Zimbabwe, shareholdings exceeding 25% in a company other than a real estate holding company are taxable in the state where the company has its seat of effective management. They may also be taxable in the other state, which will then give double tax relief by credit for the foreign tax paid.

h)   Furniture is generally treated as movable property, but in the treaties with Denmark, Ivory Coast, Luxembourg and Switzerland it is treated as part of the home to which it relates.

i)   Nationals of Austria, Bahrain, Canada, Germany, Italy, Kuwait, Qatar, Saudi Arabia, Spain, the United Arab Emirates and US citizens (who are not also nationals of France) are exempt from French wealth tax in respect of assets situated outside France on 1 January in each of the first five years after they take up residence in France. If they cease to be resident in France for a period of at least 3 years and then return to France, the 5 year tax holiday recommences. In the renegotiated double tax treaty between France and the

UK, UK nationals who are not also nationals of France will benefit from the above treatment when the treaty comes into force. Although the treaty was signed in 2004, it has not yet been ratified and is still undergoing negotiations. The date when the new treaty is expected to come into effect is uncertain at the time of going to print. The temporary exemption will only benefit UK nationals who settle in France after the new treaty enters into force.

j) In all other cases – eg for residents of Australia, Belgium, Japan and the UK, French internal law determines the taxability of French wealth and of the wealth of French residents.

5.7. Tax on the Market Value of Real Estate in France Owned by Certain Companies

5.7.1 Outline of the Tax

a) The tax of 3% per annum of the market value of any real property in France owned directly or indirectly by a company reinforces the French anti-avoidance regimes in respect of other taxes. The object of the tax, from the point of view of the French administration, is to force the disclosure of the identity of the beneficial owners of foreign companies which own real estate in France. Partly this is designed to enable the French to assess non-residents to French taxes applicable on the sale of real-estate owning companies, but mainly it is designed to discover French residents who are concealing their wealth behind foreign companies.

b) Previously the tax applied only to foreign companies owning property in France. However, following a succession of court cases in years up to 1992, all involving Swiss companies, the administration found that it could not apply the tax, and therefore force the disclosure of the identities of the owners of a company, where the company could claim the benefit of a non-discrimination clause in a double tax treaty (because French companies were not subject to the same tax). Therefore the rules were amended in the 1993 Finance Law and since then this tax applies to all companies, French or foreign, which do not benefit from one of the exemptions listed below.

c) To escape the tax, a company must either:

   i)   show that its investment in French real estate is less than 50% of its assets in France (for this purpose, any real estate used by the company itself for its own business – other than property development – is ignored); or

   ii) have its seat of effective management in a country which has concluded a treaty with France containing a clause committing the parties to provide assistance to each other in combating tax fraud, and provide details each year of:

- its real estate investments in France and

- its shareholders, or

iii) have its seat of effective management in France or be protected by a non-discrimination clause in a double tax treaty, and give an undertaking to provide on request details of:

- its real estate investments in France and

- its shareholders, or

iv) be quoted on a French stock exchange or a foreign stock exchange regulated by similar rules; or

v) be a sovereign state, international organisation or public institution; or

vi) be a French pension fund or a non-profit making organisation which justifies having the property for its operations.

d) Although the tax ostensibly now applies to French companies, as well as foreign companies, any French *société civile immobilière* should be making declarations of its property and shareholders, and should therefore be exempt.

5.7.2 Taxable Persons

The tax applies to all companies.

5.7.3 Connections

The tax applies where French real estate unconnected with a French business constitutes more than 50% of the assets of the company.

5.7.4 Jurisdiction

France is defined in 2.

5.7.5 Events

The tax is a tax on status, not dependent on any event.

5.7.6 Period

A liability to tax exists while the required proportion of the company's assets consist of French real estate and the other conditions for exemption are not fulfilled.

5.7.7 Treaty Exemption

a) The countries which have double tax treaties with France containing a clause providing mutual assistance against tax fraud and evasion are:

Albania	Cyprus	Japan	Namibia	Miquelon
Algeria	Czech Rep	Jordan	Netherlands[3]	Sweden
Argentina	Denmark	Kazakhstan	New	Thailand
Armenia	Ecuador	Korea (S)	Caledonia	Togo
Australia	Egypt	Kuwait	New	Trinidad and
Austria	Estonia	Latvia	Zealand	Tobago
Azerbaijan	Finland	Lebanon	Niger	Tunisia
Bangladesh	Gabon	Lithuania	Nigeria	Turkey
Belgium	Germany	Luxembourg[2]	Norway	Ukraine
Benin	Ghana	Macedonia	Pakistan	United Arab
Botswana	Greece	Madagascar	Philippines	Emirates
Brazil	Guinea	Malawi	Poland	United
Bulgaria	Hungary	Malaysia	Portugal	Kingdom[4]
Burkina Faso	Iceland	Mali	Quebec	USA
Cameroon	India	Malta	Romania	Uzbekistan
Canada	Indonesia	Mauritania	Russia	Venezuela
Cent. African	Iran	Mauritius	Senegal	Vietnam
Republic	Ireland	Mayotte	Slovak Rep.	Yugoslavia
Chile	Israel	Mexico	South Africa	Fed. Rep. of
China [1]	Italy	Monaco	Spain	Zambia
Congo	Ivory Coast	Mongolia	Sri Lanka	Zimbabwe
Croatia	Jamaica	Morocco	St Pierre &	

Notes:

(1) The treaty with China excludes Hong Kong and Macao.

(2) The treaty with Luxembourg excludes Luxembourg Holding companies.

(3) The treaty excludes the Netherlands Antilles.

(4) The treaty with the United Kingdom excludes the Isle of Man, Gibraltar, and the Channel Islands.

b) The countries which have concluded double tax treaties with France containing non-discrimination clauses are as follows:

Algeria	Ecuador	Kazakhstan	Poland	Turkey
Argentina	Egypt	Korea (S)	Portugal	Ukraine
Armenia	Estonia	Latvia	Romania	United Arab
Austria	Finland	Madagascar	Russia	Emirates
Bangladesh	Ghana	Malaysia	Senegal	United
Bolivia	Hungary	Malta	Singapore	Kingdom
Brazil	Iceland	Mauritius	Slovak Rep.	USA
Bulgaria	India	Mexico	South Africa	Venezuela
Cameroon	Indonesia	Mongolia	Spain	Ex-USSR
Canada	Iran	Namibia	Sri Lanka	Yugoslavia
Chile	Israel	Netherlands	Sweden	Fed. Rep. of
China	Italy	Nigeria	Thailand	Zimbabwe
Congo	Jamaica	Norway	Trinidad &	
Cyprus	Japan	Pakistan	Tobago	
Czech Rep.	Jordan	Philippines	Tunisia	

c) The following countries have a double tax treaty with France which contains a clause of equality of treatment:

Belgium	Central	Germany	Lithuania	Niger
Benin	African	Greece	Luxembourg	Switzerland
Burkina-Faso	Republic	Ireland	Mali	Togo
	Denmark	Ivory Coast	Mauritania	
	Gabon	Lebanon	Morocco	

PART 2

Computational Rules

6. INCOME TAX

6.1. General

6.1.1 The Three Kinds of Income Tax in France

a) The basic French income tax system has proved unsuccessful at raising the sums required by the French state, due both to widespread tax evasion and to myriad exemptions and allowances which have been secured by special interest groups and taxpayers generally. To make good its fiscal deficit, successive French governments have created parallel systems to collect tax by deduction at source from investment income and to by-pass the reliefs given in the income tax system. The 'social contributions' *CSG, CRDS, PS* (see 1.6.2) can effectively be treated as additional taxes on income with no nil-rate band and a wide income base.

b) Since their introduction, almost all forms of income received by French residents are subject to social contributions of 8% (for earned income) or 11% (for investment income), and are then subject to income tax either by deduction of a flat rate of tax at source (eg bank interest) or to taxation on the income tax scale (eg earned income and rental income).

c) Where income is subject to taxation at source, the tax withheld often satisfies the taxpayer's liability to income tax, so that he has no further income tax to pay in respect of that income. The tax withheld is then said to be *libératoire*. The amount of income which has been taxed at source is required to be declared on the taxpayer's income tax return, but it is not taken into account in determining the rate of tax which applies to the taxpayer's other income. For example a taxpayer with €100,000 of bank interest received under deduction of tax at source at 29% (including social contributions) and €5,600 of earned income will suffer no tax at all on his earned income because it falls within his nil-rate income tax band. So completely distinct are the two forms of income tax that they might be regarded as separate taxes.

6.1.2 The Scheme of This Book

a) It has become necessary to deal with the social surcharges and the taxation of income by deduction of withholding taxes at source before dealing with the general income tax system.

b) This is partly a consequence of the fact that part of the social contributions are deductible from income assessable on the normal scale for the purposes of computing income tax, and partly a reflection of the relative importance of the different charges. The social contributions raise more tax than the normal income tax system.

6.2.   Territorial Basis

a) For French residents, income tax is based on worldwide income.

b) The liability of non-French residents is calculated on the basis of their French source income only.

c) The social contributions are paid by French residents. Non-residents with French source income or capital gains are not liable to any of the charges outlined in 6.3., provided that their identity is known.

6.3.   The Social Contributions

a) Better known as the acronyms *CSG, CRDS and PS*, these soon become part of the vocabulary of any new resident of France and for:

CSG: *Contribution Sociale Généralisée*, or general social contribution.

CRDS: *Contribution au Remboursement de la Dette Sociale*, contribution for the repayment of the social debt.

PS : *Prélèvement Social*, (yet another) "social levy".

b) French resident individuals pay *'CSG'* on almost all forms of income, including earned income, rental income, annuities and capital gains, the main exceptions being interest on certain savings accounts described in 6.6.11(j). The *CSG* is assessed at a rate of 8.2% on most investment income, 7.5% on earned income (salaried or not), but at the reduced rate of 6.6% on pension income, unemployment benefits and social security benefits. Earned income is reduced by 3% as an allowance for expenses before calculation of the *CSG*. The only forms of income exempt from the *CSG* (and the other social contributions listed below) are interest payments on certain exempt savings accounts. In calculating the amount of income subject to the *CSG* (and the other charges listed below), the following points should be noted:

i)   the taxpayer can deduct only 3% from his earned income in respect of expenses (instead of the income tax allowances of at least 10%).

ii) the dividend abatement of €1,525 for a single person (€3,050 for a couple) and the 40% abatement are not deductible from the *CSG* base.

iii) the charges are not equivalent to social security contributions as they do not entitle the payer to any social or health benefits.

c) In addition, a French resident individual is obliged to pay the *CRDS*. This is 0.5% of the income subject to the *CSG* i.e. earned and investment income, rental income, annuities and capital gains.

d) Investment income which is subject to the *CSG* is subject to a further 'social levy' of 2.3% *('PS et contribution additionnelle de 2.3%')*. This 2.3% charge also applies to rental income, annuities and capital gains as well as other forms of investment income including French dividends covered by the taxpayer's abatement, proceeds from life assurance policies and *PEA*s.

e) In many cases, the above charges are collected by deduction at source (eg when bank interest is credited to an account owned by a French resident). Where the tax is due by direct assessment, it is not collected if the total of the charges is less than €61.

f) The rates of social contributions on types of income and gains which are taxed at fixed rates are summarised below at 6.4.2. With regard to income and gains taxed on the progressive tax scale, the social contributions payable in 2008 are as follows:

Type of Income	CSG [1]	CRDS	PS	Total
Investment [2] and property income	8.20%	0.5%	2.3%	11%
Salaries and unemployment benefits (On 97% of the gross amounts received)	7.50%	0.5%	0%	8%
Retirement or Disability Pensions	6.60%	0.5%	0%	7.1%

Notes: [1] *Part of the CSG applicable to income taxable at scale rates (rather than fixed rates) is deductible from the following year's taxable income. The deductible portion is currently fixed at 4.2% on pensions, 5.1% on salaries and 5.8% for other source income.*

[2] *The taxable amount for dividends includes the tax credit and is retained before the application of any abatement or deduction for expenses.*

[3] *Foreign pensions may be exempt from the CSG and CRDS provided the pensioner is eligible to continued health cover under one of the DSS forms (E121, E106) or another form of health cover provided by his country of origin. Foreign investment income (interest, dividends and commercial annuities) and gains are not exempt from these charges.*

g) Part of the *CSG* paid in respect of income taxed at scale rates (*barème*) as opposed to fixed rates, is deductible (see notes). This has to be considered when opting for taxation at source rates on investment income for instance.

6.4. Income Taxed at Fixed Rates

6.4.1 General

a) Fixed interest income and the redemptions from life assurance contracts, *Plans d'Épargne Populaire* and *Plans d'Épargne en Actions* are subject to withholding taxes at source. In principle, for a French resident, these withholding taxes are optional but in practice most taxpayers will wish to avail themselves of the option because their marginal rate of tax on the normal income tax scale will be higher than the withholding tax rate.

b) Withholding taxes are described in chapter 13, more specifically from the point of view of non-residents, but the rates are recapitulated here with the social contributions included, for the benefit of French residents.

c) In addition, capital gains on sales of shares and securities are taxed at fixed rates, as we shall see in chapter 8, and it is convenient to schedule these here.

d) Where the taxpayer elects to suffer the optional withholding taxes, the social contributions are deducted at source by the paying establishment.

6.4.2 Fixed Tax Rates

a) The table on the following page shows the 2008 scale of fixed tax rates.

b) In the table, 'Interest' includes interest on bank accounts (other than exempt savings accounts such as the *Livret A* etc), corporate bonds, shareholders loan accounts, and certificates of deposit.

c) The section headed 'French Life Assurance – old policies and *fonds turbo'* applies to the proceeds of life assurance policies and 'investment bonds' issued by a French insurance company or by a French branch of a foreign insurance company which correspond to:

i) premiums paid on or before 25 September 1997; or

ii) premiums paid after 25 September 1997 on contracts entered into before that date which provide for regular periodic premiums, not exceeding those prescribed in the original contract; or

iii) single premiums paid under the terms of the contract during the period from 26 September to 31 December 1997; or

iv) premiums paid during the period 26 September to 31 December 1997, over-and-above the regular premiums reserved under the contract, up to a maximum additional contribution of €30,500 per person (ie both husband and wife were able to pay additional premiums of €30,500 during this period).

and to policies issued after 25 September 1997 which are denominated in units of account (rather than in Euros) and invested in certain forms of equity-based collective investment scheme *('fonds turbo' or 'DSK' funds)*. The underlying investments must be shares issued by companies which have their registered office in France or in another EU country, and at least 50% of the underlying investments must be quoted shares. At least 5% of the underlying shares must be shares in unquoted companies (outside the financial services and property-letting sectors) or venture capital funds.

d) The proceeds of all other French life assurance contracts are subject to the rates of tax listed under 'French Life Assurance – other policies'.

e) The withholding taxes are available to policies issued by certain foreign insurance companies that do not have a permanent establishment in France (see f below).

2008 INCOME/GAIN

	Income Tax %	CSG/CRDS %	Other %	Total %
French Bank Interest	18.0	8.7	2.3	29.0
PEPs [1] withdrawals				
within 4 years	35.0	8.7	2.3	46.0
between 4 and 8 years	18.0	8.7	2.3	27.0
after 8 years	0.0	8.7	2.3	11.0
PEAs withdrawals				
within 2 years	22.5	8.7	2.3	33.5
between 2 and 5 years	18.0	8.7	2.3	29.0
after 5 years	0.0	8.7	2.3	11.0
French Life Assurance – *'old policies' and 'fonds turbo'* withdrawals				
within 4 years	35.0	8.7	2.3	46.0
between 4 and 8 years	16.0	8.7	2.3	27.0
after 8 years	0.0	8.7	2.3	11.0
French Life Assurance – *other policies*				
withdrawals				
within 4 years	35.0	8.7	2.3	46.0
between 4 and 8 years	16.0	8.7	2.3	26.0
after 8 years	7.5 [2]	8.7	2.3	18.5
Capital Gains on Shares	18.0	8.7	2.3	29.0

Notes:
[1] Since 25 September 2003, it is no longer possible to open a new *PEP*.

rate of tax applied to excess of redemptions over abatements of €4,600 per annum (single person) or €9,200 (couple).

(3) Interest paid on a *Livret Bleu* account *(Credit Mutuel)* is taxed at 9% (including social contributions).

f) The European Commission's infringement procedure against France regarding the discrimination in the application of the taxation at source option has finally led to changes in the French legislation. The benefit of the taxation at source rates now extends to the increase in value of life assurance proceeds, interest and dividends paid by financial establishments which are resident:

(i) In EU member countries

(ii) In EEA countries (excluding Liechtenstein) which have signed a double tax treaty containing a clause providing mutual assistance against tax fraud.

g) Full details of the investment or account and income have to be declared within 15 days following the end of the month in which the income is paid. The relevant form 2778 can be obtained from local tax offices. The establishment nominated by the taxpayer or the taxpayer himself has to file this form and pay the tax at the appropriate rate. In the case of long-term savings schemes such as life assurance policies, the rate of tax depends on how long the policy has been held. Foreign policies are likely to be scrutinised by the authorities to ensure that they comply with the *Code des Assurances* and cannot be considered as mere capitalisation bonds.

h) The option is irrevocable for any given payment, and in the absence of any adequate filing and tax payment, the income is taxed at normal *barème* rates.

i) Taxpayers who receive regular income from foreign financial products or companies during the tax year should check with their insurers/financial establishments how they may benefit from the option for the French "tax at source" rates and what measures the establishments have in place with regards to this. The establishment should at least produce a certificate showing the income or increase in value paid and exact date of payment.

j) The efficiency of the system dependents on the foreign financial establishments' facilities in reporting the relevant information in a format acceptable to the French authorities. Nevertheless, as far as the French administration is concerned they have now complied with EU regulations. In practice, it is really up to the taxpayer to ensure that the tax payment is made within the required time limits (see (g)), and to keep a close record of when income payments are expected. Depending on the frequency of income payments this leads to increased formalities, which often deters taxpayers from using the option on their foreign source income. It is also important to note that the option for the taxation at source leads to the loss of the deductible *CSG* and in the case of dividends, the loss of the abatements and tax credit normally granted to this type of income (see 6.6.8).

6.5. Income Taxed on the Income Tax Scale

a) Tax on earned income, business income, agricultural income, rental income, dividend income, gains on foreign life assurance contracts, some short term capital gains and capital gains on land is calculated using a progressive scale of income tax rates (the *barème de l'impôt sur le revenu*).

b) These forms of income are also subject to the social contributions, (*CSG, CRDS, PS*) which are collected, alongside the income tax liabilities, by direct assessment on the taxpayer. Part of the *CSG* charge (5.8%) is deductible from the following year's taxable income (see 6.3).

6.6. Computation of Gross Income

6.6.1 Classification of Taxable Sources of Income

Income assessable in the hands of an individual is divided into seven classes:

i) Property income (*revenus fonciers*);

ii) Industrial or commercial profits (*bénéfices industriels et commerciaux*);

iii) Certain directors remuneration (*rémunerations des dirigeants de sociétés*);

iv) Agricultural profits (*bénéfices agricoles*);

v) Wages, salaries, pensions and life annuities (*traitements, salaires, pensions et rentes viagères*);

vi) Non-commercial profits (*bénéfices non commerciaux*);

vii) Investment income (*revenus de capitaux mobiliers*).

6.6.2 Property Income

a) Property income comprises rents, income from advertising hoardings, hunting rights and most other forms of income derived from land apart from income from buildings used in the activities of a business and income from furnished lettings (which is classed as commercial income). No distinction is made in principle between property in France and property outside France, although under many of France's double tax agreements income from real estate is taxable only in the country in which the real estate is situated.

b) Certain non-resident individuals who have at their disposal a house or flat in France are subject to French income tax on a notional income (*base forfaitaire*) equal to three times the annual rental value of the house (or houses), unless their actual French source income is greater. This applies not only if they own residential property in France, but also if they rent it, have a usufruct over it or have the use of the property as a shareholder in a company which owns it. The rental value is determined by comparison with other rented properties in the area. Income tax is then computed applying the normal tax rates.

c) However for most non-residents this notional income basis does not apply, because they are either:

i) resident in a country which has concluded a double tax treaty with France which suppresses this French tax rule; or

ii) they are French nationals or a nationals of a country which has concluded a treaty of reciprocity with France and they can prove that they are subject to income tax in the country where they are resident on all of their income and that they pay tax of at least two-thirds of that which they would have suffered had they been resident in France.

iii) more generally, the French Administration do not apply this taxation to residents of a double tax treaty partner country, unless there is a specific provision for the application of the rule in the treaty.

d) This rule therefore affects residents of Hong Kong, the Channel Islands, Andorra etc, which are territories which do not have double tax treaties with France (France does not accept that its double tax treaty with China extends to Hong Kong). For residents of Monaco the position is complex. According to a doctrine of the French tax administration, French and Monegasque nationals resident in Monaco are permitted one holiday home in France without paying tax on this basis, provided the home is located in the Provence-Alpes-Côte d'Azur region. Following a Supreme Court ruling, nationals of any country which has a double tax treaty with France prohibiting discrimination against nationals of the contracting states, wherever resident, and who reside in Monaco are not subject to the taxation on national income on any one property they own in the region of Provence-Alpes-Côte d'Azur. The countries which have signed a double tax treaty with France containing a non-discrimination clause are listed in 5.8.7(b).

e) The French resident owner of a residential property is not deemed to have an income from it if he does not in fact receive any income. Equally he cannot deduct from his income any of the expenses related to the property. The same principles apply to shareholders in fiscally transparent property holding companies and time share companies.

f) Rent from lettings of furnished property is classed as commercial income and the taxable income is calculated under the rules described in 6.6.3.

g) Income from unfurnished lettings is calculated on a calendar year basis, and is generally exempt from VAT. The net taxable amount is determined depending on the level of annual rents received. If the total gross annual rental income received in 2007 does not exceed €15,000, the landlord is automatically assessed under the *Micro-Foncier* regime. Under this regime 30% of the gross rent is deducted as representing the total amount of expenses related to the rental income. The €15,000 limit applies for the whole tax year and is adjusted pro-rata temporis if the activity only takes place during part of the year. The limit is not pro-rated for the year when the letting activity started or ended.

h) The *Micro-Foncier* does not apply to landlords who benefit from other tax advantages, such as owners of historic monuments and landlords who benefit from accelerated depreciation allowances. The shareholders of an SCI who receive a share of unfurnished rental income may benefit from the *Micro-Foncier*, but only if they personally hold at least one property which is also rented out unfurnished, and if the total income together with the share of SCI rental income does not exceed €15,000.

i) Lettings outside the scope of the *Micro-Foncier* are assessed under the normal *foncier* regime, which allows the deduction of a wide range of expenses including, repairs and maintenance, improvements to residential property (but not expenses of construction, reconstruction or enlargement), management expenses and pay for *concierges*, insurance property taxes, loan interest, certain restoration works etc. The fixed general deduction of 14% was suppressed from 1 January 2006. Instead, landlords may deduct itemised management and property insurance costs as well as a €20 set amount per property for postage and telephone.

j) Landlords under the scope of the *Micro-Foncier* regime may opt for the normal regime simply by filing the necessary annex tax form 2044 when they declare their rental income. This option is irrevocable for a period of three years, after which the taxpayer may change the regime every year.

k) In order to replenish and improve the stock of dwellings offered on the rental market the French system offers a variety of tax schemes for the benefit of owners who undertake to rent their refurbished properties during a minimum period. The tax advantages of the rental schemes are usually subject to conditions such as, the length or value of the lease, the type of building and resources of the tenants. The numerous constraints and incessant amendments to the conditions or the schemes themselves often mean that in practice, they are not as attractive as anticipated. Anyone considering renting under a *"Borloo", "Robien"* etc rental scheme must obtain up to date details of the specific rules. Below is a chart summary of the main rules applicable for each scheme at the time of going to print:

Schemes	Dates of eligibility	Conditions			Advantages
		Length & type of lease	Type of building	Other conditions	
Amortissement Périssol	from 01/01/1996 to 31/08/1999	9 years unfurnished Main or second home of tenants	New		Depreciation of 10% of purchase price for 4 years. 2% for the following 20 years same depreciation for any structural work improvements are depreciated at 10%. Annual deduction of losses from general taxable income allowed up to €15,300.
Robien Classique	from 01/01/2003 to 31/08/2006	9 years unfurnished Main home of tenants within 1 year of completion of work	New	Rent/sqm² fixed between €10.51 and €21.02 depending on the situation of the dwelling	Depreciation 8% of purchase price for 5 years. 2.5% for the following 4 years, renewable twice for 3 years. Depreciation of renovation and reconstruction costs, improvements are depreciated at 10%. Annual deduction of losses from general taxable income allowed up to €10,700.
Robien recentré	from 01/09/2006	9 years unfurnished Main home of tenants within 1 year of completion of work	New build and ancient to be converted into rented accommodation	Rents/sqm² fixed between €8.76 and €21.02 depending on the situation of the dwelling	Depreciation 6% of purchase price and costs for 7 years. 4% for the following 2 years, non-renewable (max 50%). Depreciation of renovation and reconstruction costs, improvements are depreciated at 10%. Annual deduction of losses from general taxable income allowed up to €10,700.
Robien ZRR	from 01/01/2004	9 years unfurnished Main home of tenants within 1 year of completion of work	New build and ancient to be converted into rented accommodation	Situated in specific rural zones targeted for redevelopment	Specific rental income deduction of 16%. Depreciation 6% of purchase price and costs for 7 years, 4% for the following 2 years, non-renewable (max 50%), depreciation of renovation and reconstruction costs, improvements are depreciated at 10%. Annual deduction of losses from general taxable income allowed up to €10,700.
Borloo neuf	from 01/09/2006 or from 01/01/2006 *if retrospective option to Robien recentré*	9 years unfurnished Main home of tenants within 1 year of completion of work unauthorised use or rental by relatives	New build	Must have opted for the regime, *Robien recentré* rents/sqm² fixed between €7.01 and €16.82 depending on the situation of the dwelling. Means tested with a maximum annual income of a single tenant fixed between €28,672 and €42,396 depending on the situation of the building (1).	Specific rental income deduction of 30%, depreciation 6% of purchase price and costs for 7 years, 4% for the following 2 years, renewable twice for 3 years, depreciation of renovation and reconstruction costs, improvements are depreciated at 10%. Annual deduction of losses from general taxable income allowed up to €10,700.

Borloo ancien	from 01/10/2006	Unfurnished Main home of tenants	New or *ancien*	Contract with ANAH (*Agence Nationale pour l'Habitat*), same limit of rents and tenants' resources as for *Besson ancien* or if in social sectors rents/sqm² fixed between €4.76 and €16.81 and subject to lower resources limits fixed by the *Ministère du Logement*	Specific rental income deduction of 30% or 45% if in social sectors may be combined with advantages of "vacant dwellings put up for rental".
Besson amortisement	from 01/01/1999 to 02/04/2003	9 years unfurnished Main home of tenants Use or rental by relatives authorised under strict conditions	New build	Rents per sqm² fixed between €9.71 and €15.06. Means tested with same limits as for *Borloo neuf*.	Depreciation 8% of purchase price for 5 years, 2.5% for the following 4 years, renewable twice for 3 years, i.e. a total of 50% over 9 years or 65% over 15 years, same depreciation for any structural work improvements are depreciated at 10% for 10 years. Annual deduction of losses from general taxable income allowed up to €10,700.
Besson ancien	from 01/01/1999 to 30/09/2006	6 years unfurnished. Main home of tenants	Ancient dwellings	Rents/sqm², fixed between €7.95 and €16.81. Means tested with same limits as for *Borloo neuf*.	Specific rental income deduction of 26% for the first 6 years, renewable for 3 years, even if by then the tenant's income exceeds the limit. Annual deduction of losses from general taxable income up to €10,700.
Loi Malraux		6 years and within 1 year of completion of work. Unfurnished and main home of tenants	Specific buildings in designated protected zones must be kept for 6 years at least		Deduction of demolition and reconstruction or renovation and transformation costs, losses are deductible from general taxable income except loan interest.
Principal residence rented out for professional reasons	New professional activity starting between 01/07/05 and 31/12/07		Ex-principal home of landlord	The owner must have a new home (rented) within a year of starting his new job and over 200km away from the previous dwelling.	Extra 10% deduction of gross rental income up to 31 December of the 3rd year following the start of the rentals or up to the purchase date of a new principal home.
Scheme for vacant dwellings put up for rental	up to 31/12/07 and valid for 2 years	Unfurnished rentals, main or second home of tenants who may be relatives	Must have been vacant for the year prior to the start of the lease		Deduction of 30% of gross rental income up to 31 December of the 2nd year following the start of the rentals.

Notes:

1) 2008 limits. Other limits apply for couples and/or dependants and limits vary depending on the situation of the buildings.
2) The limitation of the rents and the condition relating to the tenants' resources can make these schemes unattractive and exposed to sitting tenants' complications.
3) The advantages may apply to companies (SCI, SCPI) under specific conditions.
4) The *Lienemann* scheme was suppressed from 1 January 2005.
5) The non-respect of the conditions leads to a termination of the advantages and a payment of the tax difference.

6.6.3 Industrial or Commercial Profits

a) Industrial or commercial profits cover professional, commercial and artisanal income, including the rent of furnished lettings, earned by individuals. In addition members of the *sociétés* listed in 3.2.2. and 3.3. which have a commercial, industrial, artisanal or mining activity are usually taxable under this category in respect of their shares of the profits of the *société*. Taxable profits are computed under one of three regimes:

   i) Under the *Micro-BIC* regime, a business which is not subject to corporation tax and which has a turnover which does not exceed €76,300 (for businesses which sell goods or provide furnished lodgings, which will be referred to in the remainder of this paragraph as 'the first category') or €27,000 (for all other industrial or commercial businesses, or 'the second category') can pay tax on its turnover reduced by an abatement of 71% (for the first category) or 50% (for the second category) of its turnover or €305, whichever is the greater. These turnover limits are also the limits for exemption from the requirement to register for VAT. The regime may also be used by a taxpayer when his turnover exceeds the relevant limit for the first time and for a period of 2 years maximum. But in that case the abatement is restricted to 71% of €84,000 or 50% of €30,500 (as appropriate), and the surplus turnover is treated as income. A taxpayer who qualifies for the *Micro-BIC* regime can opt for one of the 'real' regimes described below.

   ii) The 'simplified real regime' (*régime du réel simplifié*) applies to businesses excluded from the *Micro-BIC* regime (including businesses which pay corporation tax) which have a turnover of less than €763,000 (if selling goods or providing lodgings) or €230,000 (if engaged in other businesses). Computations are produced under normal principles, but the reporting and accounting requirements are simplified. A taxpayer who qualifies for this regime can elect for the normal real regime if he prefers.

   iii) The 'normal real regime' (*régime du réel normal*) is the basic business tax regime applying to all larger businesses.

b) The rules for the computation of industrial or commercial profits are also used for the computation of profits for corporation tax purposes, and are explained in greater detail in 7.3. However there are differences between the rules applicable to a company subject to corporation tax and a company in which the shareholders are subject to income tax. Clearly, where a business is carried on by a sole trader or a fiscally transparent company or partnership, a distinction has to be made between the business assets and the private assets of the proprietors for the purposes of calculating depreciation and capital gains. Beyond that the main distinctions are:

   i) Remuneration paid to the owners of a fiscally transparent company is not deductible in computing the profits of the company – this simply constitutes part of their business income.

ii) A salary paid to the spouse of a sole trader or of a partner in a fiscally transparent company is only deductible up to €13,800 (and adjustable depending on working hours), if the couple is married under community property rules or under the regime of *participation aux acquêts*. If the company's accounts are maintained by a *Centre de Gestion Agrée* (*CGA*) the wage is deductible in full.

iii) Contributions paid to compulsory pension insurances are deductible without limitation. Voluntary additional pension and unemployment contributions (*régime supplémentaire* and *régimes complémentaires de prévoyance et perte d'emploi*) are also deductible but within specific limits fixed every year.

c) Before 2006, a fiscally transparent business subject to a 'real' tax regime and registered with a *CGA* (see 1.14.3) could deduct 20% from its net profits, up to a limit of €120,100 (2005). Now the 20% abatement is integrated to the *barème* bands. Taxpayers who are not registered with a *CGA* have to increase their net taxable income by 25% to neutralise the favourable effects of the new *barème*. If registered, the taxpayer can claim a tax credit for the *CGA* registration cost, up to a maximum of €915 per annum. The registration with the *CGA* must be made within the first five months of the accountancy period, i.e. by 30 April for a 31 December year-end.

d) Fiscally transparent companies cannot benefit from the option accorded to companies which suffer corporation tax to write off their research and development expenditure (including the costs of writing computer programs) in the year in which it is incurred.

e) Investment income (eg dividends from other companies) is treated differently.

f) In general terms, taxpayers who suffer 'industrial or commercial' losses in respect of an income-tax paying business can offset the losses against any of the taxpayer's other income of the same year or the next 6 years **only if** the taxpayer or a member of his household is working full-time in the business. If the latter condition is not fulfilled, the losses are regarded as 'non-professional' industrial or commercial losses, and they can be relieved only against the taxpayer's other 'non-professional' income of the same category for the tax year in which they are incurred or the next 6 years. For taxpayers who let furnished accommodation, the new rules actually enlarge the scope for relieving losses, since a loss sustained in a new business of furnished lettings can be offset against income of any other 'non-professional' business taxed in the industrial or commercial category. For such taxpayers the existing distinction between 'professional' and 'non-professional' landlords is retained (see 18.2.2(p)).

6.6.4 Certain Directors' Remuneration

a) Several different regimes exist for the taxation of director's remuneration according to the type of company in which the office is held. Directors of fiscally transparent companies are taxed like partners in a partnership.

b) Directors of companies that are subject to French corporation tax are generally taxed under rules similar to those for any other employee (see 6.6.6. below). Salaried directors may deduct their contributions to retirement savings plans within the same limits as those for salaried employees. Other directors and in particular majority shareholder directors are subject to the rules applicable to individuals who receive professional earnings classed as non-commercial income.

c) In some cases the remuneration paid to a director can be reclassified as a distribution. There are special rules relating to controlling managers of *SARLs*. They may not deduct the allowance for expenses of 10% of their salary, which is available to other employees (see 6.6.6(b)(i)), but can claim for their real expenses. The amounts paid to such individuals are assessed as income of the year in which they are received, even if they were charged against the profits of an earlier year of the company's accounts. Similar rules apply to the income of the managing partners of a *société en commandite par actions*.

d) The members of the supervisory board or the administrative board of an *SA* are sometimes paid attendance fees *(jetons de présence)*. These are treated as investment income.

6.6.5 Agricultural Profits

a) Agricultural profits are assessable under three alternative regimes, depending on the level of turnover.

   i) A *'forfait'* regime applies to those whose agricultural turnover does not exceed €76,300 per annum on average over the preceding two years. Incidental commercial or non-commercial income from tourism on the farm, trading in produce, forestry work for third parties, etc, is taxable separately as per the *bénéfices industriels et commerciaux* or *bénéfices non-commerciaux* rules described in 6.6.3. and 6.6.7. Where the incidental income exceeds the limits for smaller company tax regimes (micro regimes), all profits (agricultural and non-agricultural) are taxed under the relevant category of 'simplified real regime' or 'normal real regime'.

   ii) The 'simplified real regime' applies to farmers with a turnover of more than €76,300 and less than €350,000. Under this regime income is calculated using normal principles, but simplified in relation to accounting provisions, stocks, the farmer's consumption of his own products and his reporting requirements.

iii) The 'normal real regimè' applies to farmers with a turnover exceeding €350,000. They must compute their income using normal accounting principles. The rules of taxation of any non-agricultural incidental income are the same as those applicable under the 'simplified real regime'.

b) Farmers assessed under a 'real' regime can declare incidental income of up to 30% of their agricultural turnover or €50,000, whichever is higher, as part of their agricultural income (ie. not as commercial or non-commercial profits taxable under another category). This limit is increased to 50% or €100,000 if the accessory income concerns the windpowered production of electricity or photovoltaïque. Any deficit origination from those side-line activities is not deductible from the overall income of the taxpayer, as from 1 January 2007.

c) Taxpayers who suffer agricultural losses can offset the losses against income of any other category provided that their total net income (excluding agricultural income) does not exceed €101,300. If so any excess losses may be carried forward for up to six years.

d) From 2006 farmers are subject to the same accounting rules as those applicable to the *Bénéfices Industriels at Commerciaux*. The 20% abatement granted up until then to those registered with *CGA* is now integrated to the *barème* income bands. Agricultural businesses which are not registered with a *CGA* now have to increase their net taxable income by 25% to compensate for the favourable effects of the new *barème*.

e) The salary paid to the spouse is deductible in full if the farmer is registered with a *CGA*. If not the deduction is limited to €13,800.

f) Farmers may deduct their compulsory pension contributions without limitation. Deductions in respect of additional voluntary contributions paid into group insurance contracts are allowed but within specific limits fixed every year.

g) Young farmers benefit from a specific favourable regime for the first five years of activity.

h) Farmers may claim a tax credit for tax years 2008 to 2010 during which they can show that at least 40% of their turnover originates from organic farming *(agriculture biologique)*. The tax credit is €1,200 increased by €200 per hectare (limited to €800 in total) used for organic farming.

6.6.6 *Wages, Salaries, Pensions and Life Annuities*

a) Wages, salaries, pensions and life annuities are taxable after deductions for social security contributions, for expenses and for interest on certain loans as described below. Benefits in kind are included in the total remuneration at their market value.

b) The employee can deduct the following expenses:

  i)   10% of his net wage or salary (subject to a minimum of €401 (€880 for those previously long term unemployed) and a maximum of €13,501) for expenses. These limits apply to 2007 earnings.

  ii) anyone may itemise their actual expenses and claim additional deductions if their actual expenses exceed their standard deductions. The expenses which may be claimed include the costs of private cars used for business purposes, which include the expenses of travelling to work.

  iii) journalists benefit from a special supplementary deduction for expenses of €7,650.

  iv) the 20% abatement applicable up to 2005, is now integrated in the income bands of the income tax scale or *barème* (see 6.11.1)

  v)   interest on loans contracted to enable the taxpayer to subscribe to the capital of a new industrial or commercial company or a cooperative resulting from the reconstruction of a company, or in the course of a management buy-out.

  vi) his pension contributions: The compulsory legal basic and comple-mentary pension contributions are deductible in full. Salaried employees also benefit from a deduction in respect of additional optional pension contributions but these are limited to maximums of €20,598 (2007) and €21,297 (2008) for *the retraite supplémentaire* and €7,724 (2007) and €7,986 (2008) for the *prévoyance complémentaire*.

c) Special rules apply to employee share option schemes. For quoted shares, the option price may not be less than 80% of the average price of the shares in the last 20 account periods of the stock exchange preceding the day on which the option is granted. The option price of unquoted shares must be equal to their value, as certified by the company in general meeting, or, if the company holds shares for attribution to employees, to at least 80% of their value. For options issued after 1 January 1990, if the option price is more than 5% below the market value, the discount is taxed as salary when the option is exercised. Otherwise there is no tax on the issue or exercise of the option.

The French tax system differentiates two types of gains relating to stock options:

  i)   The acquisition gain which is the difference between the value of the stock at the time the option is exercised, and the value of the same stock at the time the option was granted.

  ii) The gain on the disposal, calculated as the difference between the sale price and the value of the stock when the option was exercised.

  iii) The discount is the difference between the price at which the option was granted and the value of the share at the date the option was granted.

If the discount exceeds 5%, the excess is taxed as a salary at the time the option is exercised. Numerous changes to the taxation rules applicable to stock options have increased the complexity of the whole treatment. The current system is best illustrated in the following chart.

STOCK OPTIONS		GAINS ON DISPOSAL
Granting of the Options	Exercise of the Options	Sale of the shares
	Market value of the shares	
1) Sale within 5 years from the granting of the option (minimum holding period). 4 years for options granted after 27 April 2000. Taxation as a salary (income tax rates) plus social surcharges of 11%. 2) Sale 5 years <u>or more</u> after the granting of the option. 4 years for options granted after 27 April 2000.		
• For options granted before 27 April 2000: tax at 41%. • For options granted after 27 April 2002:	Taxation at rate for capital gains tax on disposals of investment holdings exceeding €25,000 (2008)	
i) 41%, up to €152,500 on gains, 51% thereafter. ii) If the shares are held for a further 2 years (after the minimum 4 year holding period), 29% on gains up to €152,500, 41% thereafter.	29% (including social surcharges)	

d) Until 31 December 1999, certain companies were able to issue 'subscription bonds' to employees. These gave the employee the right to subscribe for shares at a price fixed by the company when the shares were issued. The bonds themselves cannot be sold by the employee, but any gains on the shares issued to the employee are taxable as capital gains. This means that they escape tax if the employee's sales of shares (of all kinds) do not exceed €20,000 in 2007 and €25,000 from 2008 in the year and they suffer tax at 29% (including social surcharges) if they do. However if the employee has worked for the company for less than 3 years, the rate of tax on any gain is increased to 30% (ie 41% including the social surcharges). The gains are also exempt from the normal social insurance contributions described in 1.6.3.(c). To be able to issue subscription bonds:

i) the company had to have been registered for less than 15 years (7 years for subscriptions before 1 September 1998);

ii) the company had to be subject to French corporation tax;

iii) the company could not be engaged in banking, finance, insurance, or management or letting of property;

iv) the capital of the company had to be owned at least 75% by individuals or companies owned by individuals; and

v) the company had generally not been the result of a restructuring of a pre-existing business.

e) Every business with more than 50 employees is required to operate a profit sharing scheme for its employees. The amounts distributed to each employee are exempt from income tax in the hands of the employee if under the terms of the scheme the employee is unable to dispose of the income for at least 5 years, for example under a save-as-you-earn scheme. The payments remain subject to the *CSG*.

f) An employer's contribution towards luncheon vouchers (*titres restaurant*) is exempt from tax in the hands of the employee up to a limit of €5.04 per voucher.

g) The employer's contribution towards holiday vouchers (*chèques-vacances*) is exempt from tax in the hands of the employee up to the limit of the monthly minimum wage. Holiday vouchers can only be given to employees whose income does not exceed certain limits revised every year.

h) Two different scales of deductions from pension income apply, depending on whether the pension is received by the taxpayer in consideration for payments made by him or not.

i) When the pension is an annuity (*rente viagère*) purchased by the taxpayer either for cash or in exchange for property (eg a house), only part of the annuity received is taxable. The percentage that is taxable depends on the age of the taxpayer according to the following scale:

	%
under 50	70
between 50 and 59	50
between 60 and 69	40
over 69	30

ii) When the pension is paid by a former employer, an abatement of 10% applies with a minimum of €357 per pensioner and a maximum of €3,491 per household. Up to 2005 the net amount was reduced by a general abatement of 20% up to a maximum amount of pension of €120,100.

This abatement is cancelled as it is now integrated in the income bands of the income tax scale (see 6.11.1).

    iii) In France, the state pension, which is means tested, is exempt from tax.

i)   A French resident employee who is seconded abroad by a French employer can be exempt from tax in respect of his earnings for the assignment (see 6.6.11(f)).

j)   An expatriate working in France for a foreign company can be exempt from tax on part of the earnings he receives for this assignment (see 6.6.11(g)).

6.6.7   Non-Commercial Profits

a)   'Non-commercial profits' include profits of 'liberal professions', for example lawyers, doctors, auditors and architects and the remuneration of certain office holders, such as notaries, process servers and clerks to tribunals. There are two systems of taxation in this category:

    i)   Under the *régime déclaratif spécial (Micro BNC)*, if the taxpayer is not a public office holder (eg a *notaire*) and his receipts do not exceed €27,000 (excluding VAT) in the calendar year, the taxable income is normally calculated on the basis of the receipts less an abatement of 34% for expenses (minimum €305). The taxpayer can elect to be taxed on his actual income if he prefers. He might wish to do so in order to offset any non-commercial losses against his other sources of income.

    ii)   If the taxpayer is a public office holder, or his receipts exceed €27,000, he must declare his exact income. This is called the *régime de la déclaration contrôlée*.

b)   Self-employed professionals who are not registered with a *CGA* have to increase their net payable income by 25% to neutralise the favourable effects of the new *barème*.

c)   Self employed professionals may deduct their compulsory pension contributions without limitations and the contributions to voluntary additional schemes subject to specific limitations revised every year.

6.6.8   Investment Income

a)   'Investment income' covers only income from investments in bonds, shares, shareholders' loan accounts and cash, and gains on money funds. Income from investment in land is taxed as described in 6.6.2 above. As we have already seen, fixed interest income is generally subject to tax by withholding at source (although the income can be assessed at normal scale rates if the taxpayer prefers).

b) There are three categories of investment income for tax purposes:

    i) Dividends and distributions from French or EU companies and companies resident in a country which has signed a double tax treaty with France benefit from a 40% abatement. From 1 January 2009, this will be restricted to distributions from companies resident in a country with a treaty clause providing mutual assistance against tax fraud (see 5.8.7(a)). This leaves a few years for the non-participating countries (e.g. Switzerland) to re-negotiate the terms of their treaty with France. A dividend tax credit is also granted to French residents or residents of a country which has signed a double tax treaty with France containing an agreement on the refund of the former *avoir fiscal*. The credit is calculated as 50% of the distribution, and applies before the 40% abatement described above. It is limited to €115 for a single person and €230 for a couple.

       From 1 January 2008, dividends can be taxed at source at a rate of 18% if the taxpayer expressly opts to do so. The extra 11% social surcharges are now levied at source in all cases, that is to say, whether the dividend is taxed as *barème* rates or at source. It is very important to note that the taxation at source of dividends leads to the loss of the 40% abatement, tax credit and tax free annual abatement of €1,050 (per person). In fact the option, even if exercised in respect of a single dividend payment in the tax year, leads to the loss of these advantages. It is difficult to determine precisely the benefit of the taxation at source at the time the option must be exercised. In some cases, the *barème* rate will not be known to the taxpayer until year end when all his income is known and computed according the new rules in place. In practice dividends taxed at the 30% tax band rate suffer an effective tax rate of around 16.3% (after application of the abatements etc). This increases to around 21.7% for those subject to the 40% rate band, so the advantage of the taxation at source option seems to only concern higher rate taxpayers. The deductible *CSG* will continue to be granted in respect of dividends taxed at *barème* rates, but it does not apply if the taxation at source is opted for.

    ii) Interest received is either added to the rest of the taxpayer's income and taxed at *barème* rates, or by option, it is taxed at source (see 6.4.2). The tax withheld then constitutes a final liability *(prélèvement forfaitaire libératoire)*. In this case the interest is not included in the taxpayer's income assessable under the income tax scale.

    iii) All overseas source investment income, converted into Euros, is added to taxable income. Where the income derives from a country with which France has a double tax treaty providing credit for foreign taxes suffered on investment income, the creditable foreign tax has to be added to the net dividends or interest received. The option for taxation at source is now possible for investment income (interest, dividend,or increase in value) originating from investment companies established in EU and certain EEA countries (see 6.4.2(f)).

c) A French resident taxpayer is entitled to an annual allowance for dividends, and interest on blocked shareholders' loan accounts, received from French or qualifying foreign companies (see (b)(i) above). The allowance is €1,525 for a single person and €3,050 for a couple (per household).

d) A shareholder or partner in a business who makes finance available to the business in the form of a blocked loan account, which will within 5 years be converted into capital, can elect that the interest received on the loan will be subject to a *prélèvement forfaitaire libératoire* at the rate of 29% (18% for non-residents). The rate of interest may not exceed the maximum rate which may legally be paid to shareholders (ie 5.41% for 2007).

e) An individual who holds a deep-discount security pays income tax on the gain realised at the maturity of the investment, not on an accrued income basis.

f) Taxpayers who have foreign, i.e. non-French, bank/building society accounts and life assurance policies are obliged to declare these to the French tax authorities when filing their return. Lists should be set out on plain paper, stating the name and address of the establishment, the account/policy number and reference and the date that it was opened/taken out. Failure to provide these details could result in a fine of 25% of the value of any payments made into any policy(ies) during the tax year and €750 per undeclared account.

6.6.9 Exceptional Income

a) If a taxpayer receives an exceptional income during the tax year, he may apply a special treatment to this to attenuate the effects of the *barème* and not suffer the higher rates unduly as a result of declaring the whole amount in the relevant tax year.

b) The tax is calculated by adding one-fourth of the payment to the household's income in the year of receipt. The resulting increase in the tax due is then multiplied by four.

6.6.10 Basis Periods

a) In general income tax is assessed each year in the name of, and on the basis of the income arising to the taxpayer in the preceding year. Thus the assessment for 2007 is raised in 2008, and the 2007 tax liability is paid in 2008.

b) However if a commercial business keeps annual accounts to a date other than 31 December, the income is calculated on the basis of the accounting period ended in the year of assessment. For example the income of a year ended 30 September 2007 is assessed as the income of 2007, and the assessment will be raised and the tax will be paid in 2008.

c) Non-commercial businesses pay tax on the basis of the income of the previous calendar year. Thus in 2008 they will pay tax assessed for 2007, based on their income for the calendar year 2007.

6.6.11 *Exempt Income*

There are many forms of income which are exempt from French income tax, of which the following are examples:

a) Income accruing in a qualifying savings scheme (*plan d'épargne populaire* or *PEP*) is exempt. Provided the savings plan (which may be a life assurance contract) lasts for at least 8 years the proceeds are exempt from income tax (but not the 11% social surcharges). Earlier redemptions are taxed at fixed rates (see 6.4.2). It is no longer possible to open a new *PEP*, but the favourable tax regime continues to apply to all *PEPs* set up before that date.

b) Income accruing in a qualifying personal equity plan (*plan d'épargne en actions* or *PEA*) is exempt. Provided that the taxpayer does not withdraw funds from the scheme for at least 5 years, the income and gains accruing in the scheme are free of income tax (but the 11% social surcharges apply). Earlier withdrawals result in tax on the increase in value under the capital gains tax regime for sales of securities, so that if the total proceeds of the taxpayer's disposals of equity investments exceeds €20,000 (2007) (€25,000 from 2008) the gains are taxed at the rate of 29% (with the social surcharges). However if the redemption occurs in the first two years, the rate is increased to 33.5% (with the social surcharges). A taxpayer who redeems a *PEA* before 5 years and invests the proceeds into a newly created company or business within 3 months, may benefit from an exemption. In this instance, the proceeds are not taken into account for the purpose of the €20,000 (2007) (€25,000 from 2008) disposal limit. However, the increase in value remains subject to the 11% social surcharges.

c) Reasonable rent from the letting of part of an individual's principal residence is exempt if the property let constitutes the principal residence of the tenant.

d) Rent of up to €760 a year from short-term letting of rooms (eg as *chambres d'hôtes*) in an individual's principal residence is exempt.

e) Profits from certain new businesses are exempt (see chapter 7).

f) Salaries paid in respect of foreign service for an employer established in France can be exempt, even if the employee remains resident in France. The salary will be exempt if it suffers tax in the foreign country of at least two-thirds the amount that it would have suffered in France. If the foreign service amounts to more than 183 days in any period of 12 months and consists of construction, oil exploration or certain sales employment, the salary is exempt regardless of whether or not it is taxed in the foreign country. Even if the taxpayer's foreign service does not qualify for exemption under these heads, he is taxed in France only on the salary he would have received had the service been performed in France. Special payments for foreign service are therefore tax free. All such salary payments nevertheless remain subject to social surcharges of 8.2%.

g) Additional earnings paid to a person working in France for a foreign company may be exempt if they are paid to cover extra costs directly linked with the expatriation of the employee, such as, accommodation, travel, and generally costs associated with the change of residence, extra tax and social security charges and so on. If these are abnormally higher than the person's earnings for the normal exercise of his function in the company (by comparison to earnings for similar functions exercised in France) the difference is added to the taxpayer's taxable income. The exemption may apply for up to six years provided the employee was not fiscally resident in France at any time within the ten years preceding his expatriation. An expatriate may also deduct his national insurance contributions made in his country of origin without limitation as well as pension contributions within the same limits as those granted to French employees.

h) Amounts transferred to a special reserve for the benefit of employees under a profit sharing scheme, and retained in the business for 5 years, are exempt.

i) Part of a salary paid to an apprentice is exempt from income tax (up to the annual minimum wage).

j) Interest arising on 'Livret A' accounts at the post office (La Poste), savings banks (caisses d'épargne), and interest on LDD (ex CODEVI) accounts are exempt. The Compte d'Epargne Logement, Livret d'Epargne Populaire also allow tax-free savings under specific conditions (19.3.4).

6.6.12 Minimum Income

a) Individuals with gross income of less than €8,030 (or €8,780 if they are over 65) are exempt from income tax.

b) Taxpayers, whose main source of income (over 50%) consists of salaries, pensions or annuities, are exempt from income tax if their global income does not exceed €6,635.

6.7. Deductions from Gross Income

6.7.1 General

There are several categories of charges deductible from the taxable income:

a) Charges which are specific to the types of income listed above in chapters 6.6.2 to 6.6.8.

b) Global charges such as alimonies or allowances paid to ascendants and descendants (regardless of where they reside), deductible *CSG*, and specific charges listed below in this section.

c) General abatements from net taxable income which depend on the age, the tax household's resources and family charges.

d) Tax reductions and tax credits deductible from the *barème* liability itself described in 6.12. If the conditions required for the tax reduction or credit cannot be fully respected for the relevant period, the tax advantage is reintegrated to the future taxable income. Over the years, conditions of eligibility and qualifying expenditure have become so specific that it is almost necessary to verify the position with the local tax authorities systematically before claiming for these.

6.7.2 Personal Expenses

a) The *Code Civil* imposes an obligation of maintenance, in cases of need, between generations in a family. Maintenance payments are deductible from the income of the payer for tax purposes in certain cases. Payments may be made in cash or in kind. The following relationships can give rise to allowable maintenance:

i) An allowance paid to an ascendant (parent or grandparent etc) is deductible if it is commensurate with the needs of the recipient and the wealth of the payer. In general the taxpayer has to prove the real cost of the maintenance, but if this is paid in kind by the provision of accommodation and food in the taxpayer's home, the expenses are automatically allowed up to a limit of €3,203 per annum.

ii) An allowance paid to an adult child is deductible if it is paid in accordance with the obligation to maintain a child contained in the *Code Civil* or under the terms of a court order. There is no requirement that the child should be a member of the household of the person paying the maintenance. The amount of allowance which qualifies for relief is limited to €5,568 per child. If the child is married, the limit is doubled to €11,136 if the parents of one spouse can prove that they are the only means of support for the couple. When the maintenance is allowable, the parent cannot also claim the abatement for married children 're-attached' to a parent's household (see 6.8.(b)) or the additional *parts* under the family quota system available when a single child is 're-attached' to a parent's household (see 6.10.3(j)). The maintenance for which the parent has obtained tax relief is taxable income in the hands of the child, but, in view of the amounts which are allowable, if they are the only income of the recipient there will in practice be no tax liability in respect of them. If the maintenance actually paid exceeds the amount deductible by the payer, the taxable income of the child is limited to the amounts stated above.

iii) An allowance paid by a divorced parent for a minor child living with the other parent is deductible from the payer's taxable income, if it is paid under the terms of a court order or it is paid voluntarily and it is not 'excessive'. If the parent who does not have custody of the child pays a capital sum with a view to providing an annuity for the child, the capital sum divided by the number of years of the annuity is allowable as an annual deduction from the parent's income up to a maximum of €2,700 per annum (per child). To the extent that the payment is allowed as a deduction, it constitutes taxable income of the child.

iv) Alimony paid under a court order between an ex-husband and wife is deductible from the income of the payer if the couple are divorced or living separately. Capital sums paid from one ex-spouse to the other are not deductible. The administration also allows voluntary increases in alimony in line with inflation if no indexation is imposed by the judgement or by law and the payments are commensurate with the means of the payer and the needs of the recipient. The payments constitute taxable income of the recipient to the extent that they are deductible for the payer. Alimonies or allowances paid under a court order effective before 1 January 2006, are automatically increased by 25% for the purpose of the deduction.

b) An allowance in kind paid to a person over 75 who the taxpayer is not under a legal obligation to maintain and who is living in the taxpayer's house is deductible from the payer's income provided the annual allowance is less than €3,203 and the income of the recipient is below €7,635 for a single person or €13,374 for a married couple.

c) Owners of buildings classed as 'historic monuments' or listed as being of special historic or artistic interest can deduct the expenses related to the building from their income. If they receive an income from the property, they can deduct any losses on their property income from their total income; if they do not receive an income (eg because they occupy the property), 50% of the expenses relating to the property are deductible from the owners' income.

d) Individuals can deduct the contributions made by each member of the fiscal household to a *Plan d'Epargne Retraite Populaire (PERP)*. This deduction is limited to the greater of either:

- 10% of the professional income in the preceding tax year up to a maximum deduction of €24,854 (2007).

- or 10% of the social security ceiling revised every year, i.e. €3,107 (2007).

The lowest limit is likely to apply to individuals who do not contribute to any professional or salaried retirement scheme, whilst the first limit works as an annual limit taking into consideration any deductions claimed in respect of contributions to voluntary professional schemes or extra contributions paid into compulsory schemes.

6.7.3 Deductible CSG

a) A portion of the *CSG* (see also paragraph 6.3.) is deductible from the general taxable income subject to the mainstream income tax rates (*barème*). The rates of deductibility can be summarised as follows:

CSG applied on:	Deductible percentages
Investment and property income	5.8%
Salaries and unemployment benefits	5.1%
Retirement or Disability Pensions	4.2%

b) The *CSG* charge levied on income tax at source at 18% or capital gains and as a general rule any income which is not taxed as *barème* rates, does not give rise to any deduction. This is an aspect that must be taken into account when considering the option for the taxation at source of 29% (inclusive of social surcharges) on investment income for instance.

6.7.4 Investment Incentives

a) A French resident individual who invests cash in subscribing for shares of a company formed on or after 1 January 1994 in the context of a rescue of a failing business and who suffers a loss on the shares because the company ceases trading within five years, can normally deduct the loss from his income up to a limit of €30,000 per annum for a single person or €60,000 for a married couple. This relief cannot be cumulated with the tax incentives for investment in the film industry (see (b) below) or with certain other tax incentives, but since 1 January 1996 it is available alongside the tax reduction for investment in small and medium sized businesses. This investment incentive was suppressed from 1 January 2007, so 2006 was the last tax year in respect of which the deduction could apply.

b) Amounts invested in a *Livret de dévelopement durable (ex Codevi)* may give rise to a tax deduction limited to 25% of the annual taxable income of the household and to €20,000 per person. These accounts were created in favour of nationals of developing countries and holders of a *carte de séjour* allowing them to run a professional activity in France. Withdrawals may give rise to a withholding tax of 40% if the amounts are not invested in suitable and qualifying development schemes.

c) Individuals who carry on a professional, commercial or non-commercial activity as a small business subject to income tax can benefit from a reduction of taxable profit under certain conditions. These also apply to profits liable to corporation tax and are explained in greater detail in 7.3.

6.7.5   Loan Interest

a) The only form of interest which qualifies as a charge against income is interest paid in respect of loans granted to returning French expatriates coming from states which have gained their independence.

b) There is however a tax credit in respect of loans taken out for the purchase on a main home, see 6.12.1, and a tax credit for loans taken out to invest in certain small and medium-sized companies as described in 6.11.5.

6.8.   Deductions from Net Taxable Income

a) Taxpayers over 65 years old or who hold an invalidity card for 40% disability due to an accident at work or to war wounds may benefit from an abatement deductible from their gross taxable income. The deduction is means tested and limited to the following amounts:

Gross taxable income (2007)	Abatement applicable per qualifying person
Below €13,550	€2,202
Between €13,550 and €21,860	€1,101

There is no abatement if the household's income exceeds €21,860.

These abatements are doubled if both spouses are over 65.

b) A married or *PACS* couple, of whom at least one of the spouses is:

i)   under 21; or

ii)   under 25 and still a student.

can ask to be 're-attached' to the household of one or other set of parents for income tax purposes, in which case the income of the young couple is added to the parents' income and the parents may claim a deduction of €5,568 per person re-attached to the household. The household does not benefit from extra parts under the family quota system (see 6.10.2). For example if a young couple with a child are re-attached to the household of one of their parents, which otherwise consists of a husband and wife and two minor children, the income of the young couple is added to the household's income, and then €16,704 (ie 3 x €5,568) is deducted from it. The tax is calculated using *3 parts*, ie the basis of computation for a married couple with two minor children.

6.9. Taxable Income

a) The taxable income of the household includes the income of every member of the household.

b) The total income of the household is rounded down to the nearest 10 Euros.

6.10. Personal Allowances

6.10.1 Relief by Deduction from Income

The French tax system does not provide relief by personal allowances deducted from income. However the first band of income is taxed at 0% and as we shall see, the more members of the household there are, the more 0% bands are available against their income.

6.10.2 Relief by Division of Income

a) French income tax is assessed on the income of the household. Where there is more than one member of the household, there would be a risk that the family income was unfairly taxed at the higher rates in the tax scale, if nothing was done to reflect the fact that several people are sharing the income. The family quota (*quotient familial*) system mitigates the effects of the progressive nature of the tax rate scale by treating the income of the household as if it was the income of several separate individuals. The taxable income of the family is divided by a number of *parts* (units of the family) which is determined by:

   i)   the marital status and the number of members of the family; and

   ii) the number of dependent persons.

b) The tax per *part* is then calculated.

c) The tax per *part* is then multiplied by the number of *parts* in the household.

d) This relief is granted to non-French nationals if their country offers a similar system to French citizens. This reciprocity is presumed so that, in effect, the system is available to virtually all foreigners.

6.10.3 Calculation of Parts

a) The household consists of a single person, a married couple or an unmarried couple registered under a *PACS* and their dependants.

   i) An unmarried couple living together are taxed separately; if they have children, the children can be treated as dependants of the father or the mother as the parents please.

   ii) A married couple are only taxed separately if they are living apart and have separate estates (under their contract of marriage), or if they are in the process of divorce, or when one of the spouses has abandoned the matrimonial home and they are living on separate incomes (see 3.1.(e)).

   iii) Heterosexual and homosexual couples registered under the *Pacte Civil de Solidarité (PACS)* are treated as one fiscal household in respect of the third year following the date of registration of the *PACS* and have to file a joint return in that year.

b) The membership of the family is quantified as on 1 January in the tax year or, if it is to the taxpayer's advantage, 31 December in the tax year. If a child is born and then dies during the tax year, the administration accept the addition to the family for that year.

c) In the remainder of this section the term 'dependant' means:

   i) a child under 21; or

   ii) a child under 25 who is a student; or

   iii) an invalid child (of whatever age).

The term 'child' includes any child (whether related or not) accepted into the home and exclusively and effectively in the care of the household.

d) A single, divorced or separated person and a widow or widower are normally entitled to one *part*. However, widows or widowers who have dependants, will be entitled to 2 family shares in their own right. This should apply in respect of 2008 income onwards and regardless of their parenthood to the dependant(s).

e) However a single person who lives alone is entitled to one and a half *parts* if:

   i) he or she has at least one adult child, or had a child who is now deceased but who reached the age of 16 (or who died in a war) (but see 6.11.2(e)); or

ii) he or she has an invalidity card for 40% disability due to an accident at work or war wounds, or is in receipt of a pension as a war widow or civilian victim of war or an invalidity card for blindness or major disability; or

iii) he or she has adopted a child, under certain conditions.

f) A single person is also entitled to one and a half *parts* if he or she is invalid and has at least one dependant.

g) For most single persons, the first dependant entitles the taxpayer to one extra *part*. A second dependant entitles the taxpayer to a further half *part*, and the third and subsequent dependants each entitle the taxpayer to an extra *part*. However if the taxpayer is single or divorced, and lives with another person (*en concubinage*), the first dependant counts for only half a *part*. This rule applies equally to married taxpayers who are taxed separately and widows who do not have a child from their marriage.

h) A married or *PACS* couple without children is normally entitled to two *parts*. However:

i) if either partner to the marriage is an invalid, the couple are entitled to two and a half *parts;* and

ii) if both partners are invalids they are entitled to three *parts*.

i) The first two dependants count for half a *part* each and the third and following children count for one *part* each.

j) An unmarried child who is not otherwise a 'dependant' but who is

i) under 21; or

ii) under 25 and still a student.

can ask to be 're-attached' to his parents' household and is then a dependant person entitling the family to half a *part*.

k) Married children can also be 're-attached' to a parent's household, but in this case the parents benefit from a deduction from their taxable income (see 6.7.2). The household does not qualify for extra *parts*.

l) Any dependant who has an invalidity card counts for an extra half *part* on top of the normal allowance.

m) Divorced/separated parents can equally share the benefits of any family *parts* in the context of joint and equal custody. Each parent is now entitled to half of the family *part* benefit in respect of the child (or children) cared for under joint custody. A parent who at the same time, has full custody of one or more other children may benefit from extra family *parts*:

i) 0.25 family *part* for each of the first two "shared custody" children and 0.5 *part* from the third onwards, if the parent has no other dependent children.

ii) 0.25 *part* for the first "shared custody" child and 0.5 *part* from the second, if the parent also has another dependant.

iii) 0.5 *part* for each "shared custody" child, if the taxpayer has at least two other dependent children.

For example, in the context of a separated couple with shared custody in respect of their three children, each parent would be entitled to one family *part* (their own) plus 0.25 for the first two children and 0.5 *part* for the third, i.e. a total of two family *parts*.

In addition to the above, all relevant articles of the *Code Général des Impôts* relating to tax benefits, reductions etc, in respect of dependent children now specify that the tax advantages are shared equally by each parent in the context of shared custody. This concerns mainly the tax reductions for childminding expenses, and children's education, the increase in tax reduction in respect of equipment or installations in the principal home, the wealth tax reduction granted in respect of dependants, tax reductions relating to the *taxe d'habitation* and *taxes foncières*, etc.

6.11. Computing Income Tax Liabilities

6.11.1 Rates of Income Tax

a) For French residents, the tax per *part* is calculated by applying a progressive scale of tax rates to defined bands of income. The 20% abatement applicable to pensions, salaries and self-employed earnings (where the taxpayer is registered with a *CGA* (*Centre de Gestion Agrée*)) is included in the *barème* income bands. As a result, the total number of bands is 5 instead of 7 previously. The *barème* applicable to 2007 income is as follows:

Band of value (€)			*Rate of Tax (%)*
Less than (€)		5,687	0.0
between 5,687	to	11,344	5.5
between 11,344	to	25,195	14
between 25,195	to	67,546	30
67,546	and above		40

b) The tax per *part* is multiplied by the number of *parts*.

c) This amount is rounded to the nearest Euro, to give the crude tax liability (*impôt brut*), to which a number of adjustments are applied (see below).

d) For non-French residents who are taxable in France by reason of their French source income, the above rules generally apply subject to the modification that the tax due cannot be less than 20% of their taxable income.

e) The tax calculated as above is reduced by 40% or €6,700, whichever is the lowest, if the taxpayer is resident in French Guyana, and by 30% or €5,100, whichever is the lowest, if the taxpayer is resident in Guadeloupe, Martinique or Réunion.

6.11.2 Maximum Relief (Plafonnement)

a) Wealthy taxpayers would derive what is considered to be an excessive advantage from the *quotient familial* system. It is therefore provided that if the saving in tax resulting from the application of the system exceeds €2,198 per half *part* in the family in excess of one *part* (or two *parts* in the case of a married couple), the normal *quotient familial* system may not be used.

b) Instead the tax is calculated as if the taxpayer had only one *part* (two in the case of a married or *PACS* couple) and then €2,227 is deducted from the resulting liability for each additional half *part* claimed. For single, divorced or separately taxed married taxpayers, the amount deducted for the first child is €3,852, and the amount deducted for each subsequent child is €2,227.

c) There is a specific ceiling on the benefit obtained by single individuals who can claim an extra half *part* because they have raised one or more children who are now adult (see 6.10.3(e)(i)). The maximum tax saving procured by this extra half *part* is limited to €855 for the year in which the taxpayer's youngest child reaches the age of 26 and subsequent years.

d) For invalid taxpayers, taxpayers with invalid dependants, war veterans aged over 75 and single individuals who have raised one or more children who are now adult but the last of whom is under 25, the maximum tax saving procured by the extra half part is limited to €2,857.

e) The effects of the *plafonnement* are compensated by a tax reduction (after application of the *plafonnement*) granted to taxpayers who are invalid, who have invalid dependants, who are war veterans or single parents of one or more children who are now adults, but the last of whom is under 25. The reduction is €630 for each half part they are entitled to in excess of one part.

6.11.3 The "Décote" and the 'Franchise'

a) For a French resident, if the tax calculated as above does not exceed €838, the tax is reduced by a rebate (*'décote'*) of the difference between €419 and half of the tax liability. Eg:

Gross Tax	€710
Rebate €419 – (€710 ÷ 2)	€64
Net Tax	€646

The effect of this rule is that tax liabilities of less than €419 (half of €838) are exempted from tax.

b) If the liability after this adjustment is less than €61, it is not collected. This amount is called the *'franchise'*. The taxpayer remains liable to the tax, and his liability will be taken into account if, for example, he makes a claim for repayment of tax credits attaching to dividends. But if he merely owes tax of an amount less than the *'franchise'*, no steps are taken to collect the tax.

6.12. Tax Reductions and Tax Credits

6.12.1 Mortgage Interest for Principal Home Acquisition

a) Interest paid in respect of a mortgage taken out to finance one's principal home can give rise to a tax a tax credit for the first five annuities. In practice this concerns loans which have been taken out from 22 August 2007. However, the Government may, in accordance with its earlier announcements, grant the credit in respect of operations commenced from 6 May 2007.

b) The credit is set as 40% of the interest paid (excluding insurance premiums) in the first year of the loan and 20% thereafter. The total annual interest charge on which the credit is calculated is limited to €3,750 for a single taxpayer, €7,500 for a couple, plus €500 per dependant. If one of the spouses is disabled, the annual limit is set at €15,000.

c) The loan may be taken out to finance the building of a new property to be used as main home but not for the renovation work on an existing main home. The law does not at this stage specify if a loan taken out for the acquisition of a property to be renovated and used as a main home would qualify. Foreign loans may qualify if conditions are met and provided they originate from and EU or EEA establishment. This tax credit cannot be combined with the one granted in respect of investments in the Outre-Mer Territories described in 6.12.8.

6.12.2 Cost of Equipment or Installations in the Home

a) The cost of specific equipment or installations fitted in a principal residence qualifies for a tax credit if the building is over 2 years old. The expenditure must be incurred between 1 January 2005 and 31 December 2009, and invoiced by the building firm carrying on the work at the reduced VAT rate of 5.5%. The tax credit is calculated on the cost incurred and percentages vary depending on the nature of the eqipment, and/or the age of the building. The range of qualifying expenditure is as follows:

i) 15% tax credit for the cost of low temperature boilers.

ii) 25% tax credit for the cost of condensing boilers, equipment relating to energy-savings, heating regulation, rain water collection and re-use, heating connection. This is increased to 40% if the property was built before 1 January 1977 and the installation occurs within 2 years of the acquisition.

iii) 50% tax credit for the cost of energy-producing equipment using renewable energy sources such as wind mills, solar panels, wood-burning stoves, etc and geothermal pump.

iv) 15% tax credit for equipment to safeguard against technological risks, such as reinforcement of existing constructions, installation of shatter-proof windows etc.

v) 25% tax credit for new or replacement equipment for the elderly or disabled as well as related installation work. 15% tax credit for the costs of electric lifts.

b) The above tax credits are subject to a global limit over the period (1 January 2005 to 31 December 2009) of €8,000 for a single person and €16,000 for a couple, increased by €400 for each dependant. The taxpayer must deduct any expenses for which he has already claimed the tax credit in previous years to determine whether his deduction for the tax year will be limited. Any state grants received to finance any of the above equipment must also be deducted before applying the tax credit.

6.12.3 Charitable Donations

a) Individuals can obtain a tax reduction in respect of donations to charities (which operate at least partly in France), general and public interest associations (sports, family, cultural, humanitarian, educational and so on). Donations for the financing of political parties or elections may also give rise to the tax credit. The reduction of tax is 66% of the amounts given limited to 20% of the donor's taxable income. If gifts exceed 20% of the taxpayer's income, the excess may be carried forward for five years.

b) A special tax reduction is granted for donations to certain charities that provide food, medical care and lodging to individuals with no resources. The reduction of tax is 75% of the amounts given, limited to €488 for 2007 and €495 for 2008, and is cumulative with the above reduction.

6.12.4 Private Employment of Home-help

a) A taxpayer who employs a home help in a house in France (whether his principal residence or second home) may benefit from a tax reduction calculated as 50% of the salary and social contribution paid to this person. The qualifying services provided by the home help are defined in the *Code du Travail* and concern mainly the following: child-minding at home, tuition/homework assistance, assistance to the elderly, the disabled and the sick, housekeeping, small gardening tasks (limited annually to €3,000), and small house maintenance tasks (limited annually to €500). The cost of employing au-pairs, staff employed within or as a continuation of the taxpayer's professional activity, guardians or concierge of properties etc is excluded.

b) The tax reduction is limited annually to €12,000 increased by €1,500 per dependant or member of the tax household over 65 years old up to a total of €15,000 (ie a maximum reduction of €7,500). The main limit is €20,000 for tax household comprising someone who is disabled and in need of special assistance provided by the home employee.

c) From 2007 onwards, if the employment concerns child minding and home tuition, the tax advantage is a tax credit with the same limits as those described above, rather than tax reduction. Under the tax credit system a refund of tax is usually allowed if the amounts deducted exceed the liability. The conditions for the tax credit are as follows:

- Both parents must carry out a professional activity, and

- the employee must be paid by *chèque emploi-service universel* system.

If these conditions are not met, the employment may still qualify for the general tax reduction together with the employment of home helps for other tasks. Where a taxpayer qualifies under both the tax reduction and the tax credit, priority is given to the tax credit when applying the limits.

6.12.5 Investment in Small or Medium-Sized Companies

a) From the 2007 tax year individuals resident in France who subscribe to the share capital of certain companies may deduct from their tax liability 25% of the amount subscribed up to a maximum investment of €20,000 for a single taxpayer or €40,000 for a couple. Amounts invested in excess of the above limits may give rise to a tax reduction spread over the 4 following years. The shares must be kept for at least five years.

b) The reduction is available for investments made between 1 January 1994 and 31 December 2010. The company must be subject to corporation tax and must have its registered office in an EU or EEA country.

For the investment to qualify the company must fit the European definition of small and medium sized company that is to say:

i) Medium companies must have less than 250 employees, an annual turnover under €50 M and an annual balance sheet under €43 M.

ii) Small companies must have less than 50 employees, an annual turnover or annual balance sheet under €10 M.

iii) Micro-enterprises: up to 10 employees, an annual turnover or annual balance sheet under €2 M.

To be eligible the companies must also have more than 75% of their share capital held by individuals or qualifying small or medium sized companies.

c) A similar tax reduction was in place and is effective for the 2006 tax year. The conditions of qualifying companies are slightly different and not extended to non-French ones.

d) Tax reductions of the same amount but limited to €12,000 for a single taxpayer and €24,000 for a couple are available for investments in *fonds communs de placements dans l'innovation* ('*FCPI*') during the period 1 January 1997 to 31 December 2010, and *fonds d'investissement de proximité* ("*FIP*") from 1 August 2003 to 31 December 2010.

e) Loans taken out to finance the investment in an existing small or medium sized company can give rise to a tax reduction calculated as 25% of the interest charge paid during the tax year. This is limited to €10,000 for a single person and €20,000 for a couple. The company in which the taxpayer invests must fulfil the criteria outlined in b) above. The taxpayer must keep the shares up to 31 December of the fifth year following the acquisition. There is no time limit for the application of this reduction.

6.12.6 Investment in Listed Tourism Residences

a) Taxpayers who invest in or renovate certain listed tourism residences, new or completed before 1 January 1989 or buildings in need of renovation for that use, may qualify for a tax reduction. The property must be let unfurnished for at least 9 years to a tenant who will let it as a *résidence de tourisme*.

b) The tax reduction is calculated as 25% of the purchase price (including related costs) or 20% of the renovation costs. The reduction is limited to €50,000 for a single person and €100,000 for a couple. The limit is reduced to €12,500 and €25,000 respectively if the property is new. The limit for the reduction applicable to qualifying renovation work is €10,000 for a single person and €20,000 for a couple. Depending on the type of investment the limits above are applied over a six-year period.

c) Certain reconstruction, repairs, improvement and extension work on qualifying tourism properties may also give rise to the above tax reduction but only in the year of expenditure. The tax reduction is increased to 40% if the investment concerns dwellings which are part of a *village résidentiel de tourisme*.

6.12.7 Investment in Forestry Property

a) Taxpayers who invest for a minimum of 15 years in forest or woodland of up to 25 hectares, land destined to be planted with trees (within three years), or shares in forestry groups or companies can qualify for a tax reduction. The investment must take place between 1 January 2001 and 31 December 2010.

b) The tax reduction is calculated as 25% of the acquisition price (limited to 60% in the context of shares in forestry groups or companies). It is limited to an annual amount of €5,700 for a single person and €11,400 for a couple. The maximum annual reduction is therefore €1,425 or €2,850 depending on the family situation of the investor.

c) There is a specific tax reduction for the cost of forestry work but within a sub-limit of €1,250 (€2,500 for a couple).

d) A tax reduction is also granted in respect of contributions to qualifying syndicates for preventive work against forest fires in designated forests. The tax reduction is set as 50% of the contribution paid upon presentation of the required certificate and limited to €1,000 per household.

6.12.8 Investment in the Collectivités d'Outre-Mer

a) Approved investments by French residents in the *DOM* or the *Collectivités d'Outre-Mer*, may qualify for a tax reduction up to 31 December 2017. The scope of the qualifying investments and the conditions for the tax reduction evolve regularly and the rules set out below are those applicable to investments between 21 July 2003 and 31 December 2017.

b) The investment can be in new housing or businesses liable to income tax engaged in industry, fishing, hotel activities, tourism, boat charters, certain types of holiday accommodation, energy sources, agriculture, building and infrastructure, craftwork, maintenance for industrial concerns, film or audio productions, transport and personal services (hairdressing, beauty salons, thermal centres, and so on), maintenance and cleaning services. The following are excluded from the benefit of the scheme: retailing, restaurants, education, health, activities of the finance and advisory sector, holiday rentals, bare boat charters, leisure activities other than those directly linked with hotel and tourism services and postal services.

c) Investments in sensitive sectors or investment by non-professional individuals must be approved if they exceed €300,000, or €1 million for all other investments.

d) The reduction is calculated as 50% of the total investment (less any grants) or 60% and 70% in certain specific cases and may be spread over the following five years. Any excess in respect of a maximum total annual investment of €1,525,000 may be refunded.

e) The taxpayer must keep the investment or share in the investing business and maintain their designated use for at least 5 years.

6.12.9 Other Reductions or Tax Credits

a) Expenses relating to child-minding outside the home, in *crèches, haltes-garderies*, nurseries, qualifying leisure centers, after school establishments, give rise to a tax credit of 50% limited annually to €2,300 per child. The child must be under 7 at 31 December of the relevant tax year. Costs relating to child-minding at home can give rise to a tax credit or tax reduction as described in paragraph 6.12.4.

b) A taxpayer who has dependent children in secondary or higher education (as at 31 December of the relevant tax year) can claim the following tax reductions:

i) €61 for each at a *collège* (secondary school)

ii) €153 for each child in a *lycée* (sixth form college)

iii) €183 for each child in higher education.

c) A taxpayer may deduct a tax reduction of 25% of the costs of accommodation in a nursing home, hospital or retirement home up to a maximum of €10,000 per person.

d) Employees who do not opt for the itemised deduction of professional expenditure from their salary and thus apply the 10% set deduction may benefit from a tax reduction in respect of their financial contribution to a union. It is calculated as 66% of the sums paid limited to 1% of the salaries received net of social security charges.

e) The purchase of an environmentally-friendly vehicle gives rise to a credit of €2,000 per vehicle and increased to €3,000, if followed within 2 months by the disposal of a vehicle, put in circulation before 1 January 1997. This tax credit will no longer apply from 2008 income as it is replaced by an *ecopastille*, which is a tax added to the *carte grise* levy. The rate varies depending on the year of purchase, the rate of carbon dioxide emission and the power of the vehicle.

f) A tax credit of €1,500 is granted for those who move more than 200 km from their original home to find employment. In addition they may benefit for the first three years from a 10% reduction on the taxable rental income they may receive from the rental of their former home and this for the first three years. This applies to anyone moving between 1 July 2005 to 31 December 2007 and who remained employed for at least 6 months. This advantage cannot be used in conjunction with the *micro-foncier* regime.

g) A tax credit is offered in respect of student loans for under 25 year olds. This is calculated as 25% of the interest paid on the loan taken out between 28 September 2005 and 31 December 2008. The annual credit limit is set at €250 band the credit applies for the first five years only.

h) The cash subscription for shares in an approved film or video company (*SOFICA*) gives rise to a tax reduction calculated as 40% of the investment up to a maximum of 25% of the taxpayer's total net taxable income or €18,000 (i.e. a maximum tax advantage of €7,200). The shares must be kept for at least five years if not the tax reduction is repayable. This tax reduction is valid for investments made between 1 January 2006 and 31 December 2008.

i) Tax credits in respect of foreign tax paid on foreign source income as per the terms of the relevant double tax treaty. For instance, an 11% tax credit in respect of UK dividends is applicable under the terms of the France-UK double tax treaty and is deductible from the French liability.

j) Tax credits in respect of dividend payments (see 6.6.8) are refundable if they exceed the taxpayer's liability.

k) Companies, including those which are fiscally transparent, are entitled to a special credit for research expenditure.

l) When relief by way of credit is available under a double tax treaty to the French resident in respect of foreign taxes suffered on foreign source income, the foreign taxes paid are credited against his French tax liability.

m) Insurance against unpaid rents for certain specific social rentals may qualify for a tax credit of 50% of the premiums paid. The premiums cannot be deducted from the taxable income if claimed as a tax credit.

n) There is a tax reduction of €20 for taxpayers who submit their tax forms on line for the first time and pay their income tax liability by direct debit or on line.

This applies for the 2007, 2008 and 2009 tax years. Taxpayers who submit their tax returns on line do not need to attach the receipts for the charitable donations in respect of which they claim a tax reduction.

o) Owners of listed objects of art, collections or other such listed movable assets may have a tax credit in respect of the associated conservation or restoration costs paid from 2008. The tax credit is calculated as 25% of the costs within an annual limit of €20,000, ie a maximum tax credit of €5,000. The object(s) must be exposed to the public (museum etc) within five years of its restoration.

6.13. Minimum Tax

a) There is no minimum tax liability for French residents.

b) The tax due by a non-resident on his French income cannot normally be less than 20% of his taxable income (ignoring income subject to a *libératoire,* i.e. final withholding tax). There are three cases when the tax can be lower:

   i) if the non-resident can show that he would have suffered tax at a lower rate if his worldwide income had been taxed in France;

   ii) if the non-resident is subject to tax on the *base forfaitaire* (three times the rental value of his home(s) in France); and

   iii) if the tax computed with the minimum rate does not exceed €305, it is not collected.

6.14. Maximum Tax

a) A "tax burden" limit is set at 50% of any given household's taxable income. Known as the *"bouclier fiscal"* (tax shield), it relates to income tax (including *CSG, CRDS* and *PS*), wealth tax and local property taxes. The total of these charges cannot exceed 50% of the household's taxable income. The limitation of tax burden only applies to taxpayers fiscally resident in France.

b) The following taxes are excluded from the calculation: refuse tax, TV tax, local property taxes on second homes, taxes paid abroad or additional liabilities resulting from a tax audit.

c) The right to claim for a refund of tax exceeding the 50% limit starts on 1 January in respect of the tax paid in the preceding year. For instance, from 1 January 2008, it is possible to claim in respect of the tax paid during 2007. For the income tax element this relates to 2006 income. The claim must be filed before 31 December each year, if applicable.

d) In addition the total liability of an individual to wealth tax and income tax cannot normally exceed 85% of his income of the previous year (including any income which is exempt from tax, and allowing only certain business losses). If the sum of these taxes would exceed this amount, the wealth tax is reduced euro for euro by the excess. However, for taxpayers with taxable wealth exceeding €2,450,000, the amount of this reduction is reduced by 50%, or €11,573 if this is higher.

6.15. Payment of Income Tax

6.15.1 Payments in Advance

French income tax payers are not required to pay any tax in advance. They do not pay tax in respect of their income for tax year 2007 during 2007, other than by means of tax withheld from investment income. During 2008 they pay their income tax due for 2007.

6.15.2 Mainstream Liabilities

a) The traditional method of tax payment in France is payment in three instalments *(tiers provisionnel)*, due on 31 January, 30 April and in September during the year following the tax year which is being assessed. The first two instalments are calculated simply as one third of the tax paid in the previous year, and the third represents the balance of the liability. The taxpayer must make the first two payments before 15 February and 15 May respectively, failing which the tax due is increased by a penalty of 10%. Strictly speaking the deadlines are 31 January and 30 April, but it has become the custom to extend them by two weeks. For example in 2008 a taxpayer will normally pay two instalments, each calculated as one-third of the tax he paid in 2007 (based on 2006 income), by 15 February and 15 May 2008. These are payments on account of his 2007 liability, which will be determined by an assessment issued after the beginning of September 2008. The final instalment of tax due is payable on the last day of the month following the making of the assessment, and the 10% penalty is applied if the payment is made after the 15th day of the second month following the making of the assessment. Taxpayers whose liability in the previous year was less than €327 are exempt from the requirement to make the payments on account.

b) Alternatively the taxpayer can elect to pay his tax monthly, and 51% of income tax collected by direct assessment is now paid this way. On the 8th day of each month from January to October, he pays 1/10th of the tax he paid in the previous year by direct debit. For example the taxpayer would pay in 2008 ten instalments each equal to one-tenth of the tax he paid in 2007 (based on his 2006 income). These payments can be stopped at the request of the taxpayer if it seems to him that his liability has been satisfied before the 10th payment is made. However if he stops the payments and it turns out that his actual liability is at least 10% more than his estimate of the liability, the taxpayer has to pay the difference plus a penalty of 10% of the difference. The amount of the monthly payments can be reduced if the taxpayer's liability is more than 10% lower than the estimated liability on which the payments were calculated. If the actual liability exceeds the payments on account, the payments continue into November and December. Normally this position will be foreseen in August or September, because the taxpayer will have received his assessment for the year by then. The November payment is equal to one of the earlier payments and the December payment recovers the balance due. If the December payment will be more than double the normal monthly amount, this payment is spread over the last four months of the year, unless the taxpayer elects otherwise. If the assessment is not raised until after 31 October, the balance of tax due is recovered in the same manner as the third instalment under the normal payment system described above.

6.16. Anti-Avoidance Measures

6.16.1 Taxation on the Basis of Apparent Wealth

a) A French resident taxpayer can be asked to declare certain elements of his lifestyle if a principal tax inspector believes that there is a disparity between his lifestyle and his declared income. These elements include the taxpayer's main residence and holiday homes, permanent domestic staff, cars, motorcycles of more than 450 cc, aeroplanes, yachts of at least 3 tons, motor boats with engines of at least 20 HP, horses, racehorses, hunting rights costing in excess of €4,600 per annum, golf club subscriptions costing in excess of €4,600 per annum. The declaration also includes any declarable elements connected with any member of the household if they have improved the lifestyle of the taxpayer during the tax year, whether in France or in another country.

b) Each relevant lifestyle element has a 'notional income' value determined by a tariff. For example the taxpayer's homes are valued at five times their cadastral rental value; cars are valued at their cost when new, less 50% after three years; membership of a golf club is valued at twice the annual subscription and green fees etc. The tariff rates for yachts and motorboats are quintupled if the boat is registered in a country which has not concluded a treaty with France containing a clause providing for mutual administrative assistance in combatting fiscal fraud. The value of the taxpayer's lifestyle elements is totalled to arrive at a notional income (*revenu forfaitaire*).

c) If:

i) there is a 'marked disparity' between the taxpayer's declared income and his lifestyle, which is deemed to be the case when the notional income exceeds the declared income by more than one third; and

ii) the disparity existed not only in the tax year in question but also in the previous year; and

iii) the notional income of the taxpayer determined by the application of the tariff scale is at least €53,374 (2007).

tax is assessed, at normal scale rates, on the notional income and not the declared income.

d) If the notional income of the taxpayer is at least €106,748 (2007) and the taxpayer has at least 7 taxable 'elements', the tax is increased by 50%.

e) However the taxpayer is allowed to justify his lifestyle by proving, for example, that he inherited or borrowed the funds he is spending. If he shows that his resources cover the cost of his lifestyle this basis of taxation is not applied.

f) This system does not apply to non-French residents.

6.16.2 *Controlled Foreign Companies*

a) Individuals resident in France who own, directly or indirectly, at least 10% of the shares, profit shares, or voting rights in a foreign company, organisation, trust or similar institution are subject to income tax in France on their pro rata share of the income of the company, trust etc if:

i) the company, trust etc is subject to a privileged fiscal regime (ie it suffers no income tax or it suffers notably less income tax than it would have paid had it been subject to tax in France); and

ii) its main activity is the holding of shares, bonds and cash deposits.

b) If the company, organisation, trust or similar institution is established or incorporated in a state which has not concluded a treaty with France providing for administrative assistance in tax matters, the 'investor' is deemed to have a taxable income from his 'investment' of at least the maximum rate of interest which can be paid on shareholders' loans in France (which for 2007 was 5.41%), applied to his share of the net assets of the entity. This taxable amount is then increased by 25%. If the actual income of the entity is greater, it is used as the taxable basis.

6.16.3 *Declarations*

a) There are a number of reporting obligations designed to reinforce the tax system, or to counter drug trafficking.

b) In replacement of the exchange control system, financial institutions declare payments made between France and foreign countries to the *Banque de France*. However:

i) businesses which have transactions with foreign countries exceeding €457 million during a calendar year must send monthly declarations thereof to the *Banque de France*; and

ii) French residents must send monthly declarations to the *Banque de France* if their borrowings in foreign currency and in Euros exceed €76,225,000.

c) Individuals and non-commercial companies (ie other than an *SA, SAS, SARL, EURL, SCA, SNC,* or *SCS*) must inform the French tax authorities of the details of their accounts in foreign countries; failure to do so results in the treatment of transfers to or from the foreign accounts as taxable income in the hands of the account holder.

d) To counter drug trafficking:

i) financial institutions must report suspicious transactions to *TRACFIN,* a department of the Ministry of Finance; and

ii) transfers by hand or by mail out of or into France of funds, securities or other values of an amount of €7,600 or more must be declared to the French customs authorities. Transfers between France and Monaco are also covered by this requirement.

e) Failure to make any of these declarations results in severe penalties.

6.16.4 *Payment by Cheque*

a) The following payments must be made by crossed cheque, bank transfer, credit card or charge card, if they are made by a trader. This rule does not apply to payments made by an individual in his private capacity, who are subject to the rule at (b) below:

i) payments exceeding €750 for rent, transport, furnishing, building works, purchase of immovable or movable property, purchase of shares etc; and

ii) payments of salaries exceeding €1,500.

b) All payments of amounts in excess of €3,000 made by French resident individuals, must be made by crossed cheque payable only to the payee or by bank transfer or by a credit or charge card. Individuals who fail to respect this requirement face a penalty of up to €15,000. The payee is normally liable for half of the penalty, and both the payee and payer are generally liable for the total penalty.

c) The above rule does not apply to non-French residents, who can therefore pay any amount by travellers cheques or cash.

7. CORPORATION TAX

7.1. General

7.1.1 Sociétés de Capitaux

In general, French corporation tax applies only to the profits of a business carried on in France by a 'capital company' (société de capitaux).

a) As we have seen at 3.2., there are a large number of forms of company in France which are fiscally transparent or semi-transparent, and which are therefore prima facie not liable to French corporation tax. While it is possible for these forms of company to elect to be subject to corporation tax, or to make themselves subject to corporation tax by virtue of their commercial activities, this chapter is mainly concerned with the types of company listed in 3.2.1(a).

b) Foreign companies are similarly not liable to French corporation tax unless they can be considered as equivalent to one of the French forms of company described in 3.2.1(a).

7.1.2 Assessment of Capital

French corporation tax takes no account of the net worth of the company.

7.1.3 Relationship with Income Tax

The rules for calculating taxable profits are based on the system of income tax for industrial and commercial income. Those adjustments and tax credits which are more likely to be appropriate to a company paying corporation tax are described in this chapter, but many of them apply equally to companies which are fiscally transparent.

7.2. Territorial Basis

a) Unlike French income tax, the normal system of French corporation tax is essentially territorial in its basis, with tax being assessed on the profits of a company's trade or business in France. Profits or losses of a business carried on outside France are not normally brought into account, although a few large corporations are assessed on a worldwide income basis by agreement with the French government.

b) This principle requires definition at the boundaries. In particular the following rules should be noted:

   i) a complete cycle of operations (for example a purchase and resale) carried on in France is generally treated as a French activity;

ii) by contrast a complete cycle of operations carried on abroad by a French company may remain subject to French tax if the operation is not distinct in nature and method from the operations of the company in France;

iii) special rules apply when operations are carried on partly in France and partly abroad;

iv) transfer pricing controls apply to transactions between related companies (see 7.9.(a));

v) payments to and receipts from residents of low tax areas are subject to close scrutiny (see 7.9.(b));

vi) a French company can be subject to tax on the income of a branch or subsidiary or associated company located in a tax haven (see 7.9.(c)).

c) Under the definition of most double tax treaties, a foreign company will be subject to French corporation tax if:

i) it has a permanent establishment in France,

ii) it has a dependent agent in France,

iii) it habitually carries out a complete commercial cycle in France (e.g. purchase and sale).

It is interesting to note that foreign companies can ask the French tax authorities for a written confirmation that it does not have a French permanent establishment. The absence of any reply from the authorities within three months is treated as a tacit agreement.

7.3. Computation of Taxable Profits

7.3.1 Classification of Taxable Sources of Income

a) Taxable profits are classified in principle in the same way as income is classified for income tax purposes. In practice the main distinction made is that between:

i) trading profits; and

ii) incidental income (*profits accessoires*);

b) *Profits accessoires* include, for example:

i) income from dividends on shares (but see 7.3.5);

ii) profits from participations in companies not subject to corporation tax;

iii) rental income;

iv) interest on loans, deposits and current accounts;

v) financial profits, such as gains on the financial futures market (the *MATIF*) or equivalent foreign exchanges (see 8.2.5).

7.3.2 Gross Income

Gross income is calculated on the basis of tax adjusted accounting income, with the following main exceptions:

a) Short term capital gains are taxable as ordinary income of the year in which they are realised. The system relating to long term capital gains is described in 8.3.

b) 'Headquarters' operations of multinationals are in principle subject to the same taxation as any other company, but they can obtain a ruling from the *Direction des Vérifications Nationales et Internationales* (the *'DVNI'*) fixing (on a *forfaitaire* basis) their taxable income at (normally) 6 to 10% of their operating costs. The applicable margin is agreed on a case by case basis. Any expatriate employees of such an operation are subject to a *régime simplifié* and do not suffer 'tax on tax' when their employer reimburses the employee for additional taxes he may suffer over and above the tax he would have paid in his home country (the employer pays corporation tax on these amounts). Expenses paid by the headquarters in respect of the expatriate's foreign employment (eg housing allowances and school fees) do not form part of the employee's taxable income in France provided that the employer includes the expenses in the cost base on which its tax liability is calculated. The company can also obtain exemption from the business tax for the year in which it is created and a reduction of 50% of the business tax for the following year. If it is established in a redevelopment zone, these exemptions may be further extended.

c) A company subject to French corporation tax which holds, directly or indirectly, at least a 10% interest in a branch or company established in a foreign country where the tax regime is 'privileged' is subject to French corporation tax on its pro-rata share of the profits of the subsidiary unless it can show that the operations of the subsidiary do not principally have the effect of sheltering profits in a low tax regime. The parent company can also escape this rule if it can demonstrate that the subsidiary is mainly engaged in industrial or commercial activities in its local market, and that most of its business is conducted with independent third parties.

d) With the exception of units in certain equity and risk-capital funds, units in a collective investment scheme must be revalued at the end of the accounting period and any unrealised gain is brought into charge to tax.

7.3.3 Basis Periods

Companies pay tax on the basis of their accounting periods. The rates of tax are established for each accounting period by reference to the date on which the period commences. Therefore there is no need to time-apportion income over different tax years if the rate of tax changes.

7.3.4 Accounting Methods

'Professional gross income' is calculated under normal accounting principles, subject to the following rules:

a) The accruals basis is compulsory (but see 7.3.9(a)).

b) For maintenance and other long term contracts the income brought into account for tax purposes includes only the income attributable to the current year.

c) Gains and losses on conversion of foreign currency assets and liabilities must be brought into taxable income.

d) Stocks and work in progress are valued at the lower of cost or market value at the end of the year on a FIFO basis. Provisions for inventory price increases are not allowable unless the rate of inflation reaches 10%.

7.3.5 Exempt Income

Dividends (limited to 95%) received from French companies in which the receiving company owns at least 5% of the equity are exempt from tax (see 7.8.4).

7.3.6 Deductions Generally

a) The following taxes are deductible:

   i) salary tax (*taxe sur les salaires*), described in 1.8.(a);

   ii) apprenticeship tax (*taxe d'apprentissage*), described in 1.8.(b);

   iii) employer's participation in vocational training (*participation des employeurs à la formation professionnelle continue*), described in 1.8.(c);

   iv) construction participation (*participation des employeurs à l'effort de construction*), described in 1.8.(d);

   v) tax on insurance contracts (*taxe sur les conventions d'assurances*), described in 1.8.(f), in so far as it relates to insurance of a company vehicle;

   vi) social solidarity contribution of companies (*contribution sociale de solidarité des sociétés*), described in 1.8.(g);

vii) tax on supermarkets (*taxe sur les grandes surfaces*);

viii) land taxes (*taxes foncières*) and business tax (*taxe professionnelle*) described in 1.8.(h) and chapter 22;

ix) registration taxes described in 1.8.(j);

x) taxes on leases (*contribution sur les revenus locatifs or CRL*) described in 1.8.(k).

xi) foreign tax paid in respect of operations carried on abroad but taxable in France.

b) The following taxes are not deductible:

i) company car tax, described in 1.8.(e), when paid by a company subject to corporation tax (but deductible if paid by a fiscally transparent company);

ii) tax on insurance contracts (*taxe sur les conventions d'assurances*), described in 1.8.(f), in so far as it relates to non-motor policies;

iii) tax penalties are not deductible. From 1 January 2008, this is extended to penalties levied for non-compliance with the legislation applicable to various administrative organisations (customs, social security, European Commission…).

c) The French tax system offers greater scope than most for transfers of pre-tax profits to reserves, which significantly reduce the effective rate of French corporation tax. The following are the main accounting provisions which can be allowable:

i) provisions for bad debts and debts in litigation;

ii) provisions for repairs, maintenance and depreciation of certain assets;

iii) provisions for extra remuneration, year-end bonuses, certain benefits and holiday pay;

iv) provisions for deductible taxes not yet paid;

v) provisions for reduction in value of portfolio investments (which create a long term capital, rather than revenue, loss). Depreciation in the value of shares held as participations is only allowed exceptionally when the loss in value can be proved by reference to a number of factors including the market value, the probable sales value of the interest, and the profitability of the company in which the participation is held;

vi) provisions against a diminution in value of stocks (see 7.3.4(d)) or for price increases (if the rate of inflation exceeds 10%);

vii) certain businesses may deduct additional provisions, for example newspaper businesses, banks and credit institutions, insurance companies, oil and coal companies;

viii) a provision for replacement of assets is allowable if the company is under an obligation to renew assets which it does not own but which are leased to it or made available for its use. However the amount of the difference between the cost price and the replacement cost is now time apportioned over the period during which the asset will be used instead of being allowed immediately.

d) The deduction of charges from related parties is allowable only if the charges are justified on arms-length principles.

e) Formation expenses can be written off immediately or amortised over five years.

f) Exchange gains and losses on foreign currency loans to or from the company are taxable or deductible. The value of stocks acquired in foreign currencies can be adjusted to reflect any exchange gain or loss. Since the profits of a foreign permanent establishment are not taxable, it follows that there is no tax relief for exchange losses relating to the assets of the branch.

g) Directors' attendance fees are only deductible within certain limits. The total paid to all the directors must not exceed 5% of the average remuneration paid to the 10 highest paid employees of the company, multiplied by the number of directors.

7.3.7 Employment Costs

a) Costs of employment, including social insurance contributions and contributions to pension funds for employees, are normally deductible.

b) Every company with more than 50 employees is compelled by law to operate a profit-sharing scheme. The company and its employees can establish the terms of their own scheme (respecting the general principles of the relevant law). Alternatively there is a statutory scheme, which applies in the absence of any other arrangements. Under the statutory scheme, the amount which is contributed to a reserve for employees' participation is calculated as follows:

$$\text{Reserve} = \tfrac{1}{2} \times \left(B - \frac{5C}{100} \right) \times \frac{S}{VA}$$

where:

B = the net after tax profit,

C = the amount of the paid up capital, share premiums, reserves and accumulated profits,

S = the gross amount of the salaries paid before deduction of the employees social insurance contributions, pension contributions or 10% deduction for expenses, and

VA = is the value added by the business, calculated from its profits

c) The contributions to this reserve are fully tax deductible for the company. The contributions to the reserve are based on the profits of the previous year and therefore tax relief is normally obtained in the year following that for which the reserve is being made or increased.

d) Generally the reserve has to be retained in the company for a pre-determined period, and payments out of the reserve to employees are tax free in the hands of the employee provided the reserve is retained in the company for at least 5 years. Under the statutory scheme, the reserve is retained for 8 years.

e) As mentioned above, the company and its employees are free to negotiate their own arrangements (within limits), but in this case the tax advantages accorded to the profit-sharing scheme are only available if the amounts contributed to the scheme do not exceed one of 4 limits, chosen by the parties:

i) 50% of the accounting profits;

ii) 50% of the taxable profits;

iii) the accounting profits reduced by 5% of the capital of the company; or

iv) the taxable profits reduced by 5% of the capital of the company.

7.3.8 Depreciation

a) Fixed assets are not pooled for depreciation purposes, and depreciation is calculated on each asset separately.

b) Depreciation of fixed assets is allowed if the deterioration of the assets is caused by the passage of time or use. The depreciation must relate to a genuine diminution of the market value of the asset, and must therefore normally be borne as an expense in the accounts. The two alternative methods of depreciation are as follows:

i) The straight line method (*amortissement linéaire*) is the most commonly used. The rates are based on the normal useful life of the assets. The generally accepted straight line rates of depreciation are as follows:

	%
Industrial buildings	5
Commercial buildings	2 to 5
Office buildings	4
Residential buildings	1 to 2.5
Tools and equipment	10 to 15
Machinery	10 to 20
Furniture	10
Office equipment	5 to 20
Vehicles and rolling stock	20 to 25
Computers	33.33
Patents	20

The tax administration will accept a depreciation rate based on a useful life which does not depart by more than 20% from the industry standard.

ii) All industrial or commercial companies can choose the declining balance method (*amortissement dégressif*) to compute depreciation on equipment and all hotel investments. Except for hotel buildings and certain industrial buildings with a utilisation span below 15 years, the declining balance method may not be used for residential or business realty. It cannot be used for second hand equipment or equipment with an estimated useful life of less than three years. The rates are calculated by applying multiples to the straight line rates, i.e.

Assets with a useful life of	Multiple of straight line rate	
	before 1 January 2001	after 1 January 2001
3 to 4 years	1.5	1.25
5 to 6 years	2.0	1.75
over 6 years	2.5	2.25

For example if the straight line rate of depreciation applicable to an asset is 20% and the asset has an expected life of 5 years, the rate of depreciation calculated on a declining balance basis will normally be 35% (ie 1.75 x 20%).

However for assets acquired between 1 February 1996 and 31 January 1997, the multiples listed above are increased by 1 point. Therefore if the asset in the above example was acquired during this period, the declining balance rate of depreciation would be 60% (i.e. 3 x 20%).

c) When the depreciation calculated on a declining balance basis for any year becomes less than the residual value of the asset divided by the remaining years of its useful life, the latter sum is the charge applied for that and subsequent years. For example an asset with a useful life of 5 years costing €50,000 is acquired on 1 October 2003. The straight line depreciation rate is therefore 20% and the declining balance rate is 40%. The depreciation allowed on a declining balance basis for each of the five years of the life of the asset is as follows:

		€
2003	50,000 x 40% x 3/12 (Note)	5,000
2004	(50,000 – 5,000) x 40%	18,000
2005	(50,000 – 5,000 – 18,000) x 40%	10,800
2006	(50,000 – 5,000 – 18,000 – 10,800)/2	8,100
2007		8,100

Note: The depreciation for the first year is calculated pro-rata for the period of the year during which the asset was owned.

d) A company can change the method of depreciation it uses from one year to another, and can use different methods for different assets.

e) Assets acquired for a cost of less than €500 (excluding VAT) can be written off in the first year.

f) Depreciation in respect of cars put in circulation after 1 June 2004 may not exceed €9,000 if the CO_2 emission rate exceeds 200mg/km. The depreciation limit for other vehicles is €18,300. Other limits applied for vehicles acquired before 1 November 1996.

g) A company can elect not to take all of the depreciation to which it is entitled if it so wishes, but the depreciation claimed on its assets in total must be at least equal to the depreciation that would have been claimed on those assets on a straight line basis.

h) Special rates of depreciation apply to numerous categories of expenditure which the government wishes to encourage. For example:

   i) Materials acquired before 1 January 2009 to save energy can be written off over 12 months. For example if the materials are acquired 3 months before the end of an accounting period, one quarter of the cost will be written off in that period and three-quarters will be written off in the following period. This depreciation can equally be applied to electrically powered vehicles acquired before 31 December 1999, and it is extended to new vehicles powered by natural gas or liquid petroleum gas acquired before 31 December 2010 or vehicles powered by ethanol fuel and acquired from 1 January 2007.

ii) Buildings constructed before 1 January 2009 used in treatment of polluted air or water can be written off over 12 months.

iii) Sound-proofing materials purchased before 1 January 2006 to reduce the noise from installations which existed at 31 December 1990 can be written off over 12 months.

iv) Computer software and internet site set-up costs can be written off over 12 months. Software costing less than €500 can be written off immediately as an expense;

v) 50% of the cost of an investment in the shares of a film or video production company can be written off in the year in which the investment is made.

vi) Hotel and catering companies can depreciate the costs of materials and equipment necessary to meet hygiene, security, access to the disabled, and sound-proofing legal standards. The purchase must be made between 15 November 2006 and 31 December 2009 for an accelerated depreciation on 24 months.

vii) Small and medium companies who build, or contract the building of specific industrial or commercial property in designated revitalisation zones can depreciate the related costs by 25%.

viii) Sums invested in shares of forest preservation companies, can be depreciated at the rate of 50% within the double limit of 15% of the investor's taxable profit and €100,000.

ix) Investments in shares of rural or regional development companies also qualify for a 50% exceptional depreciation rate. This is however limited to 25% of the net taxable income and the shares must be kept for 5 years. Similarly, up to 1 January 2009, the acquisition of shares in qualifying electricity-producing companies may be depreciated at the 50% rate.

i) Equipment purchased before 1 January 2006 with certain government grants can be 'super-depreciated' (this is called *suramortissement*). The grants to which this treatment applies include the *Prime d'Aménagement du Territoire* referred to at 1.11.2(b). The depreciable base is the cost price plus half of the grant. The asset would therefore eventually be depreciated below its cost price, but the calculation is performed outside the accounts. The value of the asset in the accounts is based on its cost price and the super-depreciation does not affect the calculation of capital gains or losses.

7.3.9 Loan Interest

a) Loan interest is deductible on an accruals basis. Businesses which are subject to a super-simplified accounting regime may deduct the interest on a payments basis, but companies subject to corporation tax are not permitted to make use of this accounting system.

b) Interest is deductible even if the loan was taken out to make an investment which produces income which is exempt (for example the acquisition of shares in a subsidiary). However interest relating to investment in a foreign permanent establishment is not allowable, following the territoriality principles of French corporation tax.

c) There are three limitations on the deductibility of loan interest when the loan was provided by shareholders in the company. The first and second of these apply to any French company, but the third applies only to companies subject to French corporation tax:

i) The authorised share capital of the company must be fully paid up.

ii) The interest rate must not exceed the average rate of interest on variable rate loans with a duration of more than 2 years charged by financial establishments in France (the *Banque de France* calculates the figure on the basis of information provided by 3,000 institutions). For accounting years ending on 31 December 2007 the rate is 5.41%.

iii) In the event of thin-capitalisation within a group of related companies the deductible interest is subject to further limitations. First, thin-capitalisation is defined by three criteria:

- the loan represents over 150% of the company's share capital, and

- the interest charge exceeds 25% of the borrowers' profit before interest and tax, and

- the interest paid to related companies exceeds the interest received from these same entities.

The amount of interest which exceeds the highest of these three limits has to be included in the taxable profit, unless:

- it is below €150,000, or

- the company can prove that its total borrowings are lower than those of the group.

Any excess interest can nevertheless be carried forward, but only up to 25% of the profit before interest and tax and after deduction of any other interest charges allowable for the period. From the second year, the deduction of any remaining excess interest is reduced by 5%.

This is best illustrated in an example: A company paid €400,000 in interest to related companies in 2007. The charge is below market rate. This borrowing company is in the following situation with regards to the limits set out above:

- limit of total borrowing: €100,000

- limitation at 25% of profit before interest and tax: €200,000

- amount of interest received from the related companies: €85,000

The non-deductible portion of interest is the difference between the interest effectively paid and the highest of the previous three limits, that is to say €400,000 - €200,000 = €200,000. This sum will have to be included in the 2007 taxable profit of the borrowing company, as it exceeds €150,000. It may however be carried forward for deduction in future tax years but reduced by 5% for each year beyond the second.

This limitation is not applied when the shareholder is a holding company (*société mère*) situated in the EU, EEA, or a country with a double tax treaty with France which contains a clause of non-discrimination and which does not specifically provide for the application of the thin-capitalisation rule.

iv) Interest charges paid by corporation-tax paying companies to their directors or majority shareholders in respect of loans exceeding 150% of the share capital are not deductible. The charge of interest for the amount lent up to this limitation is deductible provided it is within the rate limit of ii) above.

v) The thin-capitalisation rules does not apply if the loans are set aside and destined to eventually be incorporated to the share capital.

d) When bonds are issued after 1 January 1993 at a discount of more than 10% ("deep discount bonds"), the annual interest is calculated on an actuarial basis, and the issuer obtains relief on the interest so calculated. For bonds issued before that date a variety of rules apply, depending on the date of issue. For bonds issued between 1 January 1984 and 31 December 1992, the issuing company obtains relief either by calculating the accrued interest or by spreading the discount in equal fractions over the life of the bond, at its own option. This applies to all bonds issued at a discount in this period, whether or not the discount exceeds 10%.

e) When convertible bonds are issued which carry a premium, the premium is only allowed if and when the bonds are redeemed and the premium is paid. A provision for the premium which may be payable if the holders do not convert is not allowable.

f) Interest on participating loans is regarded as interest rather than a distribution but is subject to the limitation of interest set out in (c) above if the loan was made by a shareholder.

7.3.10 Business Entertaining

Business entertaining expenses are normally deductible. However a company is required to justify any expenses incurred by its employees. A declaration of expenses is required for the following expense items if the relevant threshold is exceeded:

a) remuneration and benefits in kind of the 5 or (in the case of a company employing more than 200 people) 10 highest paid employees if the total paid to this group exceeds €150,000 or €300,000 respectively or if the payments to any one employee exceed €50,000;

b) travelling or removal expenses paid to the above group of employees if the expense exceeds €15,000 in total;

c) expenses of cars used partly for private purposes and of property not used for the purposes of the business which are paid to the above group of employees, if they exceed €30,000 in total;

d) gifts other than promotional items with a value of less than €30 per recipient, if the gifts exceed €3,000; and

e) entertaining expenses exceeding €6,100.

7.3.11 Dividends

Dividends paid are not deductible in computing profits.

7.4. Investment Incentives

7.4.1 Tax Privileged Companies

Certain types of company are privileged for tax purposes. These do not take a distinct juridical form, but within the forms described in 3.2.1(a) above are granted privileges because of their objects. Among these are:

a) *Sociétés d'investissement à capital variable (SICAVs).* These are public investment companies governed by a law of 3 January 1979 which are exempted from tax on income and gains arising in their portfolios. Distributions to their shareholders do not give rise to a tax credit in the shareholder's hands, but the underlying tax credits on the income of the company are passed through to the shareholders in proportion to the dividends they receive. If the company capitalises its income, the tax credits are lost.

b) *Sociétés immobilières pour le commerce et l'industrie (SICOMI)*. These are sociétés anonymes or *SARLs* which rent out properties for business use. Until 1991 they were exempted from tax on both their rental income and the capital gains arising on disposal of their properties. Over the period from 1991 to 1995 their income from simple rental agreements became progressively taxable, but their income from hire-purchase leases continues to be exempt, at their option, for contracts concluded before 1 January 1996. They have to distribute 85% of their tax-exempt income by way of dividend.

c) *Sociétés immobilières d'investissement*. These are sociétés anonymes engaged in renting out buildings in France at least three quarters of the surface area of which is used for habitation. They are exempt from tax on their rental income and short term deposit interest. Distributions to shareholders do not give rise to a tax credit in the shareholder's hands.

d) *Sociétés de capital risque ('SCR')* are venture capital companies (constituted as *sociétés anonymes* or *sociétés en commandite par actions*). Their whole portfolio must consist of shares (no less than 50% at any given time) in unquoted industrial or commercial companies, which are registered in France or another EU or EEA country. The companies must be subject to French corporation tax, or carry on such a business that they would have been subject to French corporation tax if they were carrying on business in France. *SCRs* may, by exception, own movable (other than qualifying shares) and immovable assets provided that these are necessary to their activity. Generally speaking, an *SCR* must have as its sole object the administration of its portfolio. Nevertheless, *SCRs* with assets under €10 million may carry on incidental activities such as consultancy services or providing financial expertise provided that these may be considered as an extension of their normal activities. Profits arising from the incidental activities must not exceed €38,120 and the incidental turnover must remain below 50% of the company's overall charges in any accounting period. *SCRs* with assets over €10 million need to create subsidiaries to carry out any incidental activities. No one family group may hold more than 30% of the share capital of the company. The company is exempt from corporation tax on its investment income and capital gains arising from its portfolio. Generally, individual shareholders are exempt from income tax on any dividends distributed by the *SCR* out of its dividend income, or capital gains which arise to the *SCR* more than 4 years before they are distributed. Distributions out of gains realised within 4 years are taxed as capital gains on securities in the hands of the shareholder. However, the shareholder can escape tax (but not social surcharges) on either type of dividend by reinvesting it in the company and retaining the newly acquired shares for at least 5 years. To qualify the shareholder must also ensure that he, together with his family members, does not hold more than 25% of the company's share capital within the five years preceding the acquisition of the new shares.

e) *Société Unipersonnelle d'Investissement* ("*SUIR*") is a single shareholder investment company (*société par action simplifiée à associé unique*) and functions as an *SAS*. *SUIRs* can be regarded as "business angel companies", allowing an individual investor to bring equity to EU unquoted companies carrying on a commercial, industrial or artisanal activity which are subject to corporation tax. These companies must have been in existence for less than five years at the time of the investment and must be owned at least 50% by individuals. The sole shareholder of the *SUIR* must not hold more than 25% and cannot hold any director's role in any of the companies the *SUIR* has invested in. Provided all the conditions are met a *SUIR* may be totally exempt from corporation tax and *IFA* for ten years. The sole shareholder also benefits from an income tax exemption. But he remains liable to social surcharges and (if he resides abroad) withholding taxes on his dividends. However the capital of the *SUIR* is not exempt for wealth tax purposes.

f) *Sociétés de pluripropriété* (or *multipropriété*) are time-share companies formed to facilitate the co-ownership of real or personal property – for example an apartment building, a yacht or a marina. Although such companies are subject to corporation tax – unlike *sociétés immobilières de copropriété transparentes* (see 3.2.2(c)) – they seldom have any taxable income. In general the only income they receive is the reimbursement of their operating expenses by their shareholders. The benefit in kind that their shareholders enjoy from the use of the jointly owned property is not treated as a distribution, and is exempt from income tax in the hands of the shareholders. If the assets owned by the company consist of real estate to the extent of more than 50%, a sale of the shares in the company is subject to capital gains tax as a sale of land. Such companies may not normally engage in transactions with non-members to an extent such that their receipts from third parties exceed 10% of their total receipts.

7.4.2 'New Businesses'

a) New businesses established before 31 December 2009 in specific geographic zones may benefit from a tax holiday. This system has been in place for several years but is regularly altered. The latest change was mainly introduced to meet EU regulations and in particular the rule concerning maximum aid. The designated zones and general tax advantages are as follows:

i) *Zones "d'aide à finalité régionale"* (Regional Aid Zones) also known as ZAFR: Subject to prior authorisation, businesses and companies set up in a ZAFR may benefit from a two year tax exemption. These are entities which tend to benefit from European grants and thus the overall cumulative benefits (tax breaks and grants) are now subject to limitations set under specific European legislation.

ii) *Zones de Revitalisation Rurale* (ZRR): exemption from income or corporation tax for 4 years followed by a partial exemption of 60%, 40% and 20% of the net profit for the following three years.

iii) Zones de Redynamisation Urbaine (ZRU) : exemption from income or corporation tax for 2 years followed by a partial exemption of 75%, 50% and 25% of the net profit for the following three years.

b) The ZRR and ZRU tax advantages are also limited under European legislation. The maximum exemption is calculated as the total amount of expenditure (employment or investment costs) which qualifies for European aid, multiplied by a rate which varies depending on the region and the size of the company or business. The resulting EU limitation is applied in conjunction with the general €225,000 limit (over three years) set under French tax law. The advantages described in i) to iii) above are also subject to another European rule known as *"de minimis"* whereby the tax advantage together with any grants cannot exceed €200,000 over a three year period. In practice the lower of these three limitations applies.

c) Qualifying activities are those of the industrial, commercial or artisanal sectors. Non-commercial activities may qualify provided that they necessitate at least three employees. These activities must be new and the benefit of the exemption is only granted to those assessed under a *régime réel* as opposed to a micro regime. Some activities relating to property management and rentals as well as some financial activities are expressively excluded. A business may generate part of its turnover outside the designated zones but if this exceeds 15% of the total turnover, the taxable profit realised outside the zone is excluded from the tax breaks.

d) The exemption is generally not available if more than 50% of the voting rights in the new company are held by other companies. However, corporate shareholdings are ignored unless a shareholder acts as a director or holds more than 25% of the shares in a participating company which engages in a similar activity.

7.4.3 Zone Franches Urbaines - Enterprise Zones

a) New businesses and companies created before 31 December 2007 or 31 December 2011 (depending on the location) in one of the designated *ZFU*, may be exempt from income or corporation tax for up to five years. The types of qualifying and excluded activities are largely the same as those described above in 7.4.2. There are also specific eligibility criteria relating to the size of the business or company, date of incorporation, turnover and number of employees.

b) The five years exemption is followed by a partial exemption of 60%, 40% and 20% in the following there years, subject to an annual €100,000 limitation, increased by €5,000 per new employee. The EU limitation *"de minimis"* described above in 7.4.2 also applies to ZFU benefits.

7.4.4 Research

a) Industrial and commercial companies subject to a 'real' system of taxation can benefit from a tax credit in respect of their research expenditure.

b) The credit is 10% of the annual research expenditure and 40% of the amount by which the company's research expenditure in any one year exceeds the inflation adjusted value of their average expenditure on research in the two previous years, subject to a maximum credit of €16 million. New companies receive a credit in their first and second years calculated as 50% of their first year's expenditure.

c) The tax credit can be used to settle the company's tax liabilities for the year in which it was earned. Any excess credit can be carried forward against liabilities of the three subsequent years. If there is any unused credit after three years, it is repaid to the company.

d) The credit is available to fiscally transparent companies as well as companies subject to corporation tax, but in the case of a fiscally transparent company the credit is only passed to the shareholder (in proportion to his shareholding) if he works in the business.

7.4.5 Sponsorships

a) Subject to specific rules and limitations, there are a number of tax credits to promote the following sectors:

   i) new talents in the music recording industry and production of new CDs or DVDs;

   ii) film production;

   iii) production of new video games;

   iv) distribution and production of television programmes;

   v) acquisition of shares in press companies.

b) Companies liable to corporation tax can benefit from a tax credit in respect of donations made to public interest organisations with philanthropic, educational, scientific, sporting and cultural etc objects, as well as donations made to the State to assist with the purchase of "national treasures" (works of art, museum pieces etc). The credit is calculated as 60% of the funds donated limited to 5‰ of the company's turnover. Any excess may be spread over five years.

c) Companies which purchase the works of living artists for public exhibition and musical instruments benefit from a tax credit in respect of the costs spread equally over 5 years within 5‰ of the company's turnover.

d) Companies which purchase works of art to be exhibited (for ten years at least) in a *musée de France* or public library, cultural or archaeological assets, may deduct a tax credit of either 90% (with a limitation of 50% of the tax liability) or 40% (with no limitation) of the acquisition cost depending on the object and conditions of exhibition.

e) Professionals carrying on an activity through an income-tax paying business may opt for the above in lieu of the general individual taxpayer's credit for similar donations.

7.4.6 Training and Employment

a) Small and medium companies who have set up a *Plan d'Epargne Entreprises* may claim a tax credit in respect of the training provided to their employees in matters relating to this savings scheme and any other employees shareholding opportunities. This applies in the tax years 2007 and 2008 and is calculated as 25% of the first 10 hours of training for each employee, but limited to €75 per hour. Overall the credit is limited to €5,000 (for the two year period) and is also subject to the EU *"de minimis"* limitation. The training must be carried out by specific organisations.

b) The employment of apprentices may give rise to a tax credit calculated as €1,600 multiplied by the number (annual average) of apprentices employed during the period. This is increased to €2,200 for disabled apprentices. The tax credit is limited to the employment costs of apprentices reduced by any States grants obtained in respect of these employments.

c) Similarly, the employment of work experience students also gives rise to a tax credit. This is set at €100 per student per week, limited annually to €2,600 per student.

d) There is a tax credit is respect of the continued professional training of managing directors (up to 40 hours annually).

e) The employment of individuals classed as "reserve" work force may give rise to a tax credit limited annually to €30,000 per company or business. This is valid until 31 December 2008.

7.4.7 Investment in the Départements and Collectivités d'Outre-Mer

a) Investment in the above territories can qualify for several different investment incentive schemes offering reductions of tax. Companies subject to a 'real' tax regime (whether under income tax or corporation tax) which invest in industry, the hotel business, fishing, tourism, new sources of energy, agriculture, construction, public works, transport, craftwork, maintenance for industrial businesses or audiovisual or film production or distribution can deduct the whole of their investment from their tax bill.

b) Prior approval is required for investments exceeding €300,000 in certain sensitive sectors or in excess of €1 million in other sectors.

7.4.8 Investment in Corsica

a) Smaller companies or businesses which carry on a commercial, industrial, artisanal, agricultural or self employed activity in Corsica can qualify for a tax credit. The business or company has to be subject to one of the "real" basis of assessment, created in the period from 1 January 2002 to 31 December 2011 and run for 5 years at least. The tax credit is calculated as 20% of the investment (less any public grants), and may be carried forward for the following nine years.

b) Companies which were created in Corsica between 1 January 1998 and 31 December 1999, engaged in industry, hotel operations, building, public works or certain craftwork businesses were exempt from corporation tax for the first 8 years of their life. No more than 50% of the shares of the qualifying company could be held by other companies. Equally, companies subject to corporation tax (wherever formed) which established a new business in Corsica between 1 January 1991 and 31 December 1999 in the areas of industrial, agricultural, artisanal or construction activity could be exempt from corporation tax for 8 years. The exemption is available only with the prior agreement of the Ministry of Finance and now subject to EU limitations (see 7.4.2).

7.4.9 New Innovating Businesses

a) Businesses within this newly created classification may benefit from a total tax exemption for 3 years and a tax abatement of 50% for 2 years. This applies to accounting periods showing a profit. The periods of exemption therefore do not have to be chronological.

b) To qualify the business must allocate at least 15% of its total expenditures to research and development. At least 50% of its share capital must be owned by individuals, by SCRs or designated associations. The benefit of the tax breaks is reserved to activities created less then eight years prior to the election for this status.

7.4.10 Family Tax Credit

a) Companies and small income tax businesses (assessed under a régime réel) may claim a tax credit in respect of expenditure relating to assistance they provide to their employees to facilitate the interaction between their family and professional life such as creation of crèches, maternity, paternity or child sickness leave, ad-hoc childminding expenses.

b) The tax credit is calculated as 25% of the expenditure up to €500,000 per annum.

7.5. Loss Relief

7.5.1 Carry Forward

a) Losses can be carried forward indefinitely for offset against taxable income (and long term capital gains other than gains on development land), unless the company has changed its form or merged or there has been a change in beneficial ownership.

b) Where a company has suffered depreciation in a loss making period, the unused depreciation can be carried forward indefinitely.

7.5.2 Carry Back

a) Companies subject to corporation tax can carry losses back against the undistributed taxable income of the three preceding years. This option is available to any company subject to corporation tax, except in respect of an accounting period in which the company ceases trading or merges into another company. It is a condition of the availability of the relief that the company should be up to date with its tax payments for the previous three years.

b) The corporation tax paid in the preceding years is not immediately repaid to the company when this option is exercised, but the company becomes entitled to a tax credit at the rate of tax applicable to the deficit period. This can be used to pay its corporation tax liabilities arising in the next five years. Alternatively, the tax credit can be discounted with a bank. If the credit is not used during the five years the tax is repaid.

c) If the company does not elect to use the carry back option during the tax year, the losses must be carried forward.

7.5.3 Losses in Mergers

In a merger it is rare for the losses of the acquired company to survive. Any attempt to avoid this problem by a reverse take-over (*fusion à l'anglaise!*) can be attacked as an abuse of law. The Ministry of Finance has the power, in its complete discretion, to authorise the carry over of losses of either the acquiring or the acquired company. The acquiring company may be permitted to carry over its losses if the merger was effected for bona fide commercial reasons and if the nature of the business of the acquiring company is not altered.

7.6. Computing Corporation Tax Liabilities

7.6.1 Rates of Tax

a) The rate of French corporation tax is $33^{1}/_{3}$%.

b) Gains on certain types of shareholding can be subject to tax at 19%.

c) Companies with liability to French corporation tax exceeding €763,000 are liable to a 'social surcharge' of 3.3%. This is calculated on the gross corporate tax, (i.e. before the deduction of any tax credits or *avoir fiscal*), less an abatement of €763,000.

d) Smaller industrial or commercial companies with a turnover under €7,630,000 and owned at least 75% by individuals may qualify for a reduced tax rate of 15% on the first €38,120 of taxable profit. This limit is adjusted if the accounting period is longer or shorter than 12 months. For instance, a qualifying smaller company with an accounting period of 18 months can apply the reduced rate on the first €57,180 of taxable profit. The remaining profit is taxed at the normal rate of 33.33%. Eligible companies may apply the 15% to part or all of their long-term capital gains within the above limit.

e) Certain non-profit-making organisations pay tax at 10% or 24% depending on the source of their income.

f) Companies carrying on business in the *DOM* benefit from a reduction of their taxable profits of $33^1/_3\%$. This effectively translates as a lower tax rate. Thus for example capital gains which would otherwise be taxable at 19% are taxable at $12^2/_3\%$ in the *DOM*.

7.6.2 Minimum Tax

a) Companies subject to French corporation tax in existence on 1 January in each year and which have a turnover of at least €400,000 generally pay an amount of tax in advance as a *forfait*. Some companies are exempt from this liability, for example new companies for the first three years of their existence, provided that at least half of their share capital is paid up in cash.

b) This is effectively a minimum tax liability, although the amount paid can be credited against the corporation tax due for the two following years if the liability for the year of payment does not exceed the minimum liability. The amount payable is based on the company's turnover in the previous year, and for the payment due in respect of companies existing at 1 January 2008, the amount of tax is calculated as follows:

Turnover	Forfait €
Less than €400,000	Nil
€400,000 to €150,000	€750
€150,000 to €300,000	€1,125
€300,000 to €750,000	€1,575
€750,000 to €1,500,000	€2,175
€1,500,000 to €7,500,000	€3,750
€7,500,000 to €15,000,000	€15,000
€15,000,000 to €75,000,000	€18,750
€75,000,000 upwards	€30,000

7.6.3 Tax Credits

a) If the taxable profit of a company includes investment income which has suffered taxation at source and thus carries a tax credit, the company may offset this credit against its corporation tax liability. This largely concerns income from bonds, *bons de caisse*, taxed at source at 12% or 10%. In this case it is the gross income that must be added to the taxable profit of the company. However in practice it is possible to add the net income received but then reduce the tax credit deductible from the corporation tax liability to 66,66%. If the deduction exceeds the liability or, if the company realises a loss, the tax credit is definitively lost.

b) The tax credits attaching to dividends received by a company from its participations (see 7.8.4) cannot be offset against the corporation tax liability of the *société mère* because the dividends do not constitute part of its taxable income. Equally dividends received from 95% subsidiaries within an integrated group do not carry a tax credit, because there is no liability to account for tax credits within a group (see 7.8.1(f)).

c) Credit is given for foreign taxes paid on foreign source income if provision for such credit is made in a double tax treaty. If the income is received abroad, the related tax credits must be reported on form 2066. The credits are lost if the company has no corporation tax liability.

d) The minimum tax paid in advance at the beginning of each tax year is deducted from the corporation tax liability of the same year and, if it exceeds that liability, the two following years.

7.7. Payment of Corporation Tax

7.7.1 Payments in Advance

a) The taxes withheld from distributions to shareholders are not an advance payment of the company's own tax liability.

b) The annual minimum tax (see 7.6.2) does represent a payment on account of the company's tax liability.

c) Corporation tax paying companies are required to file a tax return within 3 months of the end of their accounting year, although for companies with a 31 December year end the filing period is in practice extended to 4 May. Unlike the income tax system, companies subject to corporation tax are required to pay their corporation tax liabilities spontaneously – in most cases no tax assessment is issued.

d) The company is required to make four quarterly payments of tax on account during the tax year, and to render any balance due in a fifth payment. The quarterly payments on account are based on the profits of the last complete accounting period. They are due on 20 February, 20 May, 20 August and 20 November (regardless of the accounting year end), but penalties are not applied provided the payment is made by the 15th day of the month following the due date. For example a business with a 31 December year end should technically file its tax return by 30 April following the year end. It makes its quarterly payments in respect of 2008, based on the income of 2007, before 15 March, 15 June, 15 September and 15 December during 2008, and must pay any balance of tax due for 2008 by 15 April 2009. If the payments on account exceed the actual liability, the difference is repaid to the company.

e) In practice the first instalment is normally based on the income of the year before the basis period, and the difference is corrected when the second instalment is paid. (Eg for a company with a calendar year accounting period, the payment on 15 March 2008 would initially be based on the income of 2006). The quarterly payments are not due if the previous year's liability was below €3,000.

7.7.2 Mainstream Liabilities

a) Companies subject to corporation tax must file a tax return within 3 months of their accounting year end. Companies with a turnover exceeding €15,000,000 in 2007 must file their corporation tax returns electronically. The limit is €760,000 for VAT returns.

b) The final adjustment to the company's tax liability is made in a fifth payment, early in the year following the tax year (see above).

c) The 3.3% social surcharge on corporation tax is payable, at latest, with the final payment of corporation tax. Companies with a turnover in excess of €5M must pay charge and file the relevant paperwork on line.

d) Failure to meet any due date for payment results in a penalty increase in the tax due of 10%. This penalty is non-deductible for tax purposes.

7.8. Groups of Companies

7.8.1 The Integrated Basis

a) A company which owns at least 95% of another company (both paying French corporation tax) may file a consolidated return for the group. The parent company (*tête de groupe*) can be a foreign company with a permanent establishment in France, but cannot be a company 95% owned by another

French company. All of the companies in the group must have the same year end. The parent company has complete discretion to determine the perimeter of the group among its 95% subsidiaries, and can leave out companies that would qualify as group members if it so wishes. A 95% subsidiary of a 95% subsidiary (etc) qualifies for group membership, even though the parent owns only 90.25% of the sub-subsidiary (or less in the case of remoter subsidiaries).

b) It is not possible to consolidate the results of companies which are partially or totally exempt from French corporation tax, eg *SICOMI*, companies established in enterprise zones, *SCR* etc.

c) The parent company makes an election to constitute itself the sole taxpayer for the group. The election must be in place at the beginning of the first tax year for which it is to apply and filed at the same time as the *déclaration de résultats* of the previous year. This election lasts for five years.

d) The grouping of the results allows the offset of revenue losses in one subsidiary against profits of other group companies. Equally long term capital gains in one group company can be offset by long term capital losses in another. The parent company pays capital gains tax on the net gains of the whole group, and if advantage is to be taken of the 19% rate available on long term gains, the parent company must make the appropriate transfer to its reserves.

e) Transfers of assets within the group take place free of tax.

f) If a group member receives a dividend from another group member which is not covered by the optional participation exemption (see 7.8.4), the dividend received is excluded from the group income.

g) Losses incurred by a company before it joins a group may not be relieved against profits of other group companies. They can be offset against future profits of the same company.

h) If a company leaves the group the following consequences ensue:

   i) the results of the departing company in the year that it leaves the group are not treated as part of the income of the group;

   ii) gains or losses on assets transferred to or from the departing company while it was a member of the group become chargeable;

   iii) the departing company cannot carry forward any revenue or long term capital losses it incurred while a member of the group; nor can it carry back any subsequent losses against the profits of any period during which it was a member of the group;

iv) if capital assets have been transferred between the departing company and other members of the group at an over or under value, or if there has been any other form of hidden subsidy, such as debts forgiven, the effects of these are reintegrated into the group results for the year of departure and there are penalty increases in the amounts reintegrated.

7.8.2 The Consolidated Basis

a) With the consent of the French Ministry of Finance, a French company can add to its own worldwide income, the income of any subsidiaries in which it holds at least 50% of the voting rights. This percentage can be lower if the local taxation system prevents a company from holding as much as 50% of the voting rights. This basis is effectively reserved to a few large French multinational groups.

b) The company may be allowed credit for any foreign taxes paid by its foreign subsidiaries.

c) The calculation of the group taxable income is otherwise based on the principles applied in the normal system.

7.8.3 The Worldwide Income Basis

a) With the consent of the French Ministry of Finance, a French company may include income from its foreign operations, in its income assessable in France.

b) The company may be able to claim credit for any foreign taxes suffered on its foreign source income.

c) The calculation of its taxable income is otherwise made on the principles applied in the normal system.

7.8.4 Participations

a) Most companies subject in whole or in part to French corporation tax at the normal rate may exclude from their taxable income the dividends they receive from their subsidiaries and associated companies. However, 5% of the total amount of dividends received by the parent company is reintegrated into their taxable income. The parent company (called the *société mère*) can be a French company, a company with its head office in the *DOM*, or a French branch of a foreign company. It is not necessary for the subsidiary company to be resident in France, but it cannot be a fiscally transparent company. To qualify, the parent company must hold at least 5% of the shares in the subsidiary. This treatment is optional for the parent.

b) Dividends paid to a non-resident are still in principle subject to French withholding tax at 18%. However these distributions are exempt if they are paid to a parent company resident in an EU country. Similarly, most double tax treaties either provide a reduced rate or exemption for such distributions.

c) If the parent company is directly or indirectly controlled by one or more non-EU residents, it has to provide evidence that the main objective of the overall structure is not purely the avoidance of the withholding tax.

d) The participation exemption does not extend to the exemption of capital gains arising on a disposal of a participation.

7.9. Anti-Avoidance Measures

a) Transactions between a French and a foreign company under the same control can be recast in arms length terms under transfer pricing rules. Common control is presumed when the transfer is to a tax haven company (i.e. a company subject to tax of an amount at least one third lower than the tax it would have suffered had it been resident in France). The administration published a list of countries considered to be tax havens for this purpose on 9 October 1975. This list was neither particularly accurate nor complete when it was published, and it is now considerably out-of-date. The territories concerned were divided into three groups:

i) Countries with no taxes on income

Andorra	Bermuda	French Polynesia	New Caledonia
Bahamas	Campione	Monaco	Turks & Caicos
Bahrain	Cayman Islands	Nauru	Vanuatu

ii) Countries with no tax on certain foreign source income

Costa Rica	Liberia	Panama	Venezuela
Djibouti	Libya	Uruguay	

iii) Countries with low taxes, either in general or under particular regimes

Angola	Gibraltar	Jamaica	Solomon
Antigua	Gilbert and	Liechtenstein	Islands
Barbados	Ellice	Luxembourg	St Helena
British Virgin	Grenada	Montserrat	St Vincent
Islands	Hong Kong	Netherlands	Switzerland
Channel Islands	Isle of Man	Antilles	Tonga

b) Payments to persons resident in a tax haven, or to bank accounts in a tax haven, (as defined above) are presumed to be distributions and therefore not deductible, unless the taxpayer proves that they are bona fide commercial payments and not abnormal or excessive.

c) Article 209b of the *Code Général des Impôts* was substantially amended as a result of the 2005 Finance law. This follows the "Schneider Electric" case in respect of which the *Conseil d'Etat* held that the terms of Article 209b could not be applied in the presence of a double tax treaty unless the treaty specifically allowed it.

Article 209b now applies to French resident companies which hold directly or indirectly a participation of 50% in an entity established outside France and which benefit from a lower tax regime or *régime fiscal privilégié*. It also applies where there is a chain of companies or entities. The term "entity" in this context is very wide-sweeping and includes commercial and non-commercial companies, trusts or similar structures and organisations, partnerships, Anstalten and Stiftungen of the Lichtenstein, foundations and so on. However, the application of Article 209b varies depending on whether the income of the structure can be regarded as a profit or (in the absence of any specific terminology as a result of the entity's legal form), it is simply a revenue, income, or increase in value. In essence, the difference lies between "entities" in the broad sense of the word and more conventional "permanent establishments" (incorporated or not).

i) in the case of entities as defined above, the income is treated as investment income taxable at the level of the company established in France. The labelling of "investment income" as opposed to "company profit" eliminates the difficulties encountered when applying the old dispositions of Article 209b in conjunction with any double tax treaty. Indeed most treaties stipulate that investment income is taxable in the country of residence of the beneficiary as opposed to company profits usually taxable where the company is incorporated.

ii) in the case of profits of a permanent establishment, France may tax these in proportion to the level of participation held by the French company, if

- there is no double tax treaty, or

- if the treaty expressly authorises the application of Article 209b (see 5.2.7(c)), or

- the treaty provides that profits from a permanent establishment may be taxed both in the jurisdiction where the establishment is situated and the state of the registered office.

d) French resident employees of a non-French resident company are jointly and severally liable for the tax due by their employer if:

i) they control the employer; or

ii) the employer is not mainly engaged in an industrial or commercial business other than the provision of services; or

iii) the employer is resident in a tax haven as defined in (a).

When the services are provided by non-French resident employees of the foreign company in the above circumstances, payments to the company are subject to withholding taxes of 15% if the payments are in respect of the services of artists or sportsmen, or 33⅓% in all other cases.

8. CAPITAL GAINS TAX

8.1. General

a) In recent years the French capital gains tax regime has undergone a number of in-depth reforms. The system differentiates between the gains realised by individuals assessed under the *plus-values des particuliers* regime and those realised by a business (self-employed) or a company, which are assessed under the *plus-values professionnelles.*

The *plus-values professionnelles* (or business capital gains tax regime), makes a further distinction between:

i) income tax paying businesses assessed under the *bénéfices industriels et commerciaux, bénéfices non-commerciaux or bénéfices agricoles.*

ii) entities liable to corporation tax and described in 3.2.1(a).

For ease of reference the term "business" designates the income tax paying category, whilst the term "companies" relates to entities liable to corporation tax.

b) The rules usually differ depending on the nature of the asset sold (immovable or movable).

c) There is an exception for unquoted companies the assets of which mainly consist of real estate. These are classed as *sociétés à prépondérance immobilière* if more than 50% of their assets consist of immovable property (including rights or shares in immovable assets). The disposal of shares in such entities is treated as a disposal of real estate. For the purpose of applying this test, property required for the company's industrial, commercial, agricultural or non-commercial professional activities is ignored, with the exception of properties which are simply rented out (whether furnished or unfurnished). From 1 January 2008, the relevant article defining the *prépondérance immobilière* stipulates that it is <u>immovable assets situated in France</u> that are taken into account. If the 50% limit is exceeded, any gain resulting from the disposal of the share is treated as French source income.

The *prépondérance immobilière* (or property-holding nature of the company) is studied by reference to the assets recorded on the balance sheets at the end of the previous three accounting periods (or less depending on the length of existence of the company). If no accounting period has been finalised at the time a gain is realised, the situation is appreciated based on the closing balance sheets at that time.

Capital gains arising from the disposal of shares in a *société à prépondérance immobilière* by a French resident taxpayer are subject to:

i) the *plus-values des particuliers* for real estate gains, if the property-holding company is liable to French income tax. This typically concerns *SCI*s and the regime is described in 8.2.2(f).

ii) the regime applicable to the disposal of shares and other securities if the property-holding company is subject to corporation tax (see 8.3.4).

d) Finally, the French capital gains tax rules differ depending on the residence of the individuals or entities realising the gain. Direct sales of French properties or sales of shares in French property-holding entities by non-residents of France are subject to the specific regime described in 8.4. This applies regardless of the tax regime applicable to the entity (corporation or income tax). It should be noted that transfers of shares of entities classed as *prépondérance immobilière* whether French or foreign attract French registration duties at around 5%. However, the application of the registration duties to the share transfer of foreign entities was recently successfully challenged. In practice, the French authorities rely on the 3% tax reporting requirements, annual form 2746 (see chapter 12) to identify any changes in the shareholding of such foreign entities, which can lead to assessments in arrears of registration duties and capital gains tax.

8.2. Capital Gains of Individuals

8.2.1 Classification of Gains

a) Non-business related gains are classified according to the nature of the asset sold:

i) land, buildings or rights in real estate and shareholdings in unquoted property holding companies;

ii) shares and securities (other than shares in unquoted property holding companies);

iii) other movable goods;

iv) precious metals, jewels, antiques and works of art;

v) gains on the financial futures market (the '*MATIF*' – *marché à terme d'instruments financiers*), or equivalent exchanges in other countries.

8.2.2 Gains and Losses on Land and Buildings

a) In several important cases, gains on real estate are exempt. These are gains on:

i) a sale of a main residence;

ii) a sale of any residential properties held for over 15 years;

iii) a sale of one or two properties in France by certain non-residents (see 8.4);

iv) a sale of agricultural or forestry land if the price per square metre does not exceed certain limits;

v) sales of real estate totalling less than €15,000 in any one year;

vi) expropriations if the compensation received by the former owner is used to buy another property within one year;

vii) gains realised on a sale of real estate directly held by old age pensioners or individuals who hold a specific invalidity card, provided that the taxpayer has not been liable to wealth tax in the tax year two years (N-2) before the year in which the disposal was made. In addition, the net taxable income of the taxpayer in N-2 must not exceed €9,437 plus €2,520 per extra half family part (2007 income).

b) Gains on sales, exchanges and expropriations of real estate and interests in real estate (such as an usufruct in a piece of land) are computed as the difference between the purchase price (plus costs of acquisition) and the selling price (less costs of sale). If the property was inherited rather than purchased, the purchase price is deemed to be the valuation used for inheritance tax purposes.

i) The standard allowance for the costs associated with the purchase is 7.5% of the purchase price but the taxpayer has the option to itemise his costs if they were greater.

ii) The standard allowance for the cost of construction, reconstruction, extension and improvements to the house is 15% of the purchase price. This standard allowance is only granted if the property has been owned for five years at least. The taxpayer has the option to itemise these expenses if they are greater but the deductions will only be granted if the work was carried out by registered building firms and relevant invoices and evidence of payment are provided. It should be noted that the cost of replacing existing features or items of the property is not allowable.

iii) The taxpayer may deduct any inheritance or gifts tax paid at the time of acquisition of the property.

c) The gain is then reduced by 10% for each complete year of ownership after the fifth year (taper relief) and therefore totally exempt after fifteen years.

d) The taxpayer is entitled to a deduction of €1,000 (per property owner) from all of his gains arising in the year.

e) There are generally no provisions for relieving a loss realised by an individual in his private capacity on a sale of real estate. The loss cannot be relieved against other gains or income, in the same or subsequent tax years. The only exceptions are for returning expatriates and in cases where a block of land which has been acquired piecemeal is sold as one lot, realising gains on some units and losses on others. In the latter case the taxpayer is allowed to net off the gains and losses.

f) A transfer of shares of an unquoted property-holding company classed as *société à prépondérance immobilière* is treated as a sale of real estate but only if the company is liable to income tax and not corporation tax. Typically this is likely to concern shares of *SCI*s. Any gain arising on this type of share transfer is taxable under the rules described above in (b). If the shares have been held for over 15 years, the gain is exempt through the application of the 10% abatement described above in (c). If the underlying property of the company is used as one of the shareholders' main residence, he will benefit from the principal private residence exemption in respect of his shareholding.

g) The taxation of gains arising on a sale of shares by French tax residents in an unquoted property company liable to French corporation tax follows the rules applicable to the disposals of stocks and shares described below in 8.2.3 (a) and (b). The property-holding nature of the company is simply ignored, but not in the case of non-resident shareholders (see 8.4). It should be noted that the €25,000 (2008) exemption threshold does not apply and costs of improvements to the underlying property do not qualify as a deduction from the net taxable gain. Acquisition costs are only allowed if they relate to the acquisition of the shares and if they are paid by the shareholder.

h) When real estate is expropriated (by a compulsory purchase order), any gain is taxable as a gain of the year in which the compensation is received. However the gain is completely exempt if the taxpayer reinvests the proceeds within one year in other real estate assets.

i) Taxable capital gains realised by French resident individuals on the disposal of real estate are subject to a fixed rate of 27% (including 11% social contributions) on the net taxable capital gains they realise during the tax year. The tax is payable within two months of completion and must be accompanied by the tax form 2048 IMM. In practice it is the *notaire* who deals with the capital gains tax formality except for non-residents who usually need to appoint a fiscal representative for this purpose (see 8.4.).

8.2.3 Shares and Other Securities

a) Gains on sales of securities are only taxable if the total proceeds of sales made by the taxpayer and his family exceed €20,000 (2007) and €25,000 (2008).

b) Gains arising on a sale of securities are calculated as the difference between the purchase price (plus costs of acquisition) and the selling price (less the costs of sale and the tax on stock exchange transactions). If the securities were inherited, the purchase price is taken to be the valuation used to compute the inheritance tax. The rate applicable is 29% (including 11% social contributions).

　　i) The gain benefits from an abatement of one-third per full year of ownership beyond the fifth, leading effectively to a total exemption after 8 years. Because of the time condition, this abatement will only be effective from 1 January 2012, and total exemption possible from 1 January 2014.

　　ii) By exception and under strict conditions, this new abatement started applying on 1 January 2006 (to 31 December 2013) in respect of gains realised by retiring managing directors of certain small and medium companies.

iii) If the shares were bought before 1 January 1979, there is an option to take the highest value at which the shares were quoted in 1978 as the purchase price.

iv) If a sale is made from a holding of shares bought over a period at different prices, the average purchase price is taken as the purchase price of each share.

v) On a sale of share rights, the taxpayer's cost is taken as nil.

vi) Where shares are quoted in a foreign currency, the acquisition and sale value must be converted at the exchange rate of the date of acquisition and the date of sale. This effectively means that the taxpayer suffers tax on any currency gains, or will be able to set any currency loss against his overall taxable gain.

vii) If the shares were inherited or acquired by lifetime gift, the taxpayer may increase the acquisition value by any inheritance or gifts tax paid at the time he acquired these shares, thereby reducing the taxable amount.

c) Losses realised on a disposal of securities in this category can be relieved against gains realised on other disposals of securities in the same tax year or the ten succeeding tax years. Gains from the early closure of a *PEA* and profits on the *MATIF* are treated as securities of this class for this purpose.

d) When shares in one company are exchanged for shares in another as a result of a public offer, the replacement shares take on the base cost of the original shares, so any gain is rolled-over into the new shares.

e) Tax under this heading applies to foreign companies as well as all individuals (whether resident in France or not), subject to the terms of any double tax treaty provision to the contrary.

f) Gains arising on shares in property companies (*sociétés immobilières*) liable to income tax are subject to the system described in 8.2.2. Non-residents are subject to a specific withholding tax (see 8.4).

g) The 'permanent' rate of tax on a disposal of securities by an individual is 18%. In addition French residents pay social contributions totalling 11%, making a total tax rate of 29%.

8.2.4 Movable Assets

a) Capital gains on furniture, cars and home appliances are exempt. Examples of assets taxable under this heading are yachts, race-horses, wines, precious metals, jewels, antiques and works of art.

b) The gains of a tax household are also exempt if the total sales do not exceed €5,000 in a tax year.

c) The tax is computed in the same way as for the capital gains tax on real estate (see 8.2.2), except that if an asset is held for more than two years, the gain is reduced by 10% for every year of ownership after the second year. For a racehorse, there is an additional abatement of 15% of the gain for each of the first 7 years of ownership (or until the gain is eliminated). The €1,000 general deduction does not apply to this type of gain. The relevant tax return to declare such disposals is form 2048M. It has to be submitted within one month from the sale.

d) There is no relief for losses arising on disposals of assets in this category.

e) Non-residents are exempt from tax under this heading.

8.2.5 Gains on the MATIF

a) Gains on contracts made on the French financial futures exchange (called the *MATIF*) or any foreign futures exchange which relate to quoted securities, commodities etc are taxed at the rate of 29% for French residents (including the social contributions).

b) Losses in this category can only be offset against gains on the same type of assets, which includes gains of the class described in 8.2.3.

c) Habitual investors are taxed under the non-commercial income rules, at normal scale rates. Their losses can only be relieved against other income of the same kind received in the loss making year or the next six years.

d) Professional investors can opt to be taxed under the business income rules and thus can relieve their losses against their total income of the loss-making year and the next six years. For businesses created on or after 1 January 1996, the losses can only be relieved against the taxpayer's total income if he or a member of his household works full time in the 'business'.

8.2.6 Roll-Over Relief

a) Subject to prior approval from the administration, an individual may roll over a gain on the disposal of shares in a company in which he has worked for at least three years prior to the sale. For this he must re-invest the proceeds before 31 December in the year of the disposal, in a small or medium business, owned at least 75% by individuals and created less than fifteen years before. Neither the taxpayer nor any members of his household may be existing shareholders of the new company at the time of the investment. In addition they cannot exercise any director's function or hold more than 25% of the shares in the new company for at least five years.

b) If real estate is expropriated (by compulsory purchase order), any capital gain is exempt if the proceeds are reinvested in real estate within one year.

8.3. Capital Gains of Businesses *(Plus-Values Professionnelles)*

8.3.1 General Principles

a) "Business capital gains" or *plus-values professionnelles* are gains realised on assets registered as fixed assets in the balance sheet of a business or a company.

b) Businesses liable to income tax and assessed under the *bénéfices industriels et commerciaux, bénéfices non-commerciaux* or *bénéfices agricoles* are also liable to capital gains tax under the *plus-values professionnelles* regime. However in practice, small and medium businesses benefit from a number of exemptions described below.

c) Under the *plus-values professionnelles* regime, capital gains are largely treated as part of the taxable income or profit. The gains may result from planned operations such as sales, contribution of assets, exchanges, donation, activity cessation, and so on. However, gains may also arise from unforeseen events such as expropriation or forced cessation of activity, for instance.

d) As long as a gain or loss remains unrealised, it has no fiscal effects. There is however the possibility to account for the depreciation of fixed assets in the provision account.

e) Gains on the sale of certain forms of intellectual property, such as certain patents or patentable inventions, and fees from licensing such intellectual property, are treated as long term capital gains provided that the property concerned has the character of a capital asset for the company receiving the proceeds or income. It must not have been purchased within the preceding two years. This treatment does not apply to trade-marks, know-how, computer software or designs.

f) Capital gains or losses are normally taxable only when they are realised, eg by sale or exchange. However companies subject to corporation tax which hold investments in collective investment schemes, other than certain equity or risk capital investment funds, are required to revalue their holdings at the balance sheet date and pay tax on any resulting gain. Similarly insurance companies (other than those mainly providing life assurance or life insurance) are required to revalue their holdings of collective investment schemes annuallly and to include the resulting surplus or deficit in their taxable income.

g) Royalty income arising from an exclusive licence to use a patent is taxed as a long term capital gain if the patent forms part of the business assets of an industrial, commercial or agricultural company and the licence is granted for a period of at least five years (whether the income is subject to income tax or corporation tax). This rule does not apply unless the patent concerned amounts to a fixed asset of the licensing company and it has not been purchased within the previous two years.

h) When business assets are destroyed or expropriated, the payment of capital gains tax can be spread over a number of years equivalent to the number of years over which the asset has been depreciated.

8.3.2 Computation of the Taxable Gain

a) Gains (or losses) under this regime are computed as the difference between the sale price and the depreciated cost of the asset. There is no adjustment for inflation. Costs directly linked to the operation such as commissions, taxes and disbursements are deductible from the taxable gain. However, other expenditures such as costs of surveys, advice etc are treated as running costs.

b) The price is the value reflected in the relevant deed. However the authorities may contest this if:

i) they can prove that the parties involved have deliberately reported a lower value than the effective price paid for the asset; or if

ii) they can prove that the market value of the transferred asset is in fact higher.

c) The gain (or loss) is taken into account in respect of the accounting period in which it is realised. The exact date generally coincides with the date of the asset's transfer. For a sale, it is the day of the agreement of both parties on the price and the nature of asset transferred, even if the transfer is formalised and the price paid at a later date. When an asset is brought to a new company, the date of the transfer is deemed to be that of the company's registration at the *Registre du Commerce*. When an asset is transferred out of a company or business, the relevant date for the computation of the gain can be the date of the first balance sheet recording the transfer, or the date when the activity ceased.

8.3.3 Businesses Liable to Income Tax

a) Some capital gains tax rules are specific to individuals who realise business gains within the exercise of a commercial, non-commercial or agricultural activity, or through an income tax paying company such as those described in 3.3.2.

b) This regime still makes a distinction between long and short term gain, but in practice the scope of this differentiation is limited since many small and medium businesses benefit from specific exemptions (see below).

c) Short term gains (or losses) are:

    i)   gains on sales of assets held for less than two years; and

    ii) the portion of gain due to the depreciation claimed on assets held for two years of more.

Such gains are simply added to the business profits of the relevant accounting period or to the taxable income of the individual taxpayer. A net short term gain (after netting off any losses for the period) may be spread over three years in equal instalments - the year in which the gain is realised and the following two years. Net short term gains are subject to normal income tax rates.

d) Gains other than those listed above are classed as long term gains. These are computed as the excess sale price over the original acquisition value. They are netted off against any long term losses realised on the same tax period. The net taxable gain is subject to a tax rate of 27% (including 11% social contributions).

e) Taxable long term gains realised since 1 January 2006 within an industrial, commercial or agricultural activity benefit from a 10% reduction for each complete year of ownership after the fifth year. Such gains are therefore exempt after fifteen years.

f) Capital gains realised by small businesses liable to income tax are exempt if the average turnover of the two years preceding the sale does not exceed:

    i)   €250,000 for industrial businesses, businesses which sell goods or provide furnished lodgings (professional landlords), and agricultural businesses (category one).

    ii) €90,000 for businesses that provide services taxable as industrial or commercial income and businesses generating non-commercial income (category two).

The activity must have run for at least 5 years for the above exemptions to apply.

Where the average turnover is between €250,000 and €350,000 for businesses in the first category, or €90,000 and €126,000 in the second category, a part of the gain is exempt. The exempt portion of the gain is the ratio resulting from subtracting its average turnover from €350,000 (category one) and dividing the result by €100,000. For category two it is the ratio resulting from subtracting the average turnover from €126,000 and dividing the result by €36,000.

For example, a business in category one with a taxable gain of €20,000 and a turnover of €320,000 will benefit from an exemption of: €350,000 - €320,000 = €30,000/€100,000 = 0.30 i.e. 30% of its gain (€6,000).

g) From 1 January 2006, the chargeable or free disposal of a complete branch of activity or whole individual business (commercial, professional, industrial, agricultural or artisanal) of five years of activity or more, may qualify for an exemption under strict conditions. This exemption applies to income-tax paying businesses as well as small and medium corporation-tax paying companies. The value of the assets transferred must be below €300,000. If it is between €300,000 and €500,000, a percentage of the transfer may be exempt. This is calculated as €500,000, less the transfer value divided by 200,000. If the transfer is a sale, the vendor must not own more than 50% of the financial or voting rights in the business. Transfers of real estate (other than that used for the activity) or companies classed as *société à prépondérance immobilière* are excluded from the measure.

h) Transfers of business assets for no consideration by an individual, during his life or on death, do not result in capital gains tax, provided at least one of the new owners continues the activity for at least five years. It is the value of the asset at the date of transfer which is used as the new base cost for future depreciation purposes.

i) When assets are transferred by an individual to a company in exchange for shares, gains arising on the non-depreciable assets are not charged to tax until the shares are sold or the company sells the assets contributed. Any tax on gains arising on depreciable assets is payable by the company, rather than the individual, and can be spread over five years. The company can calculate depreciation on the assets based on their value at the date they were contributed to the company.

j) Gains on sales of shares in fiscally transparent (income tax paying) companies are treated as business capital gains if the shareholder plays an active role in the company. Therefore the gains are exempt if the turnover of the company does not exceed the thresholds set out in 8.3.3(f). It should be noted that *SCI*s carrying on furnished lettings are liable to corporation tax. Therefore the gains on the sale of shares in these companies are not eligible for the exemption mentioned above. They may nevertheless qualify under the small and medium company exemption described in (g).

k) Gains realised by professional landlords may be exempt under the conditions set out in 8.3.3(f). The qualifying criteria to be considered as a professional landlord are outlined in 18.2.2(p). Gains realised by non-professional landlords are subject to the capital gains tax rules applicable to individuals described in 8.2.

8.3.4 Companies Liable to Corporation Tax

a) Most capital gains realised by French resident companies are added to their taxable profit and taxed at the normal corporation tax rate of $33^{1}/_{3}\%$ plus the 3.3% social surcharge due by larger companies, if applicable. The tax on the gain is thus paid at the same time as the tax on the other profits of the company.

b) The distinction between long term and short term gains for entities liable to corporation tax is now of much reduced importance. Generally speaking, the differentiation was based on whether assets were held for less or over two years. The reference to long term gains now simply designates a reduced rate of tax of 19% applicable in certain circumstances. The regime applicable to gains on the disposal of stock and shares held by entities liable to corporation tax can be classed in four groups:

i) 'participations' in other companies (see 7.8.4) are generally exempt.

ii) shares in *SCR*s or *fonds communs de placements à risques (FCPR)*, which have been held for at least five years, benefit from the reduced 19% rate.

iii) a reduced rate of 16.5% on gains realised on the disposal of shares they hold in <u>quoted</u> companies classed as *sociétés à prépondérance immobilière*.

iv) gains realised on the disposal of other stock and shares are taxed at the normal corporation tax rate of $33^1/_3$. This also concerns any gain arising on the disposal of shares in <u>unquoted</u> *sociétés à prépondérance immobilière* (see 8.1.(c)).

c) Royalty income arising from a licence to use a patent, concepts, inventions or manufacturing and industrial processes which are registered as assets of an industrial, commercial or agricultural company. If purchased by the company granting the use, the rights must have been acquired at least two years before.

d) Smaller industrial or commercial companies may apply the reduced corporation tax rate of 15% to their taxable gains subject to the €38,120 limit (see 7.6.1(d)). The excess is taxed at the normal corporation tax rate.

8.3.5 *Losses*

a) A net short term capital loss is deductible from the current year's taxable income and long term capital gains. If it exceeds the current income of the company, it becomes an ordinary loss (*déficit*) and is carried forward or back (see chapter 7).

b) A net long term capital loss can generally be relieved as follows:

i) It can be carried forward to be offset against long term capital gains arising in the next ten years;

ii) For a company subject to corporation tax, the loss can be set against any reserve for long term capital gains, thus effectively obtaining relief against the gains of previous years;

iii) The loss can only be deducted from current income if the company is in liquidation and then only part of the loss is deductible, reflecting the differential between the ordinary corporation tax rate and the rate of tax on long-term gains.

c) A long term capital gain can be used to offset a trading loss or a short term capital loss:

i) of the year in which the long term gain is realised; or

ii) of a previous year if the loss can still be carried forward (six years for losses which do not represent depreciation).

8.3.6 Tax Free Exchanges

a) The following share-for-share exchanges, in which the gain of a company is rolled over into the new shares which it acquires, are tax-free:

i) mergers and demergers of collective investment schemes (*organismes de placement collectif en valeurs mobilières*), such as *SICAVs*. The gain is rolled over provided that any cash consideration does not amount to 10% or more of the nominal value of the shares received;

ii) exchanges of shares in the course of a public offer. Once more the gain is only rolled over if any cash element of the offer is less that 10%;

iii) mergers and demergers;

iv) nationalisation or privatisation.

b) An individual who transfers business assets to a company in exchange for shares can roll over any gain on the assets.

8.4. Gains Realised by Non-Residents

8.4.1 Exposure to French Capital Gains Tax

a) Individuals and companies resident outside France and not trading in France through a permanent establishment are liable to French income tax on gains on the disposal of assets situated in France, but with an exemption for movable property other than shareholdings exceeding 25%. Thus they are liable for capital gains tax, subject to any double tax treaty, only on gains arising from the disposal of:

i) real estate in France;

ii) shares in unquoted property holding companies (*sociétés à prépondérance immobilière*), other than *SICOMIs,* more than 50% of the assets of which consist of real property in France. For the purpose of applying this test, property required for the company's industrial, commercial, agricultural or non-commercial professional purposes is ignored except for properties which are simply rented out (furnished or unfurnished). This applies subject to any relevant double tax treaty.

iii) holdings of shares in French companies which are subject to French corporation tax if more than 25% of the capital has been owned by the taxpayer, together with his family, at any time in the 5 years preceding the sale; and

iv) holdings of shares in fiscally transparent professional companies with a turnover exceeding €250,000 or €90,000 (depending on the activity) if the shareholder plays an active role in the company. It is thought that he is exempt from French tax on any gain on a sale of his shares if he simply provides capital to the company, but the point is unclear.

b) Non-French residents trading in France through a permanent establishment are liable to French taxation on the business capital gains connected with their French branch.

8.4.2 Tax Rates for Non-Residents

a) Non-resident are subject to specific withholding tax rates in respect of gains arising on the disposal of French real estate or shares in French property holding companies (French or foreign) which are classed as *sociétés à prépondérance immobilière* (see 8.1.(c)). The payment of tax (usually handled by a fiscal representative) must be accompanied by the tax form 2048-IMM or 2048-M.

b) The general rate is $33^{1}/_{3}$. It applies to:

i) individuals resident outside the EU or EEA (regardless of their nationality),

ii) companies or individuals who are resident outside the EU or EEA and whare shareholders of French registered companies (or company groups) belonging to the fiscally transparent *Sociétés Civiles* categories as defined in 3.3.2.

iii) all foreign companies or entities liable to corporation tax, registered outside France (whether in the EU and EEA or not) and which hold real estate in France directly or through a *société de personnes* (*SCI, SNC* etc).

c) A reduced 16% rate applies to gains realised by:

i) individuals who reside in the EU and EEA.

ii) individual EU or EEA resident shareholders of "fiscally transparent" companies (the profits of which are taxed in the hand of the shareholders).

iii) holders of shares in *fonds de placement immobiliers (FPI)*, who are resident of the EU or EEA.

d) Gains on the sale of French real estate or shares in French property holding by property-traders (individuals and companies) resident outside France are taxed at 50%.

8.4.3 Exemptions

a) Non-residents may be entitled to an exemption in respect of a gain realised on the first two sales of a French property under the following conditions:

i) They must be EU or EEA nationals or nationals of a country which has signed a double tax treaty with France containing a clause of administrative assistance, or nationals of a treaty-partner country provided the treaty contains a clause of non-discrimination.

ii) They must provide evidence that they have been fiscally resident in France for at least two continuous tax years at some stage in the past.

iii) The property must constitute the French home of the non-resident taxpayer and as such it must have been available for his use at least from 1 January of the year preceding the disposal.

b) The exemption of the second sale is only granted if the above conditions are met and if the first sale took place over five years before. This applies to sales from 1 January 2006 and previous disposals are therefore ignored.

c) Non-residents nationals of territories described above can benefit from the exemption for old age pensioners or individuals who hold a specific invalidity card (see 8.2.(a) vii).

8.4.4 Computation of Gains for Non-Resident Individuals

a) A non-resident individual computes his taxable gain following the rules described in 8.2.2(b) to (f). This regime also applies if the non-resident sells shares of an income tax paying *SCI* or partnership.

b) The taxable gain realised by a non-resident individual selling shares of a corporation tax paying entity or "opaque" structure, is computed as the difference between the purchase price and the sale price. The gain thereby obtained benefits from the 10% reduction per year of ownership but only to the extent that the taxpayer can prove the exact date of acquisition and sale. This supposes a registration of the share transfer in France giving rise to the 5% registration duty mentioned in 8.1(d). If the date of acquisition of the shares cannot be adequately confirmed, the administration is likely to disallow the 10% taper relief.

c) If the sale price exceeds €150,000, non-residents have to appoint a fiscal representative in France to establish the capital gains tax return, calculate and collect the liability. Disposals of shares in property-holding companies (French or foreign) require a fiscal representative regardless of the disposal value.

8.4.5 Computation of Gains for Non-Resident Companies

a) A foreign company or entity which does not have a permanent establishment in France pays tax on capital gains realised in France.

b) Gains realised on the disposal of French real estate are computed as the difference between the sale price and the cost of the asset after depreciation of 2% per annum on the value of the building(s). The cost of construction, reconstruction and extension (but not replacement) which can be classed as capital expenditure is deductible provided that there is sufficient evidence that these were effectively borne by the company and subject to the presentation of the relevant invoices and evidence of payment.

c) The net taxable gain is subject to a withholding tax of $33^1/3\%$ or 50% if it is property-trading company as explained in 13.5(b).

d) Gains on the sale of shares in <u>quoted</u> companies classed as *sociétés à prépondérance immobilière* or shares in a *SIIC* are taxed at 16.5%. The shares must have been held for at least two years. In addition the vendor must hold at least 10% of the share capital in the company of which the shares are being disposed of.

e) Gains on the sale of shares in an <u>unquoted company</u> classed as a *société à prépondérance immobilière*, is taxed at $33^1/3\%$. The taxable gain is determined as the difference between the sale price and the acquisition value. There are no deductions or taper relief to reduce the taxable amount and the obligation of appointing a fiscal representative applies from the first Euro of proceeds.

f) Subject to double tax treaties, the gains on the sale out of shareholdings exceeding 25% in a French company (other than a *société à prépondérance immobilière*) is taxed at 18%. Gains on the sale of smaller shareholding are not normally taxable.

9.   GIFTS TAX

9.1.   General

a) Gifts tax is payable in connection with formal transfers of property, such as gifts made by declaration of the donor or by a legal deed. The mere transfer of an asset by hand is generally not taxable unless it is declared to the tax administration, although it may become taxable if the parties subsequently enter into a taxable gift or the donee figures among the beneficiaries of the donor's estate.

b) Given that the tax is only payable on transfers requiring a certain amount of legal formality, there is no need for a special declaration by the parties.

c) Gifts tax is payable on gratuitous transfers of value between living persons. In principle the taxes suffered are the same as those suffered by an estate on death, with the difference that transfers of land during life attract an additional local tax of 0.6%, plus 2.5% of the tax due. There are however several differences in the forms of abatement which are available.

d) Most importantly, certain lifetime gifts can qualify for a reduction of tax (see 9.6.2).

9.2.   Territorial Basis

a) French residents are taxable on transfers out of their worldwide estate.

b) Non French residents are taxable on transfers of assets situated in France.

c) A gift is taxable if the donee is resident in France, and has been so resident for at least 6 of the 10 tax years prior to the year in which he received the gift. While such a gift may be protected from French tax by a double tax treaty, in practice France has only 7 double tax treaties covering gifts taxes (see 5.4.7).

9.3.   Taxable Transfers

9.3.1   Valuation

a) The assets transferred are valued by the parties. Where jewellery and art objects are gifted, the value cannot be less than 60% of the insured value.

b) Deduction of debts is not permitted.

9.3.2 Exempt Assets

The assets which are exempt from gifts tax are the same as those exempt from inheritance tax (see 10.3.3).

9.4. Exempt Transfers

a) Manual transmission of assets is exempt from gifts tax unless it is disclosed to the tax administration. One reason why a gift may be so disclosed is that the donee may have to reveal the gift to explain why his lifestyle is not supported by his declared income (see 6.16.1(e)).

b) Transfers between husband and wife are not exempt, so that where property belonging to one spouse is given to the other, gifts tax is payable. However where property which is community property under the terms of the couple's marriage contract becomes the property of one spouse as a result of a liquidation of the community (eg because of the death of one spouse), the only tax payable is a registration tax of about 1.6%.

9.5. Exempt Amounts

The exempt amounts of transfers are the same as those applying on death (see 10.5.) and are renewable every 6 years. In other words the gift is a potentially exempt transfer. If the donor passes away within the 6 year period the portion or all of the abatement used for the gift is not granted again when calculating the inheritance tax liability. There are a few exceptions or specific allowances reserved for lifetime gifts which are as follows:

a) Lifetime gifts between spouses or partners of a *PACS* benefit from a tax-free allowance of €76,988.

b) capital payments to children resulting from a divorce settlement are exempt up to a limit of €2,700 per year for each year remaining until the child reaches 18;

c) the abatement of €1,520 allowed against transfers to non-relatives does not apply; and

d) transfers in full ownership of small artisanal/commercial businesses or goodwill of individual businesses or shares thereof, are totally exempt provided the value does not exceed €300,000. The value in excess of this limit is subject to normal gifts tax rates.

e) Lifetime gifts from grandparents to grandchildren carry an abatement of €30,390 per grandchild.

f) Gifts from Great-grandparents to their great-grandchildren benefit from a €5,065 abatement per share.

g) Outright gifts of money to a descendant (grand/great-grandchild), or in the absence of any descendant, to a nephew/niece (or great nephew/niece) are exempt up to €30,390. The donor must be over 65 years old and the donee over 18 years old and independent.

h) Outright gifts of money made between 1 January 2006 and 31 December 2010, to a descendant, or in the absence of any descendant, to a niece or nephew, to fund an acquisition of share capital or business assets are exempt up to €30,000. The investment must be made within two years of the gifts and the donee may only benefit once from the exemption.

9.6. Computing Gifts Tax Liabilities

9.6.1 Rates of Tax

a) The rates of tax are the same as those for inheritance tax (see 10.6.1).

b) The following rates apply to lifetime gifts between spouses or partners of a PACS after the tax-free allowance stated above:

Band of Value	Rate of Tax %
Less than €7,699	5
€7,699 to €15,195	10
€15,195 to €30,390	15
€30,390 to €526,760	20
€526,760 to €861,050	30
€861,050 to €1,722,100	35
€1,722,100 upwards	40

9.6.2 Reductions of Tax

a) The tax which would otherwise have been due on a lifetime gift by a person may be reduced by specific abatements. Various rates of abatement have been available over recent years, usually depending on the age of the donor.

b) Gifts made in full ownership or life interest benefit from a 50% tax reduction if the donor is less than 70 years old, reduced to 30% if the donor is between 70 and 80 years old.

c) Gifts of bare-ownership (i.e. with a retained life interest) attract a tax reduction of 35% if the donor is under 70, and 10% if the donor is over 70 but under 80.

d) There is no reduction of tax specifically for a lifetime gift of business assets.

9.7. Payment of Gifts Tax

a) The liability for the gifts tax falls on the donee.

b) The tax is normally paid at the same time as the transfer is registered (by the notary public, registrar etc), but when the gift is the transfer of a company, the tax can be spread over five years, subject to a charge for interest.

c) It is generally not possible to pay the tax by instalments, except where the assets being transferred are a business or the shares of an unquoted company, in either case engaged in an industrial, commercial, artisanal, agricultural or professional activity. In this case payment of interest may be made in 6-monthly instalments over a period of up to 5 years, followed by the payment of the tax charge due spread over 10 years. If the assets transferred are shares in a company, the recipient must receive at least 5% of the shares transferred by the donor. The rate of interest is reduced by two-thirds if the amount received by the donee is at least 10% of the capital of the business or if, globally, more than one-third of the business is transferred. If any donee sells more than one third of the shares/assets that he receives during the deferral period, the gifts tax originally due becomes payable immediately.

10. INHERITANCE TAX

10.1. General

a) French inheritance tax is paid by the inheritors of the estate of a French resident or the French assets of a non-French resident.

b) A declaration giving a description and valuation of the assets received must be sent to the administration within 6 months of the death (12 months if the deceased was resident outside France) by the donees, unless the value of the legacy is less than €50,000 and the transfer is to a direct ascendant or descendant or between spouses, or under €3,000 in all other cases.

10.2. Territorial Basis

a) If the deceased was resident in France when he died, all of his assets on a worldwide basis are taxable.

b) If the deceased was not resident in France, only his assets situated in France are subject to tax. French assets include any shares in unquoted companies which own real estate in France, to the extent that the value of their shares derives from French real estate. Only the proportion of the value of the shares that the French real estate of the company bears to the total assets of the company is taxable.

c) An inheritance may be taxable if the recipient is resident in France and has been so resident in at least 6 of the 10 tax years prior to the year in which he inherits the assets.

d) These liabilities may be modified by a double tax treaty. For example the shares in a non-French company which owns real estate in France are not treated as French situated assets in the hands of a UK resident, by virtue of the France – UK double tax treaty.

10.3. Taxable Transfers

10.3.1 Valuation

a) The assets in the estate of the deceased are valued at market value on the date of death. Gifts made by the deceased to any of the legatees within the last 6 years of the life of the deceased are also taxable.

b) There are special rules relating to the valuation of certain assets:

    i) If real estate has been valued for the purposes of any adjudication in the two years preceding or following death, the value of the property cannot be lower than the value determined in that process;

ii) Quoted securities are valued at their average price on the day of death;

iii) Decorative furnishings are valued at their sale price if sold within two years of death, at an amount determined by a legal valuation if not, or, in the absence of a valuation, at a 'forfeit' value of 5% of the total value of the remainder of the estate;

iv) Jewellery and works of art are valued at their sale price if sold within two years of death, or at a valuation if not (subject to the condition that the value cannot be less than 60% of the insured value of the assets) and in the absence of a valuation on the basis of a detailed estimation by the parties.

c) Debts are generally deductible from the value of the estate if their existence can be proved, but debts in favour of heirs and certain other debts are not allowable. Expenses incurred in treating the illness which caused the death are deductible, as are funeral expenses up to a limit of €1,500.

10.3.2 *Proceeds of Life Insurance and Life Assurance Policies*

a) Before 1 January 1999, the proceeds of life insurance policies were excluded from inheritance tax, except to the extent that any premiums paid by the insured on or after his or her 70th birthday exceeded €30,500. This excess is subject to inheritance tax for contracts entered into after 20 November 1991 for deaths occurring after 2 January 1992, and the rates of tax applied are those applicable to a gift from the life insured to the beneficiary of the policy.

b) The 1999 Finance Law introduced a new charge on the proceeds of life insurance or life assurance policies (but not 'survivorship insurance' policies (*'contrats de rente-survie'*)) paid in respect of policies entered into and premiums paid on or after 13 October 1998. When such payments are made in respect of a death occurring on or after 1 January 1999, a beneficiary of the life insurance or life assurance contracts is liable to pay tax at 20% of the total amounts paid to him, to the extent that those amounts exceed €152,500. The rate of tax is unaffected by the relationship between the life insured and the beneficiary of the policy except for payments to the surviving spouse (or *PACS* partner) which are exempt from the charge from 22 August 2007. If a payment under a contract is subject to the tax charge described in (a) above, it is not subject to the new charge, whether the new charge would result in the payment of a higher or lower amount of tax.

c) The 20% tax charge is withheld at source by French life insurance companies. Residents of France who take out a life insurance policy with a company established outside France are obliged to declare, with their income tax returns, the policies they have taken out, the date they came into effect, the duration of the contracts and the amounts subscribed under the contract or withdrawn during the tax year.

d) Both the new rule and the old rule apply to payments made on death. It therefore remains possible for a French resident to take out a single premium term assurance policy, at any age and in any amount, in favour of another individual. If the policy pays out during the life of the insured, but more than 6 years after the premium is paid, no gifts tax is payable.

10.3.3 Exempt Assets

a) The reversion of a *rente viagère* is exempt. Also exempt is the reversion of a life interest right for the benefit of a spouse, *PACS* partner or a sibling in the situation described in 10.4.(b).

b) Up to 75% of the value of certain forestry assets are exempt.

c) 75% up to €76,000, 50% thereafter of the value of certain agricultural assets can be exempt if the assets are let out on long-term leases.

d) Land and sites included in specially designated areas 'Sites Natura 2000' carry a 75% exemption subject to the production of the relevant certificates. The heirs (or donees) must undertake to maintain the requisite conditions for 18 years.

e) Works of art etc. given to the state (with its agreement) are exempt.

f) Historic monuments which are open to the public are exempt, subject to certain conditions. The furniture and works of art which form an integral part of the monument can also be exempt.

g) Newly built houses acquired during the period 1 June 1993 to 31 December 1994 benefit from an abatement of gifts or inheritance tax on the occasion of their first transfer by gift or on death, on condition that they are used as a principal residence for at least five years from the date of their acquisition (not necessarily by the owner). The abatement is €46,000 per donee, which can be cumulated with the donee's other abatements.

h) 75% of the value of business assets or shares in a company carrying on an industrial, commercial, artisanal, agricultural or professional activity can be exempt from inheritance tax. The deceased must have held the assets or shares for more than 2 years. This condition does not apply to businesses inherited or received as a gift or created by the deceased. The inheritors must undertake to keep the assets or shares for at least 6 years and at least one of the heirs must either work full-time in the business or exercise the function of a director for five years. The undertaking to keep the assets inherited must cover, in the case of shares in a quoted company, at 20% of the equity, and in the case of an unquoted company, at least 34% of the equity.

i) Newly built houses acquired during the period 1 August 1995 to 31 December 1995 benefit from an abatement of gifts or inheritance tax on the occasion of their first transfer by gift or on death, on condition that they are used as a principal residence for at least 2 years since the date of their acquisition (not necessarily by the owner). The donee or heir must undertake not to change the use of the home from residential accommodation (whether as a principal or secondary home) for at least 3 years from the date he receives the gift. The abatement is limited to €46,000 per donee, which can be cumulated with the donee's other abatements.

j) Certain rented housing acquired between 1 August 1995 and 31 December 1996 is exempt from gifts or inheritance tax on a first transfer within the limits of 75% of its value and €46,000 per part. The property has to be leased for 9 years or more within 6 months of its acquisition, and must have been held by the donor for at least 2 years. The tenant must occupy it as his principal residence and there are conditions as to the level of rent and the income of the tenant.

k) Real estate situated in Corsica is exempt from French inheritance tax if transferred in the period from 1 January 2002 to 31 December 2010. For transfers from 1 January 2011 to 31 December 2015, the exemption will no longer apply but there will be a 50% inheritance tax reduction on the property transfer. There will be no tax advantages on transfers from 2016.

10.4. Exempt Transfers

a) From 22 August 2007, no inheritance tax applies to amounts transferred by succession to a surviving spouse or partner of a *PACS*.

b) Amounts inherited by a brother or sister of the deceased can be exempted from inheritance tax if the sibling is single, divorced or widowed, over 50 years old or invalid, and he or she has lived with the deceased for the five years preceding the demise. This exemption applies also from 22 August 2007.

c) Gifts to the state, its territorial subdivisions, scientific and educational establishments, and organisations of public utility are exempt.

d) No inheritance tax is paid on the estate of war victims or victims of acts of terrorism or in respect of compensation paid to AIDS victims or victims of Creutzfeldt-Jakob disease.

10.5. Exempt Amounts

a) When a transfer is made to ascendants or descendants, the tax is computed on the net sum received by each donee less an abatement of €151,950.

b) The abatements available without special qualifications on transfers arising on death between other individuals are as follows:

   i) siblings are entitled to an abatement of €15,195 each.

   ii) Nieces and nephews may benefit from a €7,598 abatement on amounts received from an uncle or an aunt who has no descendants.

   iii) in all other cases the donee is entitled to an abatement of €1,520.

c) A handicapped person is entitled to an abatement of €151,950 on any gift or inheritance, whatever his relationship to the deceased may have been. This abatement is cumulable with the abatements for ascendants or descendants or brothers and sisters.

d) Any gifts made more than 6 years before the death are ignored in calculating the abatement available on death. On the contrary if the death occurs within 6 years from the making of the gift any relevant abatement applicable for inheritance tax will be reduced by the amount already claimed.

e) If the donor pays the gifts tax, in lieu of the donee, the tax paid is not regarded as an additional gift for tax purposes, and thus constitutes an amount exempt from gift tax.

10.6. Computing Inheritance Tax Liabilities

10.6.1 Rates of Tax

The rates of tax are the same for both inheritance tax and gifts tax.

a) The rates for transfers between parents and children etc in direct line are:

Band of Value	Rate of Tax %
Less than €7,699	5
€7,699 to €11,548	10
€11,548 to €15,195	15
€15,195 to €526,760	20
€526,760 to €861,050	30
€861,050 to €1,722,100	35
€1,722,100 upwards	40

b) The rates for transfers between brothers and sisters are:

Band of Value	Rate of Tax %
Less than €23,299	35
€23,299 upwards	45

c) The rates for transfers between relations of up to the 4th degree are:

	Rate of Tax %
Any amount	55

The relations who are covered by this tax rate can be seen from the following genealogical table. (The masculine includes the feminine throughout).

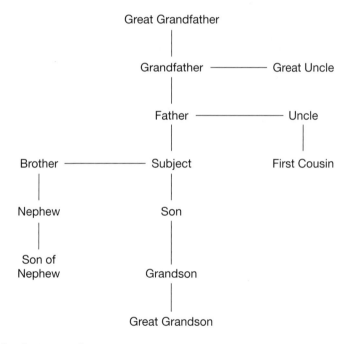

d) Transfers between others:

Band of Value	Rate of Tax %
Any amount	60

10.6.2 Reductions of Tax

a) If the inheritor or recipient of the gift has three or more children living at the date of the gift or succession, or represented by surviving children of their own, he benefits from a tax reduction of:

    i) €610 per child in excess of two if the gift or inheritance is made in the direct family line (eg from a parent or grandparent); and

    ii) €305 per child in excess of two if the gift or inheritance is made by a collateral relative or non-relation (eg an uncle or a friend).

b) War invalids (with at least 50% disability), are entitled to a reduction of 50% of any inheritance and gift taxes for which they are liable up to a limit of €305.

10.7. Payment of Inheritance Tax

a) The tax is due before the declaration is registered, but it can be spread over a maximum of five years, subject to a charge for interest. It may be extended to 10 years in total for successions in direct line if the inheritance comprises at least 50% of non-liquid assets.

b) Inheritance tax, gifts tax, wealth tax and the tax due on the termination of an indivision can, by agreement, be settled by transfer of land or buildings in coastal or estuary areas to the authority which protects these areas, if their position or ecological interest justifies this.

11. WEALTH TAX

11.1. General

Wealth tax is paid by individuals who have taxable wealth in excess of the nil-rate band for wealth tax, ie currently in excess of €770,000. The only people who have to make a return of their wealth are those who are liable to pay the tax. Taxation is based on the wealth of a household, including spouses and minor children. The assets of an unmarried couple openly living together are similarly aggregated, whether or not the couple has entered into a *PACS* agreement.

11.2. Territorial Basis

a) Individuals resident in France are taxable on their worldwide assets, subject to the terms of any relevant double tax treaties.

b) Individuals resident outside France are subject to tax on their taxable assets situated in France (but see 11.3.2(m)). These include shares in any company which owns real estate in France, to the extent that the value of its shares reflects its French real estate interests as opposed to other assets.

11.3. Taxable Wealth

11.3.1 Taxable Assets

a) The main categories of taxable assets are as follows:

   i) real estate;

   ii) furniture;

   iii) other personal property including jewellery, cars, yachts, aeroplanes and horses;

   iv) shares and bonds;

   v) the redemption value of life assurance policies or life assurance bonds;

   vi) debts owed to the taxpayer and interest accrued thereon.

b) Any debts of the taxpayer (with limited exceptions) are deductible from the taxable base. Such debts include individual income tax and local tax liabilities.

c) When property has been 'dismembered' into a life interest (*usufruit*) and bare ownership (*nue-propriété*), the property is treated as the property of the person with the life interest (the *usufruitier*).

d) A person who enjoys the income from shares or who deals with the shares in any manner, eg by exercising the voting rights attached to them, is treated as the owner of the shares.

e) Literary and artistic rights are taxable if the taxpayer is not the original author or artist.

11.3.2 Exempt Assets and Abatements

a) Assets necessary to a business conducted by its owner or his spouse are exempt. The business can be industrial, commercial, agricultural or professional. However, if the business consists of furnished lettings, the rented assets qualify as business assets only if:

   i) The taxpayer is registered as a *loueur en meublé professionnel* (professional landlord), and

   ii) the taxpayer received more that €23,000 per annum in rent, <u>and</u>

   iii) the furnished rental income represents over 50% of the households earned income.

   Finally, to qualify for exemption, the property must be directly owned by the taxpayer and not through a company.

   The business asset exempt can apply in respect of shares held by a taxpayer in a company or business in which he carries on his main professional activity may also be treated as exempt business assets. As with the conditions above the shareholder must prove that the shares relate to his principal professional activity. In the case of income-tax paying businesses, evidence is provided in that the net profit is taxed in the name of the taxpayer.

   In the case of corporation-tax paying entities, the taxpayer must exercise an executive role in the company. The qualifying roles which depend on the type of company are specifically listed in Article 885 O bis of the CGI.

b) Up to 75% of the value of shares in industrial, commercial or agricultural companies may be exempt in the following situations:

   i) Under the *Pacte Dutreil*: this exemption is subject to a joint under-taking by one or several shareholders and their beneficiaries (assignees/successors) to hold their shares for at least 6 years. Undertaking must relate to a total shareholding (in voting rights or value) of at least 20% of the share capital of a quoted company, or 34% of an unquoted company. These limits must be respected throughout the 6 years and at least one of the signatories must exercise an executive role in the company.

ii) Shares held for at least 6 years, by salaried employees or *mandataires sociaux* in a company in which they carry out their principal professional activity.

c) Subject to certain conditions, investments in the share capital of small and medium (PME) European companies (other than property investment companies) are exempt. The small and medium company criteria are as follows: less than 250 employees, an annual turnover below €50 million, or total annual balance sheet under €43 million, and 75% of the shareholding held by individuals and/or small and medium companies.

d) Pictures, tapestries, statues, sculptures, lithographs etc are exempt from the tax. However historic monuments are not exempt.

e) Shares in *SCIs* which own historic buildings can also be exempt to the extent that their value reflects antiques, works of art or collections (but not the buildings themselves).

f) Objects over 100 years old are exempt.

g) Literary and artistic rights are exempt in the hands of the artist, and patents or trademarks are exempt in the hands of the inventor.

h) French or foreign retirement annuity pension schemes (foreign or French) paid in respect of past professional activities do not normally hold any commercial value. Indeed they cannot be sold or transferred, except sometimes by reversion (survivorship pensions). There are therefore exempt, but only if:

i) The capitalisation value of the pension annuities has to have been constituted through regular premium payment during over a period of at least 15 years.

ii) The payment of premiums substantially larger than the preceding one can bring the total pension fund into the scope of wealth tax.

iii) The first pension annuity coincides with the retirement age of the taxpayer as defined in the Social Security Code or with the date fixed within a compulsory pension retirement regime.

By exception, the 15 years premium payment condition does not apply to the relatively new pensions plans (*Plan d'Epargne Retraite Populaire* (Perp), *Plan d'Epargne Retraite Collectifs* (Perco), and *Plan d'Epargne Retraite d'Entreprise* (Pere), taken out before 31 December 2008.

i) The value of life <u>insurance</u> policies (i.e. payable upon death only such as term insurance) is not generally assessable as these have no resale value. However, for policies taken out after 20 November 1991, the value of premiums paid after the holder's 70 birthday, is added to his wealth. The value of life assurance policies (French of foreign) or investment bonds is fully taxable.

j) Woodlands, forests and forestry companies are exempt to the extent of 75% of their value under certain conditions.

k) Agricultural land, and the shares of *groupements fonciers agricoles* which own agricultural land, can be exempt if the land is let out to a relative (within defined limits) of the owner on a lease of at least 18 years, and the land is used by the tenant in the exercise of his main business activity. If the land is let to someone unrelated to the owner on an 18 year lease (or if the tenant is a relative who does not use the land in his main business), the exemption is restricted to 75% of the first €76,000 of the value of the land and 50% of the balance.

l) The value of a principal residence can be reduced by an abatement of up to 30% to reflect the fact that it is occupied by a 'sitting tenant'.

m) Portfolio investments (eg bonds, cash deposits, and shareholdings of less than 10% in French companies) held by non-residents are excluded from their taxable assets.

11.4. Exempt Amounts

There are no exempt amounts, but the first €770,000 of taxable assets is taxed at a rate of 0%.

11.5. Computing Wealth Tax Liabilities

a) The rates of tax applicable to wealth owned on 1 January 2008 are:

Taxable Wealth	Rate %
Less than €770,000	0.00
Between €770,000 and €1,240,000	0.55
Between €1,240,000 and €2,450,000	0.75
Between €2,450,000 and €3,850,000	1.00
Between €3,850,000 and €7,360,000	1.30
Between €7,360,000 and €16,020,000	1.65
Above €16,020,000	1.80

b) The bands of taxable wealth are updated every year by reference to the first income tax rate band.

c) The total of the wealth tax calculated using this scale is reduced by €150 per dependent child or invalid in the household of the taxpayer (but not adult children re-attached to the household). This is halved in cases of joint custody.

d) The total of wealth tax and income tax payable in any year cannot normally exceed 85% of the income of the taxpayer for the preceding year (including tax exempt income). If the sum of these taxes would exceed this amount, the wealth tax is reduced euro for euro by the excess. However for taxpayers with wealth exceeding €2,450,000, the amount of this reduction is reduced by 50%, or €11,573, whichever is the greater.

e) As a result of the Loi TEPA published on 22 August 200, taxpayers who invest directly or indirectly in the share capital of small and medium companies may deduct up to 75% of their investment from their wealth tax liability. This applies up to a limit of €50,000 and is subject to specific reporting requirements.

11.6. Payment of Wealth Tax

Those subject to the tax are required to make a declaration of their taxable wealth as at 1 January each year, accompanied by payment of the tax due. For French residents the return has to be submitted by 15 June, for other EU residents it has to be submitted by 16 July and for non-EU residents it has to be submitted by 1 September.

12. TAX ON THE MARKET VALUE OF FRENCH REAL ESTATE OWNED BY CERTAIN COMPANIES

a) This tax applies to any company which owns real estate in France.

b) It is paid by companies and calculated on the market value as at 1 January following the year of assessment of any real estate which they own directly or indirectly in France unless either:

   i) their real estate in France constitutes less than 50% of their assets in France. For the purpose of this calculation any real estate in France which is connected with the company's own industrial, commercial, agricultural or non-commercial professional activities is ignored; or

   ii) they have their registered office in a country with which France has concluded a treaty for the suppression of tax evasion and they make a declaration of their French real estate holdings and their shareholders as at 1 January each year; or

   iii) they either have their seat of effective management in France or they benefit from a double tax treaty containing a non-discrimination clause and they either give an undertaking to supply details of their real estate holdings in France and their shareholders on request (which undertaking has to be given within 2 months of their acquisition of the property) or they make the annual declarations described in (ii) above; or

   iv) they are quoted on a French stock exchange or a foreign stock exchange regulated by similar rules; or

   v) they are international or sovereign state organisations; or

   vi) they are non-profit making organisations which justify their ownership of French real estate on the grounds of their social, philanthropic, educational or cultural activities.

c) When the real estate is owned by a chain of companies, the company immediately owning the real estate is examined to see if it is exempt. If that company is exempt, the next company up the chain is examined to see if it is exempt, and so on. However each company in the chain is jointly liable for the tax due by any other company in the chain, so in practice if any one of the companies is liable to pay the tax, it is the company which owns the real estate which will bear the cost.

d) The company subject to the tax remains liable to French corporation tax (or income tax depending on its form) on its income from the real estate. However it is not deemed to have an income from the property if the property is not in fact let (in contrast to the position of certain non-French resident individuals with residences in France – see 6.6.2(b)). It remains possible, however, that one or more shareholders of the company may have a liability to income tax on the basis of the notional income. The tax on market value, which is a capital tax, is not deductible from any income which the company does receive.

e) The *Tribunal de Grande Instance* of Nice (21 February 1995) ruled that the shares in a private marina company (the marina at Cap d'Ail) constitute real estate for the purposes of this tax. The court reasoned that the owner of the shares had the use of the quays, buildings, service roads etc of the marina.

f) The rate of tax is 3% of the market value of the French real estate owned by the company, with the exception of any property inscribed in the balance sheet of a property dealing company or in the balance sheet of a property development company as trading stock.

g) No deduction is allowed for any debts related to the property.

h) If a company owns (directly or indirectly) only a fraction of a piece of real estate, the tax is based on the percentage of the value of the real estate which it owns.

i) The tax authorities may assess non-compliant companies up to 10 years in arrears, and the outstanding liabilities in this instance are increased by late interest and penalty charges.

j) In practice, the 3% tax was specifically brought in to defeat the holding of French real estate through offshore companies, by taxpayers (resident or non residents of France) eager to get around French wealth tax. This tax has never been well received by double tax treaty partner territories such as Switzerland and more recently Luxembourg. In fact, the European Court of Justice recently judged (October 2007) that the difference of requirements and obligations to obtain a 3% tax exemption which clearly depends on whether the seat of the holding company is in France or in another EU member territory, is contrary to the EU freedom of capital movement principle. As a result, changes are expected in this field and the conditions of application of the 3% tax may well be altered in the not too distant future.

13.   WITHHOLDING TAXES

13.1.   General

a) There are two terms for 'withholding tax'. *Prélèvement forfaitaire* is a general term applied to numerous forms of withholding tax on everything from construction profits to deductions on account of tax from wages and salaries. In many cases the payment of a *prélèvement* relieves the recipient of the income from any further liability to French income tax. The *prélèvement* is then said to be *libératoire*. The second term is *retenue à la source*, and tax withheld in this form is also sometimes *libératoire*. The differences of terminology are not generally of practical significance. In cases where the withholding tax is not *libératoire*, the tax withheld is merely a payment on account, and the taxpayer is liable for any further tax that may be computed on his French source income.

b) The amount of French tax suffered on dividends, royalties and interest received by a non-French resident may be restricted by a double tax treaty. The applicable rates of withholding tax are set out in 14.3.

c) French tax suffered on dividends, royalties and interest may be allowed as a credit against the tax suffered by the non-resident in his own state under a double tax treaty.

13.2.   Dividends

a) Subject to any double tax treaty, the payment by a French company of a dividend to a person resident outside France is subject to withholding tax of 18% of the gross dividend, including tax credit. The withholding tax is *libératoire* for the non-resident.

b) The rate of withholding tax is often reduced to a lower level under a double tax treaty. Typically a rate of 15% applies on payments of a dividend to a non-resident individual shareholder (see 14.3.).

c) There is no withholding tax on dividends paid to parent companies resident in other EU member states by a French company which is wholly or partially subject to French corporation tax.

    i) The subsidiary company must be an *SA, SAS, SARL* or *société en commandite par actions*.

    ii) The subsidiary must be subject to French corporation tax, and not exempt from it. If it is partially exempt from corporation tax, the exemption from dividend withholding tax applies to dividends paid out of the taxable part of its profits.

iii) The 'parent company' must directly own 15% (10% from 1 January 2009) or more of the share capital of the company paying the dividend and have held the shares for at least 2 years at the date of the payment of the dividend. Alternatively, for dividends paid on or after 1 January 1997 the parent company may give an undertaking to retain a shareholding of at least 15% for a continuous period of at least 2 years, and must then designate a fiscal representative who will be responsible for paying the withholding tax in respect of the dividend if the undertaking is not honoured.

iv) The parent company must have its 'seat of effective management' in an EU-member state.

v) The parent company must take one of the forms of 'capital companies' listed in the annex to the EU directive of 23 July 1990.

vi) The parent company must be subject to corporation tax in the country where it has its seat of effective management, without any possibility of option or exemption. However it does not matter if the recipient company is subject to a reduced rate of corporation tax or if the tax system of the state in which it is is resident offers a 'participation exemption' in respect of dividends from subsidiaries. For example Netherlands companies which benefit from a participation ruling and the Luxembourg *SOPARFI* qualify.

vii) Where an exemption from the taxation at source is granted under the terms of a double tax treaty and under more favourable conditions, it is of course this treaty measure that will apply. This is the case for instance of the treaties with Austria, Denmark, Finland, Germany, Spain and Sweden.

viii) If the parent company is directly or indirectly controlled by one or more non-EU residents, it has to provide evidence that the main objective of the overall structure is not purely the avoidance of the withholding tax.

d) Profits realised in France by foreign companies carrying on an activity in France and distributed, are deemed distributed to shareholders resident outside France. These profits are thus subject to the taxation at source for distributions from French companies to non-residents. Companies established in an EU country are dispensed from this tax provided that they are fully subject to corporation tax. This taxation at source may be limited or cancelled all together through the terms of double tax treaties. Where it applies the company must pay the tax on a provisional basis determined as the total amount of profits and capital gains subject to corporation tax. It may nevertheless be revised and the excess refunded if:

i) the total distribution effectively falls below the original assessment of available profits, or

ii) if the company can demonstrate that all or part of the effective distributions were made to French residents.

In order to avoid a double formality, companies in this situation may ask to have the amount of tax limited to the assessable base they can reasonably predict given the distributions they anticipate to make and the residence of the beneficiaries. However, if the tax is insufficient they will have to pay the excess including an interest charge. When it is due, the tax at source must be paid at the non-resident tax office by the 15th of the month following their levy. The tax is accompanied by form 2754.

13.3. Interest

a) Where interest is paid to a French resident, there is an optional withholding tax system which often works to the taxpayer's advantage because the rates of withholding tax are comparatively low, and payment of the withholding tax usually discharges the income tax liabilities of the recipient of the interest. The payment of the withholding tax does not, however, discharge the tax liabilities of the recipient of the interest if the recipient is an industrial, commercial, artisanal, agricultural or professional company. Generally, such companies will not, therefore, opt to suffer the withholding tax.

b) The optional rates of withholding tax applicable to French residents are set out at 6.4.2. However this chapter is primarily addressed to non-French residents, and in general terms the withholding taxes (but not the social contributions) are compulsory in respect of payments to non-residents. This rule is subject to numerous exceptions in respect of payments of interest, which are set out at (c) below, but the basic withholding tax rates are as follows:

	Withholding Tax on interest or increase in value %
i) *bonds, government loans and other negotiable instruments*	18
ii) *Treasury bonds, savings bank bonds*	
issued between 1.1.83 and 31.12.89	45
issued between 1.1.90 and 31.12.94	35
issued since 1.1.95	18
iii) *PEPs[1] (plans d'épargne populaire) – including French life assurance contracts issued within PEPs*	
withdrawals during first 4 years	35
withdrawals after 4 and before 8 years	18
withdrawals after 8 years	0

continued

	Withholding Tax on interest or increase in value %
iv) *Most French life assurance contracts issued on or after 26 9.97*	
withdrawals during first 4 years	35
withdrawals during next 4 years	16
withdrawals after 8 years	7.5[2]
v) *French life assurance contracts issued on or after 1.1.90 and before 26.9.97*	
withdrawals during first 4 years	35
withdrawals during next 4 years	16
withdrawals after 8 years	0
vi) *bank deposit interest*	18
vii) *Livret Bleu (Crédit Mutuel) interest*	6

[1]   *From 25 September 2003 it is no longer possible to open a new PEP.*

[2]   *After first €4,600 of redemptions per annum for a single taxpayer, or first €9,200 of redemptions per annum for a married couple, which amounts are exempt from income tax (but subject to social surcharges of 11% in the hands of a French resident).*

[3]   *2008 rates.*

c) Subject to the effects of any double tax treaty, the above withholding tax rates apply compulsorily if the interest is paid to a non-resident. However, tax does not need to be withheld from the following types of interest:

i)   interest on French corporate bonds issued since 1 January 1987;

ii)   interest on French government loan stocks issued since 1 October 1984;

iii)   interest on French bank accounts;

iv)   interest on certificates of deposit;

v)   interest which is exempt from tax, such as interest on a *Livret A* or *Livret de dévelopement durable*;

vi)   interest on bonds issued in France by international or foreign organisations.

d) Even in the rare cases where French domestic law may require tax to be withheld (eg on interest from an old corporate bond), the requirement may be overruled by a double tax treaty. Moreover, even when interest is paid on an old corporate bond to a recipient not protected by a double tax treaty, the French tax administration has unilaterally decided to limit the tax to be withheld to 10% for bonds issued since 1 January 1965.

e) One situation in which withholding tax will be exigible is the case where the recipient refuses to reveal his identity to the payer of the interest. In this case a withholding tax of 60% applies (plus the social contributions of 11%). In addition, if the interest derives from certain kinds of bonds, there is an annual tax of 2% of the capital value of the bond. This tax is collected from the interest on the bond at the same time as the withholding tax on the interest.

13.4. Royalties

a) The withholding tax on royalties paid by a person carrying on a business in France to a non-resident who does not have a permanent establishment in France is 33^{1}/$_{3}$%.

b) The tax withheld is not *libératoire*, but is merely a payment on account of the tax liability of the non-resident. The tax withheld is also non-refundable so that if the liability of the non-resident is less than the tax withheld, the difference is simply lost.

c) The rate of withholding tax is often reduced under a double tax treaty, typically to nil (see 14.3.).

13.5. Capital Gains

a) Subject to any double tax treaty, capital gains realised by non-residents on occasional sales of French real estate suffer a withholding tax of 16% if they reside in an EU country or 33⅓% if they reside in another territory. However, certain individuals are exempt from French tax on a capital gain arising on their first two disposals of a home in France (see 8.4.). Non-residents have to appoint a fiscal representative who is responsible for the calculation and collection of the liability. If the sale price is under €150,000, or the property has been held for over 15 years there is no obligation to appoint a fiscal representative.

b) Subject to any double tax treaty, profits realised by non-residents from a trade in French property, from a business of sub-division of French property for sale in lots, or from habitual construction in France suffer a withholding tax of 50%.

c) Gains on real estate include gains on disposal of shares in unquoted companies (other than *SICOMI*) the assets of which mainly consist of real estate in France. For determining whether or not the French real estate assets of a company amount to more than half of its assets, any property in France used by the company for its industrial, commercial or agricultural purposes is ignored, except property rented out furnished or unfurnished. These gains are subject to the withholding of tax rates described above and require the appointment of a fiscal representative.

d) Gains on the sale of French property by a fiscally transparent company (*SCI* subject to income tax, for instance) which has its registered office in France are assessed under the rules described in 8.4.

e) When the gain is realised by an individual the withholding tax is a final liability.

f) When the gain is realised by a commercial company including an *SCI* liable to corporation tax, the tax withheld at the appropriate rate (50%, 33⅓% or 16%) is imputed against the French corporation tax due by the company, and any excess may be claimed for refund.

13.6. Independent Personal Services

a) Subject to any double tax treaty, payments made:

i) by a person carrying on a business in France

ii) to a non-resident who does not have a permanent establishment in France

iii) in respect of services provided or 'used' in France;

are subject to a withholding tax. The tax withheld is imputed against the French tax liability of the non-resident, but is not refundable.

b) The rates of withholding tax are as follows:

i) 15% if the payment is made in respect of artistic or sporting services;

ii) $33^{1}/_{3}$% if the payment is made in respect of any other kinds of service.

c) Payments for independent personal services are often exempt under a double tax treaty if the recipient does not have a fixed place of business in the other country. In general payments made to treaty partner residents are not subject to withholding tax, and are only assessed by direct assessment if the recipient has a fixed place of business in France.

13.7. Dependent Personal Services

a) Withholding tax is deducted from net salary and pension payments (after deduction of the 10% abatement for expenses) made to non-residents at the following rates (2008):

	%
Below €13,583	0
Between €13,583 and €39,409	12
Over €39,409	20

This withholding tax is only *libératoire* in respect of salaries of up to €39,409 paid to French nationals or nationals of countries that have treaties of reciprocity with France. Otherwise it is a payment on account of the final liability.

b) Directors attendance fees paid to a non-resident are subject to a withholding tax of 25%.

c) Pensions received by a non-French resident are often exempt from French tax under a double tax treaty.

13.8. Rental and Leasing Income

a) There is no withholding tax on rental income from lettings of French real estate.

b) By contrast, lease premiums paid by a French resident to a non-resident for the use of a movable asset in France are subject to a withholding tax at $33^{1}/_{3}\%$.

13.9. Alimony and Child Maintenance

There is no withholding tax on alimony or child maintenance payments.

14. DOUBLE TAXATION RELIEF

14.1. Relief for Non-Residents

14.1.1 Treaty Relief

a) Income from French real estate is almost invariably taxable in France. In a decision of 22 May 1992, the *Conseil d'État* ruled that an Italian company could not be assessed to French tax on its income from French real estate, under the terms of the old France – Italy double tax treaty (which was replaced with effect from 1 May 1992), because the income constituted business income of the Italian company and the company did not have a permanent establishment in France. Although the treaty to which this decision related has been replaced, it resembles the French treaties with Denmark and Luxembourg, and possibly Lebanon, Morocco and most of francophone Africa. It should be noted that the treaty with Luxembourg was modified with effect from 1 January 2008 to cancel the effects of the above decision. The same changes are expected for the treaty with Denmark in the not too distant future. Under France's other double tax treaties, rental income is usually exempt from tax in the taxpayer's country of residence or the taxpayer receives credit for the French tax paid.

b) Business profits earned by a non-French resident are normally exempt from French taxation under a double tax treaty, unless the non-resident carries on a business in France through a permanent establishment there.

c) Profits from the operation of ships and aircraft by a non-French resident are often exempt from tax in France under a double tax treaty.

d) Income from independent professional services performed in France by a non-French resident is often exempt from French tax under a double tax treaty if the taxpayer does not have a fixed base regularly available to him in France.

e) Remuneration from an employment derived by a non-French resident is often exempt from French tax under a double tax treaty unless the employment is exercised in France.

f) Pensions for service in the private sector received by a non-French resident are normally exempt from French tax under a double tax treaty. However France has the right to impose tax on certain occupational pensions paid to residents of Argentina, Australia (unless the taxpayer opts to pay tax in Australia), Canada, India, Italy, Korea (South), Pakistan and Thailand. France can also assess pensions paid by the French social security system to residents of Algeria, Argentina, Austria, Bahrain, Bangladesh, Bulgaria,

Canada, China, Congo, Cyprus, Egypt, Germany, Hungary, India, Indonesia, Italy, Japan, Jordan, (S) Korea, Kuwait, Luxembourg, Malta, Mauritius, Mongolia, New Zealand, Nigeria, Norway, Oman, Pakistan, Philippines, Qatar, Russian Federation, Sri Lanka, Thailand, (if the pension is paid to a French national) Trinidad and Tobago, United Arab Emirates, USA and Venezuela. Normally France has the right to tax pensions for public service paid to non-residents (unless they are nationals, or in some cases residents of the treaty partner country), but this is precluded under the following treaties: Australia (where the recipient has opted to pay tax in Australia or is Australian), Austria, Benin, Burkina Faso, Central African Republic, Gabon, Ghana, Ivory Coast, Japan, Mali, Mauritania, Mayotte, Namibia, New Caledonia, Niger, Russian Federation, Senegal, South Africa, Sweden, USA, Vietnam, and Zimbabwe.

g) The French withholding tax on dividends may be eliminated or reduced by a double tax treaty (see 14.3.) or, in the case of an EU parent company, by French domestic law. There is generally no withholding tax on dividends paid by a French subsidiary to an EU parent company, provided that the following conditions are satisfied:

i) the payer company is an *SA, SARL, société par actions simplifiée* or *société en commandite par actions*, and subject compulsorily to French corporation tax;

ii) the recipient company must have directly owned at least 25% of the shares of the paying company for at least 2 years, or, if it has not owned the shares for that long, for dividends paid on or after 1 January 1997 the recipient company must give an undertaking to keep at least 25% of the shares of the paying company for at least 2 years;

iii) the recipient company must have the seat of its effective management in an EU state;

iv) the recipient company must take one of the forms of corporation listed in an annexe to the EU Directive of 23 July 1990;

v) the recipient company must be subject to corporation tax in the state where it has its seat of effective management without the possibility of any option and without being exempt from corporation tax in that state;

vi) the recipient company must not have the right, under any double tax treaty, to a payment from the French Treasury of which the amount, equal to the French dividend tax credit or a fraction thereof, is greater than the withholding tax reserved by that treaty.

In addition, if the parent company is directly or indirectly controlled by one or more residents of countries which are not members of the EU, the parent company must prove that the chain of ownership was not created with the main object of obtaining the benefit of this exemption from French withholding tax.

However, if a double tax treaty provides for a treatment which is more favourable than that available under French domestic law, the treaty provisions prevail. Under the treaty with Denmark, no French tax is withheld from dividends, whatever the size of the holding of the Danish parent company (but Danish residents do not benefit from the French dividend tax credit). Under the treaties with Austria, Finland, Germany and Sweden, there is no withholding tax if the parent company owns at least 10% of the French subsidiary. In none of these cases is there a requirement that the shareholder should have owned the shares for any particular period.

If any French tax is withheld from a dividend, under most French double tax treaties the tax authority of the country where the recipient is resident will give credit for the tax withheld against the tax due in that country in respect of the dividend.

h) No French tax is withheld from payments of interest on corporate bonds issued since 1 January 1987. Equally non-residents do not suffer any French withholding tax on interest arising on Euro accounts at French banks. However, where French tax would otherwise be withheld from payments of interest to non-residents (eg on debts which are not constituted as negotiable instruments), the rate of withholding tax may be restricted by a double tax treaty (see 14.3.).

i) French withholding tax on royalties is often reduced by a double tax treaty (see 14.3.).

j) Non-French residents may be exempt from French tax on capital gains arising on French assets, other than immovable property situated in France and movable property forming part of the business property of a permanent establishment in France. Shares or rights in companies, the assets of which consist mainly of immovable property in one of the treaty-partner states, are usually treated as immovable property situated in that state. For example residents of the UK or USA who sell shares in a company (wherever incorporated) the assets of which consist mainly of French real estate are liable to French capital gains tax on the gain arising on the disposal of those shares.

14.1.2 Non-Treaty Relief

a) The non-resident may be allowed to deduct any French tax suffered on his French source income from the income for the purposes of taxation in his home country, under the domestic laws of that country.

b) The non-resident may be entitled to unilateral tax credit relief in the country of his residence for any French tax suffered. Unilateral credit relief is available in both the UK and USA in cases where no double tax treaty applies.

14.2. Relief for French Residents

14.2.1 Treaty Relief

a) Income from foreign real estate is often exempt from French taxation under a double tax treaty. Nevertheless it may be taken into account to determine the rates of tax applicable to the income sources taxable in France. This is commonly called the *taux effectif rule*.

b) Business profits earned by a French resident are often exempt from tax in another state under a double tax treaty, unless the French resident carries on a business in the other state through a permanent establishment there.

c) Profits from the operation of ships and aircraft by a French resident are often exempt from tax in another state under a double tax treaty.

d) Income from independent professional services performed outside France by a French resident is often exempt from foreign tax under a double tax treaty, if the taxpayer does not have a fixed base regularly available to him in the other state.

e) Remuneration from an employment derived by a French resident is often exempt from tax in another state under a double tax treaty, unless the employment is exercised in that other state.

f) Pensions received by a French resident are often exempt from tax in another state under a double tax treaty. Pensions for government service in the other state usually remain taxable in the other state, but may still have to be declared in France for the *taux effectif* (see above).

g) France very often exempts from French tax income which, under the terms of a double tax treaty, is taxable in the other state. For example Article 24 of the France – UK treaty exempts a French resident from French tax on UK source income which has been taxed in the UK, other than dividends and income derived by public entertainers). In these cases the income may nevertheless be taken into account in determining the rate of tax suffered by the French resident in France on his other sources of income.

h) Foreign tax suffered on dividends, royalties and interest may be allowed as a credit against the French tax suffered by the French resident under a double tax treaty.

i)   Where this is the case, if the foreign tax exceeds the French tax on the same source of income, the excess credit is lost. It cannot be credited against the French tax on any other source of income, passed to a fellow group member or carried forward or back against French tax suffered on the same source of income in previous or subsequent years.

ii) Under the terms of some French double tax treaties, any tax 'spared' by the foreign country (under investment incentive schemes for example) are treated as having been paid in that country, so that the tax saving realised by the French investor is not simply recouped by the French tax system.

i)   The amount of foreign tax suffered on dividends, royalties and interest received by a French resident may be restricted by a double tax treaty. The applicable rates of withholding tax are set out in 14.3.

j)   French residents may be exempt from tax in another state on capital gains arising on assets in that state, other than immovable property in that state and movable property forming part of the business property of a permanent establishment in that state.

14.2.2 Non-Treaty Relief

a)   French resident companies are not subject to tax in France on their foreign branch profits until they are distributed by the French company. On the other hand, foreign branch losses are not deductible in France unless the world-wide income basis is used.

b)   French *sociétés mères* are exempt from tax on the dividends they receive from French or foreign affiliates (see 7.8.4). Provided a French company owns at least 5% of a foreign company it can be exempt from French corporation tax in respect of the dividends which it receives from its subsidiary.

c)   France does not offer residents a general unilateral tax credit relief in respect of income. Unilateral credit relief is available in respect of gifts and inheritance tax suffered on assets situated outside France.

14.3.   Treaty Withholding Tax Rates

a)   The table commencing hereafter shows the maximum rates of withholding taxes reserved under France's double tax treaties.

b)   Where the domestic rate of tax is lower, or a lower rate is available under the EU parent-subsidiary directive, the lower rate will apply. For example, interest paid on Euro accounts by French banks, and interest paid on French corporate bonds issued after 1 January 1987, does not suffer withholding tax in France. The rates of withholding tax quoted under the 'Interest' column are therefore superfluous in the case of such payments.

c) Consistent with the perspective of this book, the table focuses on the rates of French withholding tax paid by non-French residents. Thus where the treaty states that domestic law rates are to apply, the French withholding tax rate is quoted. The rate of withholding tax suffered by a French resident on income from the other state is likely to be different in such cases.

Country	Dividends		Royalties	Interest
	Parent Company[1] %	Other Shareholders %	%	%
Albania	5	15	5	10/0
Algeria	0[2]	0[2]	10/5	15/0[3]
Argentina	15	15	18	15/0[4]
Armenia	5	15	10/5[77]	10/0
Australia	15	15	10	10
Austria	0	15	0	0
Azerbaijan	10	10	5/10	10
Bahrain	0	0	0	0
Bangladesh	10	15	10	10
Belgium	0	15	0	15
Benin	25	25	0	15/0[5]
Bolivia	15	15	15	15/0[6]
Botswana	5	12	10	10
Brazil	15	15	25/15/10[7]	15/10/0[8]
Bulgaria	5	15	5	0
Burkina Faso	15	15	0[9]	15/0[10]
Cameroon	15	15	15	15/0
Canada[11]	10/5[12]	15	10/0[13]	10/0[14]
Central African Republic	25	25	0[9]	15/0[10]
China (People's Republic of)[15]	10	10	10	10/0
Congo[16]	15	20	15	0
Croatia	0	15	0	0
Cyprus	10	15	0	10/0

Country	Dividends		Royalties	Interest
	Parent Company[1] %	Other Shareholders %	%	%
Czech Republic	0	10	5/0[69]	0
Denmark	0	0	0	0
Ecuador	15	15	15	15/10/0[17]
Egypt	0	0	25/15[18]	15
Estonia	5	15	10/5	10
Finland	0	15/0	0	10/0[19]
Gabon	25	25/15	10/0[20]	10/15
Germany	10/5/0[21]	15/0	0	0
Ghana	7.5/5[22]	15	10	12.5/10[22]
Greece	0[23]	25[23]	5[24]	12/10/0[25]
Hungary	5	15	0	0
Iceland	5	15	0	0
India	10	10	0	15/10/0[26]
Indonesia	10	15	10	15/10/0[27]
Iran	15	20	10	15/0[28]
Ireland	0	15	0	0
Israel	5[29]	15	10[20]	10/5/0[30]
Italy	0	15	5	10/0[31]
Ivory Coast	18/15[32]	15	10	15/0[33]
Jamaica	10	15	10	10/0
Japan	5/0[34]	15	10	10/0[35]
Jordan	5	15	25/15/5[7]	15/0[36]
Kazakhstan	5	15	10	10
Korea (S)	10	15	10	10/0[35]
Kuwait	0	0	0	0
Latvia	5/0	15	10/5[78]	10/0[31]
Lebanon	0	0	33.3	0
Lithuania	5/0	15	10/5[78]	10/0[31]
Luxembourg	5/0	15/25[75]	33.33/0[75]	15/10
Macedonia	0	15	0	0
Madagascar	15	25	15/10	15/0[38]

Country	Dividends		Royalties	Interest
	Parent Company[1] %	Other Shareholders %	%	%
Malawi	5/15	15	0	15
Malaysia	5	15	33.3/10[39]	15/0[40]
Mali	25	25	0[9]	15/0[10]
Malta[76]	5	15	10[20]	10/0[41]
Mauritania	25	25	0[9]	15/0[10]
Mauritius	5	15	15/0[42]	15/0[43]
Mayotte	25	25	0	0
Mexico	0/5	15	15/0[44]	15/0[45]
Monaco[46]	25	25	33.3	15/0
Mongolia	5	15	0/5[69]	10/0
Morocco	15/0[47]	15/0[47]	10/5[48]	15/10[49]
Namibia	5	15	10[20]	10/0
Netherlands	0	15	0	10/0[50]
New Caledonia	5	15	10[20]	0
New Zealand	15	15	10	10/0[51]
Niger	25	25	0[9]	15/0[10]
Nigeria	12.5	15	12.5	12.5/0[52]
Norway	5/0[53]	15	0	0
Oman	5	0	0	0
Pakistan	10	15	10	10/0
Philippines	10	15	15	15/10/0[54]
Poland	0	15	10[20]	0
Portugal	0	15	5	12
Qatar	0	0	0	0
Romania	10	10	10	10/0[55]
Russia	10/5	15	33.3	0
Saudi Arabia	0	0	0	0
Senegal	15	15	0[9]	15/0[10]
Singapore	10	15	0/33.3	10/0[56]
Slovak Republic	10	10	5[69]	0
South Africa	5	15	0	0
Spain	0	15	5/0[57]	10/0[58]

Country	Dividends		Royalties	Interest
	Parent Company[1] %	Other Shareholders %	%	%
Sri Lanka	25	25	10[20]	10/0[60]
St Pierre & Miquelon	5	15	10[20]	0
Sweden	0	15	0	0
Switzerland	0[61]	15	5	0
Thailand	20/15[62]	25/15[62]	15/5[63]	10/3/0[64]
Togo	25	25	0[9]	15/0[10]
Trinidad and Tobago	10	15	10[65]	10/0[66]
Tunisia	25	25	20/15/5[67]	12/0
Turkey	15	20	10	15/0[68]
Ukraine	5/0	15	10/5[77]	10
United Arab Emirates	0	0	0	0
United Kingdom	5/0	15	0	0
USA	5	15	0/5[69]	0
Ex-USSR/Russian Federation[70]	15	15	0	10/0[71]
Uzbekistan	5	10	33.3	5
Venezuela	0	15	5	5/0[72]
Vietnam	5	15	10	0
Ex-Yugoslavia [73]	5	15	0	0
Zambia	0/15	15	0	0
Zimbabwe	10	15/20[74]	10	10/0

Notes

1. The term "parent company" does not necessarily imply voting control. Generally speaking the dividend qualifies for the lower rate of withholding tax if the recipient company owns at least 10% of the capital of the paying company, but in the following cases the shareholding qualification is higher:

   a) 15%: Bulgaria and Japan

   b) 25%: Czech Republic, Hungary, Indonesia, Iran, Madagascar, Oman, Thailand and Ex-Yugoslavia

   c) 50%: Malawi, Ukraine and Zambia

2. Treaty does not cover dividends, and withholding tax rates for royalties are the domestic rates in force at the time treaty was concluded – rate quoted is the French rate.

3. Nil in respect of interest paid by one state, to the other, or its local authorities or central bank or in respect of interest paid on a loan financed by an export credit agency or similar body of the other state; in other cases domestic law rate – rates quoted are French rates on corporate bonds issued since 1 January 1987 (nil) and on shareholders loan accounts (15%).

4. Nil if the interest is paid by a state or public entity to the other state or a public entity thereof, or if it is paid for a loan given, guaranteed or insured by specified public entities of the other state; 15% in other cases.

5. Treaty allows each country to levy withholding taxes in accordance with its domestic law. Rates quoted are French rates on corporate bonds issued after 1 January 1987 (nil) and on shareholders loan accounts (15%).

6. Nil for interest paid to the Bolivian State or to French public bodies or institutions; 15% in all other cases if the recipient is the beneficial owner.

7. 10% or 5% in respect of literary artistic or scientific works, including films and tapes; 25% in respect of trademarks; 15% in all other cases.

8. Nil in respect of government loans; 10% in respect of loans for a period of at least 7 years from banks with participation from certain public bodies; 15% in all other cases.

9. Nil on royalties paid for use of patents, trademarks, secret processes, formulae and cinematographic film; domestic rate of tax of the country of the payor on 'royalties' for use of immovable property, working of mines etc (there is no French withholding tax on income from renting real estate).

10. Interest taxable in country of source. Rates quoted are French rates in respect of corporate bonds issued after 1 January 1987 (nil) and shareholders loan accounts (15%).

11. There is a treaty between France and Quebec, the benefits of which do not generally extend beyond the benefits of the Canada – France treaty.

12. 5% if the beneficial owner is subject to corporation tax and controls 10% of the voting power (in a Canadian company) or capital (in a French company); 10% if the Canadian company is a non-resident owned investment corporation.

13. Nil in respect of literary, dramatic, musical or artistic work (not including film or videotape), computer software or any patent or the right to use industrial, commercial or scientific information, or any payment to the government of the other state or organisations approved by the competent authorities; 10% in all other cases.

14. Nil if the interest is:

    i)   a penalty charge for late payment; or

    ii) paid by the central bank of one state to the central bank of the other; or

iii) paid with respect to indebtedness resulting from the sale or furnishing on credit of any equipment, merchandise or services (except where the transaction is one between associated enterprises); or

iv) paid in respect of a government or public authority bond; or

v) paid in respect of a loan provided or guaranteed by the export credit agencies of either country.

10% in other cases.

15. France takes the view that the treaty with China does not cover Hong Kong or Macau.

16. This treaty has been revoked by Congo, but is still applied unilaterally by France.

17. Nil if the payer of the interest is one of the governments or its local authorities, or if the interest is paid to one of the governments or one of its local authorities or an institution owned by one of the governments, or if the loan was contracted in connection with an intergovernmental program of economic development; 10% if the interest arises from the financing of sales of industrial, commercial or scientific equipment or from a loan of any nature granted by a bank or from the financing of public works; 15% in all other cases.

18. 25% in respect of trademarks; 15% in all other cases.

19. Nil in respect of loans or contracts for deferred payment relating to sales of industrial, commercial or scientific equipment or the construction of industrial, commercial or scientific installations or the carrying out of public works, or for interest paid on a loan made by a bank or for interest paid as a penalty for late payment; 10% in other cases.

20. Nil in respect of literary, artistic or scientific works, including film or tape; 10% in all other cases.

21. Nil in respect of dividends paid by a company resident in France to a company resident in Germany which owns more than 10% of the French company. Where dividends are paid by a company resident in Germany to a company resident in France which owns more than 10% of the paying company, the withholding tax is 5% if the dividend is paid after 1 January 1992.

22. In each case the lower rate applies to payments from France to Ghana and the higher rate applies to payments from Ghana to France.

23. Dividends are taxable in country of source. Rates quoted are French rates of dividend withholding tax (NB parent companies can benefit from the EU parent/subsidiary directive).

24. General rate is 5% but sums paid for the use of cinematographic films are treated as business income.

25. 12% for French source interest on negotiable instruments; nil on other French source interest; 10% on Greek source interest.

26. Nil if paid by or to a contracting state or one of its political sub-divisions, or certain banks and government agencies; 10% if paid to a bank which owns at least 10% of the paying company; otherwise 15%.

27. Nil if the interest is paid to the other contracting state or a statutory body thereof or to an enterprise of the other state on loans granted with the participation of public institutions of the other state, under certain conditions; 10% in respect of interest paid by a financial, agricultural, industrial, tourist etc. business to a bank or another enterprise; 15% in all other cases.

28. Nil in respect of loans arranged by agreement between the governments to finance tax exempt activities; 15% in all other cases.

29. 5% if the beneficial owner is a company which holds at least 10% of the capital of the paying company; 10% if the beneficial owner is a company which owns at least 10% of the paying company but the paying company is a resident of Israel and the dividends are paid out of profits which are subject to a lower than normal rate of tax in Israel; 15% in all other cases.

30. Nil if the interest is paid to the other contracting state, a local authority thereof or to its central bank or to any resident of the other state in respect of loans guaranteed, promoted or financed by the other state or certain of its agencies. 5% if the interest is paid in connection with the sale on credit of industrial, commercial or scientific equipment, or in connection with the sale on credit of any merchandise by one enterprise to another or on a loan of any kind granted by a credit institution; 10% in other cases.

31. Nil if the interest is paid in connection with a sale of industrial, commercial or scientific equipment or in connection with a sale of goods by one enterprise to another enterprise, or if the payer is one of the states or a local subdivision of one of the states, or if the loan is granted or guaranteed by one of the states, its local subdivisions or public bodies, or if the interest is paid in connection with an intergovernmental agreement; in all other cases the withholding tax on interest will be 10%.

32. 18% if the dividends are paid by a company which is resident in the Ivory Coast and which is exempt from tax or subject to tax at a rate lower than the standard rate; 15% in all other cases.

33. Nil if the recipient is the beneficial owner of the interest and:

i) the recipient is a contracting state or a local or statutory authority thereof; or

ii) the interest is paid by a person referred to in (i); or

iii) the interest is paid in connection with a sale on credit of industrial commercial or scientific equipment or in connection with the sale on credit of merchandise or the furnishing of services by an enterprise of one state to an enterprise of the other.

15% in other cases.

34. 5% if the dividend is paid to a company which owns over 15% of the French company. Nil for certain companies defined in the treaty.

35. *Nil in respect of interest received by central banks, government export finance agencies etc.; 10% in all other cases.*

36. *Nil in respect of bank loans, loans between enterprises and loans to finance the sale of industrial etc equipment; 15% in all other cases.*

37. *15% in respect of literary, artistic or scientific works including films; 10% in respect of trademarks, industrial or commercial equipment or know-how etc.*

38. *Nil in respect of interest received by central banks, government export finance agencies etc.; 15% in all other cases.*

39. *Royalties for use of cinematographic films or works recorded on tapes for television or broadcasting are subject to taxation in source country according to domestic rules (ie 33.3% in France); 10% in other cases.*

40. *Nil in respect of interest paid to a resident of France on an approved loan; 15% in other cases.*

41. *Nil in respect of interest on loans granted by one of the states or a statutory body thereof; 10% in all other cases.*

42. *Nil if the recipient is the beneficial owner and the royalties are paid for literary, artistic or scientific work including film and recordings for broadcast; 15% in other cases.*

43. *Nil if the interest is paid to the other state or a public body of that state or a banking institution of that state; otherwise subject to taxation at source in accordance with the law of the source state (rates quoted are French rates on interest arising on shareholders' loan accounts (15%) and corporate bonds issued after 1 January 1987 (nil)).*

44. *Nil if the royalties are paid to an author of a literary, dramatic, musical or artistic work (excluding film and television works); 15% in all other cases.*

45. *Nil if the payor or payee is one of the states or a sub-division of one of the states, or the interest is paid on a loan of at least 3 years duration granted or guaranteed by an export credit guarantee institution; 15% in all other cases.*

46. *Treaty does not provide for reduced withholding taxes. The rates quoted are French withholding tax rates on dividends, royalties, interest on corporate bonds issued after 1 January 1987 (nil) and interest on shareholders loan accounts (15%).*

47. *Nil if the dividends are paid from a company resident in France to a person resident in Morocco if that person is taxable in respect of the income in Morocco; in other cases where the recipient is the beneficial owner of the dividend, the rate is 15%.*

48. *5% in respect of literary, artistic or scientific works, not including film; 10% in respect of patents, trademarks, know how etc.*

49. *15% on term deposits and cash vouchers; 10% on other interest.*

50. *Nil in respect of interest paid under a financing contract or a contract for deferred*

payment relating to the sale of industrial, commercial or scientific equipment or the construction of industrial, commercial or scientific installations or the carrying out of public works, or if the interest is paid on a loan from a bank or if it is paid as a penalty for late payment; 10% in other cases (except 12% in respect of French bonds issued before 1 January 1965).

51. Nil in respect of interest paid to the other state or a local or public authority of that state, or on a loan made or guaranteed by the other state; in other cases 10%.

52. Nil if the interest is paid to the government of the other state or one of its territorial subdivisions, or an establishment or organisation of that government or its subdivisions, or in connection with a loan granted, guaranteed or aided by the government of the other state; in all other cases 12.5%.

53. Nil if the recipient is a company resident in France and owns at least 25% or the capital of the paying company or if the recipient is a company resident in Norway which owns at least 10% of the company paying the dividend. 5% if the recipient is a company resident in France which owns at least 10% of the paying company; 15% in all other cases.

54. Nil in respect of interest on government loans and local authority loans if the interest is beneficially owned by a resident of the other state, and in respect of loans made guaranteed or insured by an export credit agency etc ; 10% in respect of interest paid to French residents in respect other public issues of bonds by Philippines companies; and 15% in other cases.

55. Nil in respect of loans made or guaranteed by one of the states or a public body thereof; 10% in all other cases.

56. Nil in respect of interest paid to one of the states, the central bank of either state, or agreed government owned institutions; 10% in all other cases.

57. Nil for literary or artistic work (excluding film and sound or picture recording); 5% in other cases if the recipient is the beneficial owner.

58. Nil if the recipient is the beneficial owner and the interest is paid

   i)   by the other contracting state or one of its territorial authorities;or

   ii) by an enterprise of one state to an enterprise of the other; or

   iii) in connection with the sale on credit of industrial, commercial or scientific equipment; or

   iv) on any loan granted by a credit institution.

   10% in other cases.

59. Nil in respect of copyrights and films; 10% in all other cases.

60. Nil in respect of interest paid to a bank, interest paid on loans made to finance sales of industrial, commercial or scientific equipment or for public works and interest on

loans made to one of the states; 10% in all other cases.

61. *The 0% tax rate is available to parent companies owning at least 10% of the foreign subsidiary, but not if the parent is majority-owned by persons who are not residents of Switzerland or one of the EU states.*

62. *15% if the dividend is paid to a company and paid by an industrial company; 20% if the dividend is paid to a company by any other company; domestic law rates in all other cases.*

63. *5% in respect of literary, artistic or scientific work; 15% in all other cases.*

64. *3% on loans granted for 4 years or more with the participation of a public finance organisation etc or an enterprise of the other state and which are tied to the sale of plant and machinery or studies relating to the supply of industrial, commercial or scientific installations, as well as public works; 10% in respect of interest paid to any financial establishment which is a company of the other state; otherwise domestic law rates.*

65. *Nil in respect of payments for literary, dramatic, musical or artistic work (excluding film or video tapes) beneficially owned by a resident of the other state; 10% in other cases.*

66. *Nil if the interest is beneficially owned by the government of the other state, or a local authority thereof or any agency of that government or local authority, or the central bank of the other state; 10% in other cases where the recipient is the beneficial owner.*

67. *5% in respect of literary, artistic or scientific work, not including film; 15% in respect of patents, know how, technical studies etc.; 20% in respect of trademarks, films and equipment; sums paid to public broadcast bodies for the use of films and broadcasts exempt.*

68. *Nil in respect of interest paid to a government or central bank, or paid in connection with a loan guaranteed by a government; 15% in other cases.*

69. *Nil in respect of literary, artistic or scientific works, film sound or video recordings and software (except for software for Italy); 5% in all other cases.*

70. *This treaty applies to the member states of the Russian Federation, pending negotiation of new treaties with each state, but it does not apply to the 3 Baltic states of the former USSR.*

71. *Nil if the interest is paid to or by a contracting state, one of its local authorities or a public body or for finance agreed within the frame of agreements for public aid for external trade or other agreements between the states; 5% in all other cases.*

72. *Nil for interest from commercial credits and bank loans; 10% in other cases.*

73. *This treaty applies to Slovenia, Serbia, Montenegro and Bosnia-Herzegovina pending the negotiation of replacement treaties.*

74. *15% if the dividend is paid by a French company to a Zimbabwe resident; 20% if the payment is in the other direction.*

75. *25% for dividends, 15% for interest, and 33.33% for royalties paid to Luxembourg holding companies.*

76. *From 1 September 1997 companies registered in Malta under a privileged tax treatment cannot benefit from the terms of the France-Malta double-tax treaty.*

77. *5% on trademarks, design or models; 10% in other cases.*

78. *5% on the use of industrial, commercial or scientific equipment.*

PART 3

Practical Detail

15. TYPICAL INCOME TAX COMPUTATIONS

15.1. Salaried Executive

a) Robespierre is a French resident individual employed as a salaried executive. In 2007 his salary was €150,000, from which his contributions to the social security and unemployment insurance schemes totalling €37,500 were deducted. He received dividends from French companies of €12,000 in 2007, and he realised a taxable gain of €6,000 on a disposal of shares for a total sale price of €22,300. He received bank interest of €3,200 during the year, which was taxed at source. He employed a home helper through *chèque-emploi-service* and paid €7,000 in wages and employer's social contribution. He is married with two minor children.

b) The tax that he will pay in 2008 is calculated as follows:

Income of 2007	€	€
Salary		150,000
Less: deductible social security charges,		(37,500)
		112,500
Less: allowance for expenses (10%) (6.6.6(b)(i)),		(11,250)
Note: allowance of 20% no longer applies as integrated in the barème income bands		101,250
Rental income (real regime)		
Note: the loss of €400 can only be carried forward against future rental income		–
Dividends from French companies	12,000	
Less 40% abatement,	(4,800)	
	7,200	
Less abatement (6.6.8(c)),	(3,050)	
Net taxable dividends		4,150
		105,400
Deductible portion of *CSG* (see note)		(8,032)
		97,368

continued

Income of 2007	€	€
Tax Payable Based on 3 Parts (6.10.3)		
Income per *part* (taxable income divided by 3)	32,456	
Tax per *part*:		
first 5,687 at 0%	Nil	
5,687 to 11,344 at 5.50%	311	
11,344 to 25,195 at 14%	1,939	
25,195 to 67,546 at 30%	2,178	
Tax per *part:*	4,428	
Tax per *part* x number of *parts*	13,284	
Plafonnement (6.11.2)		
If the taxpayer had been entitled to only 2 *parts*, and €2,227 was deducted from his liability for each extra half *part*, the tax would be:		
Income per *part* (taxable income divided by 2)	48,684	
Tax per *part*:		
first 25,195 (above)	2,250	
25,195 to 67,546 at 30%	7,047	
	9,297	
Tax per part x number of *parts*	18,594	
Less: (€2,227 x 2),	(4,454)	
Total liability after *plafonnement*		14,140
Since the calculation applying the *plafonnement* produces a higher tax liability than the standard calculation, the *plafonnement* applies		14,140
Tax reduction for employment of home help		
50% of €7,000		(3,500)
		10,640
Add: tax on capital gain of €6,000 (at 27% including social contributions, ie 16%+8.2%+0.5%+2.3%) *(29% from 2008)*		1,620
Less: tax credit on dividend (50% of dividends limited to €230)		(230)
Add: tax at source on bank interest of €3,200 (at 27% including social contributions, ie 16%+8.2%+0.5%+2.3%) *(29% from 2008)*		864
		12,894

continued

Income of 2007	€	€
Add: *CSG* on above (6.3.(b))		

CSG base $\begin{cases} \text{7.5\% of 97\% of €150,000} & \text{10,912} \\ \text{8.2\% of €12,000 dividends} & \text{984} \end{cases}$

0.5% *CRDS* on same basis as the *CSG*	787	
2.3% *PS (prélèvement social)* on dividends	276	
Total social contributions		12,959
Total tax liability		25,853

Note:	*Deductible portion of CSG:*	
	5.1% of 97% of €150,000 (salary)	*7,420*
	5.1% of €12,000 (dividend)	*612*
Total		*€8,032*

15.2. Property Rental by a Non-Resident

a) William is a non-French resident individual who owns a home in Normandy. The value of the property (buildings only) is €122,000. The property is in fact rented out on a furnished basis from time to time and produced a rental income of €18,300 in 2007 for a total of 3 months of lettings. William occupied the property himself for 1 month, for which the rental value is estimated at €732. William paid €915 in *taxes foncières,* €610 in *taxe d'habitation* and €3,800 for repairs and maintenance during the year. He has no other French sources of income, but substantial income from sources outside France. He is married with two minor children. His country of residence has concluded a full double tax treaty with France (*Note 1*).

b) Because he is letting his property on a furnished basis, William's French source income will be assessed under business income rules and not as rental income. But since his rental income does not exceed €76,300, William will be able to use the *micro-BIC* regime for calculation of his taxable income.

c) William will not be considered to be a 'professional landlord' because his rental income is less than €23,000 per annum and it does not constitute the greater part of his income. Apart from certain consequences in terms of the availability of relief for any losses on the lettings, which are unlikely to concern William, the main consequence of not being a 'professional landlord' is that any gain on an eventual disposal of the property will be taxed as a private capital gain and not as a business gain.

d) Theoretically, if he elected to have his business income calculated under the rules for the 'real' regime, William would still be able to claim depreciation on the buildings as a business expense, provided that the property was recorded in the balance sheet of the business. However, in this case, he would have to declare a rent for the period that he occupied the property. On the assumptions that he chooses to be assessed under the *micro-BIC* rules, his income tax liability for 2007, payable in 2008, will be computed as follows:

Income of 2007	€	€
Rental income (*Note 2*)		18,300
Less: Global deduction for expenses (71%),		(12,993)
		5,307
Minimum income tax liability for non-residents at 20% (*Note 1*)		1,061

Note 1. *Because William is resident in a country which has concluded a full double tax treaty with France, he is not subject to tax on a notional income of three times the annual rental value of the property. Correspondingly, however, his liability is subject to the minimum tax rate of 20%. If his liability calculated at scale rates exceeded the minimum liability, the normal scale rates would apply, but this will clearly not be the case in this example.*

Note 2. *William is not liable to pay any social contributions because he is not resident in France.*

Note 3. *It does not matter whether the rent is paid to William by non-French residents or into a bank account outside France. The income is still French source income, and subject to tax in France.*

e) Generally a business of furnished lettings is subject to the business tax (*taxe professionnelle*), unless the local government authorities have resolved that such businesses should be exempt.

15.3. Property Owned by a Tax Haven Resident

a) Sarah is a resident of Andorra/Bermuda/Cayman/Channel Islands/Hong Kong/ Isle of Man/Monaco, who owns a villa worth €600,000 in France. The annual rental value of the villa is estimated to be €24,000. She is married with three young children. She has no significant income from France, but receives interest on an account which she maintains for convenience at a French bank.

b) Sarah is liable to French income tax on the basis of three times the market rental value of her home(s) in France (6.6.2(b)) because this notional income exceeds her actual French source income. Her liability will be calculated as follows:

Income of 2007	€	€
Notional income (€24,000 x 3)		72,000
Income per *part* (4 *parts*)	18,000	
Tax per *part* €		
first 5,687 at 0%	nil	
5,687 to 11,344 at 5.5%	311	
11,344 to 25,195 at 14%	932	
	1,243	
Tax per *part* x number of *parts*	4,972	

Plafonnement test

If the taxpayer had been entitled to only 2 *parts*, and €2,227 was deducted from her liability for each extra half *part*, the tax would be:

	€	€
Income per *part* (2 *parts*)	36,000	
Tax per *part*		
first 5,687 at 0%	nil	
5,687 to 11,344 at 5.5%	311	
11,344 to 25,195 at 14%	1,939	
25,195 to 67,546 at 30%	3,242	
	5,492	
Tax per *part* x number of *parts*	10,984	
Less €2,227 x 4	(8,908)	
	2,076	

Therefore *plafonnement* does not apply.		
Income Tax Liability		4,972

15.4. *Bouclier Fiscal*

The *bouclier fiscal* is a system which allows taxpayers to cap their tax burden at a maximum of 50% overall. The excess is refunded upon the filing of form 2041.

Mr and Mrs de la Tacse paid the following taxes during 2008:

	€	€
Available income		
Income 2007		165,000
Tax paid during 2008		
Income tax on 2007 income [1]		46,000
Social contributions (*CSG, CRDS* and *PS*) on 2007 income		18,000
Taxes foncières 2008 on main home		1,700
Taxe d'habitation 2008 on main home		1,200
Wealth tax 2008		36,000
Total taxes		**102,900**
Bouclier fiscal: 50% of income	82,500	
Tax refund [2]		**20,400**

Note: [1] *this includes income taxed at barème rates and income and gains taxed at fixed rates.*
[2] *A claim in respect of an excess of tax paid in 2008 on 2007 income will have to reach the tax office before 31 December 2009.*

16. TYPICAL CAPITAL GAINS TAX COMPUTATION

SALE OF HOLIDAY HOME IN FRANCE

a) Mr and Mrs Norman are UK residents with two independent children. They acquired a home in France in May 2001 for €305,000. They have not kept a record of the expenses connected with the purchase. They spent €70,000 on improvements to the property. In June 2008 they sold the property for €588,000. They have never been residents of France, and this is the first time that they have sold a property in France.

b) The gain on the sale is not exempt, because Mr and Mrs Norman have not been resident in France for at least two years. Therefore the gain will be taxed as follows, and Mr and Mrs Norman will have to appoint a fiscal representative.

	€	€
Sale price		588,000
Cost price	305,000	
Expenses of purchase (7.5%)	22,875	
	327,875	
Improvements	70,000	
Base cost deductible from sale value		(397,875)
Net		190,125
Abatement for period of ownership		
(7 – 5 years) x 10% = 20%		(38,025)
		152,100
Fixed abatement (€1,000 per owner)		(2,000)
		€150,100
Tax at 16%		€24,016

c) *Note:* The rate is increased to 33⅓% for residents of non EU countries. The cost of replacement of existing features is not deductible.

17. TYPICAL WEALTH TAX COMPUTATION

a) Mr and Mrs Prospero and their four-year-old son are resident in France. They have listed their assets and liabilities as at 1 January 2008 as follows:

Assets	€	Taxable amount €
Main property	450,000	315,000 [1]
Holiday house by the sea	200,000	200,000
Property in England (let on a long term basis)	350,000	297,500 [2]
Investment portfolio	680,000	680,000
Life assurance policy	80,000	80,000
Balance on accounts (foreign and French)	124,000	124,000
2 cars	27,500	27,500
Yacht	30,000	30,000
Furniture (of which antiques estimated at around €50,000)	88,000	38,000 [3]
Total assets		1,792,000

Liabilities	€
French income tax and social surcharges	18,000
UK income tax on UK rental income	2,500
Local taxes on French properties	3,000
Rates on UK property	950
Outstanding credit card amounts	500
Outstanding invoices	200
Outstanding mortgage	110,000
Total liabilities	*135,150*
Net Taxable Wealth	**1,656,850**

Taxable Wealth		Rates	Liability
Below €770,000	ie €770,000	0%	0
Between €770,000 and €1,240,000	ie €470,000	0.55%	2,585
Between €1,240,000 and €2,450,000	ie €416,850	0.75%	3,126
Total	€1,656,850		

Total liability	5,711
Deduction for a dependent child	(150)
Net liability	5,561

Taxable wealth less wealth tax liability 1,656,850 – 5,561	1,651,289

Taxable wealth		*Rates*	*Liability*
Below €770,000	ie €770,000	0%	0
Between €770,000 and €1,240,000	ie €470,000	0.55%	2,585
Between €1,240,000 and €2,450,000	€411,289	0.75%	3,085
Total	€1,651,289		
Total liability			5,670
Deduction for a dependent child			(150)
Total Net liability			**5,520**

(1) *The taxpayer is entitled to reduce the value of his main home by 30% to reflect the fact that it is occupied.*

(2) *The value of rented property may be reduced depending on the terms of the lease and the permanence of the tenancy.*

(3) *Antiques are exempt from wealth tax.*

(4) *Deduction for dependent child.*

18.   FOREIGN OWNERSHIP OF REAL ESTATE

18.1.   Acquisition of Real Estate

18.1.1 The Legal Process

a) Transfers of real property in France have to be witnessed by a quasi-public official called a *notaire* (notary public). In many cases, the *notaire* also acts as an estate agent, and will be the only person involved in the transaction apart from the buyer and vendor. While he has a duty to act professionally, the notary is appointed by one of the parties (the buyer has the prerogative to appoint the notary, but the estate agent will often insert the name of the vendor's notary in the contract).

b) It is possible for the buyer to appoint his own *notaire* in addition to the one offered by the vendor or the estate agent. In this case the two *notaires* share the fixed fee for their services. However the *notaires* are allowed to charge double the fixed fee for advice on contentious matters, and where two or more *notaires* are sharing the fee the parties to the transaction should be aware that the *notaires* are motivated to find disputes where none exist. Examine the clause in the *acte de vente* relating to the *notaires'* fees with great care.

c) Alternatively, the buyer may wish to be represented by a lawyer, who will represent his interests exclusively. This however does not avoid the need for a *notaire* to transact the conveyance.

d) The first stage in the process of buying an existing residence is normally a preliminary contract. There are two forms of contract, one being called a *compromis de vente* which is an agreement signed by both parties (a bilateral agreement) which is subsequently reiterated by a deed called an *acte de vente* before a *notaire*. This form of contract is mainly used in provincial or rural areas. In Paris the transaction is more commonly framed in a one-sided document called a *promesse de vente* (which is like a call-option granted to the buyer). On signature of the contract by the buyer a deposit of 10% (5% if the property is less than 5 years old) of the purchase price is payable. This is deposited with the *notaire* witnessing the conveyance, or the estate agent if he is authorised to accept deposits. The deposit is a part payment if the contract is completed, and it is called a *réservation*, but it is forfeited if the buyer withdraws from the contract. Similarly the vendor must pay the buyer the same amount (as well as refunding the deposit) as damages if he withdraws from the contract. Nevertheless the contract will usually contain conditions, such as that it is subject to the buyer obtaining finance, and if these conditions are not fulfilled the deposit is refundable. Because of the penalty of the amount of the deposit, it is rare to see vendors breaking a sale agreement to accept a higher offer.

e) Once the conveyancing documents have been completed by the notary, normally after 4 – 6 weeks, the buyer is asked to pay to the notary the balance of the purchase price. The notary is personally liable for the registration taxes on the sale and will insist on having all of the purchase price before proceeding.

f) The buyer and vendor have to be present before the *notaire*, in person or through an attorney, for the signature of the 'deed of sale' (*acte de vente*).

g) If the property to be acquired is unfinished, the parties will sign a 'contract of reservation', and the purchaser will pay a deposit of 5% if the property is to be completed within a year, 2% if the property is to be completed within 1 – 2 years and no deposit if the property will be completed after more than 2 years.

18.1.2 Joint Ownership

a) In many cases the non-resident buying property in France will be buying it jointly with his or her spouse, or in partnership with other non-residents. The purchasers will therefore be keen to arrange their ownership so that they each have appropriate rights to the property, especially after one of the partners has died. When property in France is acquired by two or more persons jointly, the deed of purchase (the *acte de vente*) identifies the parties acquiring the property, the type of joint ownership and, if they are married, their matrimonial regime. If they are acquiring the property *en indivision* (see (d) below), the *acte* states the proportions owned by each of them.

b) Persons who are domiciled in France enter into a marriage contract when they get married, and will either own their property:

   i) under community property rules (*régime communautaire*), in which case it does not matter who signs the contract or pays the purchase price, the couple usually own it in equal shares (there are a number of different forms of community property regime, some covering all of the assets of the couple and some covering only some of them, for example assets acquired during the course of the marriage); or

   ii) as separate estates (*régime de la séparation de biens*), in which case one or other of the parties may own the property entirely, or they may own the property in unequal shares according to whatever arrangements they make between themselves.

c) Couples from most common law countries and states are treated as married under rules substantially identical to the separation of estates system, unless they have entered into a marriage settlement. (It should be noted however that some states in the USA have community property rules). A property acquired in the name of one of the spouses will therefore belong to that spouse, and if it is simply acquired in joint names they will own the property *en indivision* (see (d)) below in the proportions in which they contributed to the cost. However a couple from a common law country who are buying property in France can enter into a marriage contract specifically for the purposes of their French property (notwithstanding that they are already married). Equally a couple who already have a marriage contract can change it.

d) The main forms of joint ownership are:

    i) ownership *en indivision* (equivalent to a tenancy in common in England and Wales); and

    ii) ownership *en tontine* (or, more technically, under a clause *d'accroisement*) (the nearest equivalent to an English joint tenancy). This form of ownership is highly unusual among French nationals, and involves inserting clauses in the *acte de vente* which create a legal fiction that the property belongs, from the outset, to whichever of the purchasers survives the longest.

e) In practical terms the difference is that when property is owned by two people as tenants in common, and one of them dies, his or her share devolves to his or her heirs, who, in France, are likely to include the children or parents of the deceased. When property is owned *en tontine,* as noted above the survivor of the owners is deemed to have owned the whole property from the beginning. It may be observed in passing that ownership *en tontine* is an effective defence against the claim of a creditor, because until one of the parties dies there is no way of knowing which of them has any interest in the property. The vast majority of joint registrations of title in France are purchases by French married couples within a community property matrimonial regime, but when a property is purchased in joint names outside the matrimonial relationship, the purchase is almost invariably an acquisition *en indivision*. Indeed for much of the early part of this century the concept of the purchase *en tontine* was thought to be unconstitutional, and even today many notaries in France regard it as tantamount to a fraud upon the children.

f) Nevertheless the purchase *en tontine* is extremely popular with buyers from common law jurisdictions because it avoids leaving the surviving spouse as a co-owner of the property with the children of the deceased spouse. If the partners have been married before, these children may not be the children of the surviving spouse and he or she may feel no moral obligation towards them. An important factor which is often overlooked when individuals choose to buy *en tontine* is that from a French tax point of view it is inefficient. This is especially true if two or more *tontine* co-owners are unrelated or not united through marriage or a *PACS* agreement. Indeed in this instance, any transfer to the surviving party(ies) would attract a 60% inheritance tax charge.

When property is held *en tontine* tax is charged upon the death of a co-owner as if the deceased's shares passes to the survivor(s). Nevertheless the recent inheritance tax exemption (22 August 2007) for transfers between spouses or *PACS* partners has increased the efficiency of the *tontine* as an estate planning tool where the protection of the survivor is the ultimate objective. The only downside is a greater tax-exposed portion upon the demise of the surviving spouse or partner.

Another point to bear in mind is that if the parties to an acquisition *en tontine* subsequently fall out, the position can be extremely messy, and it may not be easy for one of the parties to extricate himself or herself from the investment.

g) An *indivision* will exist in either of two cases:

    i) a 'common law' *indivision* results whenever two or more persons buy or inherit property jointly without making any written agreement or articles of association between themselves. The resulting relationship is governed by the Civil Code, which prescribes preemption rights (rights of first refusal), rights of management etc. Under this regime, none of the parties is bound to remain in the *indivision*, and any of them can apply to the court at any time for severance;

    ii) the parties themselves may enter into an agreement in writing prescribing their respective shares in the property, which may be stated to be effective for a fixed period of time or an indefinite period. If the agreement is limited to a fixed period, the period must be 5 years renewable either by express agreement or in the absence of notice to terminate. The parties appoint a manager (*gérant*) to look after the property.

h) The advantage of entering into such an agreement is that the parties can provide for their own rules of tenure and for the devolution of the property in the events of death, bankruptcy and incapacity. It is possible to create an *indivision* between two couples who, as between themselves, intend to own *en tontine*.

i) Non-residents acquiring real estate in France should normally create a French will to deal with the property. This can be used to prevent reserved heirs (see 21.3.2) from converting the surviving spouse's life interest into an annuity, or from buying the surviving spouse out.

18.1.3 Costs

a) The vendor will normally pay the estate agent's commission, but it is customary for the buyer to pay the *notaire's* fees.

b) The notary's fees (excluding VAT) are calculated according to the following scale:

Purchase Price	%
For that part of the purchase price:	
between €0 and €6,500	4
between €6,500 and €17,000	1.65
between €17,000 and €30,000	1.10
above €30,000	0.825

18.1.4 Taxes on Purchase

a) *TVA* at 19.6% is paid on a purchase of a new property. A sale of a building will be subject to this tax in either of two cases:

   i) if the house is sold before it is completed; or

   ii) if it is sold within 5 years of its completion, and it has not previously been sold by a non-trader.

b) When the property acquired is less than 5 years old, *TVA* is paid by the vendor, but in practice this means it is added to the sale price. A further registration tax of 0.6% is also chargeable.

c) If the property is more than 5 years old, no *TVA* is payable but the transaction is subject to registration tax. The registration tax paid to the *département* is 3.6% of the value of the property, plus a surcharge of 2.5% of the tax due to the *département*. In addition an element of 1.2% of the value of the property is paid to the local *commune*, so the registration taxes normally total 4.89%. However they are restricted in some cases, for example, in certain 'rural revitalisation zones' the amount on which the *départemental* duties are paid is reduced.

   The registration tax is paid by the purchaser unless the parties agree otherwise.

d) When a building plot is acquired by a private individual for the purpose of constructing a residence for himself (or the property consists of buildings to be demolished to make way for a new dwelling to be constructed by a private individual) the purchase is subject to the registration taxes described in (c) above. However if a plot (or a building to be demolished) is acquired by a developer the transaction is subject to *TVA* at the normal rate – which is usually borne by the purchaser. The transfer is also subject to a 'publicity tax' of 0.6% based on the net of VAT value. Work performed by building contractors is subject to *TVA* at 19.6%. In larger communities and in the Ile-de-France there may be an additional local building tax of between 1 and 5%.

18.1.5 Underdeclaration of Price

a) Because of the registration taxes and the possible capital gains tax liability of the vendor, the purchaser will often be asked to pay a portion of the purchase price 'under the table' (*sous la table*). The *acte de vente* will show a lower price paid. This may eventually present the buyer with a capital gains tax problem, because his cost basis is artificially low. However, even if he can avoid this problem (eg because he is likely to be exempt from tax on the gain), other problems will result if the deceit is discovered:

   i)   The registration taxes underpaid will be payable;

   ii) Interest will be charged on the registration taxes underpaid at the rate of 0.75% per month, and a penalty of 50% of the registration taxes underpaid will be levied;

   iii) The secret agreement will be null and void;

   iv) There are criminal sanctions against the authors of the fraud and their accomplices.

b) One fact which needs to be taken into account by anyone considering agreeing to an underdeclaration of the purchase price is that the French land registry (*le Cadastre*) exists primarily for the collection of taxes, and is part of the French tax administration. Similarly the registration of mortgages (*la Conservation des Hypothèques*) forms part of the function of the tax administration. The staff of these offices are usually tax inspectors. For example the head of each of the 353 mortgage registries is a category A agent of the exterior services of the *Direction Générale des Impôts*. This means that the tax administration is very well informed on the value of property in France.

c) The degree of risk accepted by a purchaser who agrees to pay part of the purchase price in cash will obviously depend on the size of the cash portion. The only advice which a professional adviser can give a client who is faced with this problem is not to make a cash payment.

18.2. Ownership of Real Estate

18.2.1 General

a) The onus is on the taxpayer to complete and submit the returns which the law obliges him to make. This applies to non-residents as much as to French residents, and every non-resident who has French source income or a home in France is obliged to send a tax return to the Paris tax centre for non-residents each year containing all of the information necessary to determine his tax liability.

b) The non-resident can be asked to designate a tax representative in France.

c) If the non-resident does not submit a return, the administration may send him a return with a *demande de déclaration* asking him to complete and submit it. The next step is that the administration sends a reminder to him (called a *mise en demeure*). If he then fails to regularise the position within 30 days the administration can issue an estimated assessment (*taxation d'office*). The onus is then on the taxpayer to disprove the assessment. Interest on overdue tax is charged at 0.4% per month and there is a penalty of 10% if the taxpayer has made his return late but before he received the *mise en demeure*, or if he responded within 30 days of receiving the *mise en demeure*. The penalty increases to 40% thereafter and to 80% if the taxpayer does not respond to a second *mise en demeure*.

18.2.2 Taxes on Income

a) Ownership of French real estate constitutes a French source of income. If the taxpayer does not have French source income of a greater amount, an individual who has a home in France at his disposal and who is not protected by a treaty or French nationality may be taxed on an amount of 3 times the annual rental value of the property (see 6.6.2(b)). This does not affect most non-resident owners of French property because of France's double tax treaties with many territories. However if the taxpayer concerned is unable to benefit from the exceptions to the charge, it does not matter whether he owns the property, rents it, has the use of it as the shareholder of a company which owns it or through any other structure. Nor does it matter whether he had the use of the property for only part of the year. If he rents the property, the rental value is that specified in his lease unless this appears artificially low. If he has more than one property in France, the charge is based on 3 times the total rental values of all of the properties. The income so determined is the final taxable income, and the non-resident cannot claim to deduct any home ownership expenses or other charges against income, or any losses on rented properties. Tax on the notional income is calculated using the *quotient familial* system and the normal income tax scale rates. The only silver lining to this cloud is that the minimum income tax rate of 20% is not applied to non-residents assessed on this basis (6.13).

b) A non-resident individual who owns residential property in France and who is protected by a treaty from the notional income basis of assessment will not normally have a liability to French income tax unless he rents the property out. However if he owns the property through the medium of a company, it is possible that he may be assessed to tax on the benefit in kind of the rent free use of the property (see 18.5.3).

c) So, for a non-resident who is resident in a French treaty partner country and who does not rent out his home in France and who has no other French sources of income, there will be no liability to French income tax. Even if he does have other French sources of income, the fact that he owns a home in France will not affect the calculation of his French tax liability. French residents are entitled to tax reductions for various home ownership expenses in respect of a principal residence, but these tax reductions are not normally available to non-residents.

d) If an **unfurnished property** is let commercially by an individual, either directly or through the medium of a fiscally transparent or semi-transparent company (such as a *société civile immobilière* or a *société immobilière de copropriété transparente*), the rental income is assessable under the rules for property income (*revenus fonciers*). This means that the basis period is the tax year.

e) If the rental income is less than €15,000 a year, the landlord is assessed under the *Micro-Foncier* rules, which means that his income will be computed as 70% of the gross rental income. The *Micro-Foncier* is compulsory if the €15,000 limit is not exceeded. The taxpayer can opt to calculate his rental income under the normal rules if he prefers. This is simply done by filing annex form 2044.

f) Shareholders of a transparent or semi-transparent company (eg *SCI*) may apply the *Micro-Foncier* in respect of their share of rental income obtained through the unfurnished letting of the company's underlying asset(s), but only if they also declare unfurnished rents obtained through the rental of at least one property they own directly.

g) Under the normal rules, the expenses that may be deducted from gross rental income, as and when they are paid, are as follows:

   i) repairs and maintenance;

   ii) improvements (such as the cost of installing central heating, lifts, telephones etc);

   iii) management expenses;

   iv) interest on all debts incurred in the acquisition, construction, repair or improvement of the property, and also interest on debts incurred to preserve the owner's title to the property, for example interest on a loan taken out to pay inheritance tax on the property. There is no limit to the amount of interest that is deductible or to the period of time during which interest on the loan may be deducted. The costs of borrowing (eg bank facility fees) are equally deductible. If the interest is incurred in the course of constructing a property and before the property is let, it can be offset against rental income from other properties let by the taxpayer, or it can be carried forward as a loss against future rental income;

v) local property taxes.

h) An individual who owns a *château* or listed building, whether as a principal residence or as a second home, may be permitted to deduct part or all of the property expenses listed above from his total income (normally property expenses can only be deducted from property income) subject to the agreement of the Ministry of Finance. This situation is not as uncommon as the reader may suppose, since there are many apartment buildings in the traditional centres of French towns that are listed as being of architectural or historical importance. If the owner opens the property to the public, he is entitled to an additional *forfait* deduction of €1,525 from the admission receipts if the *château* does not have a park or garden, or €2,290 if it does. The cost of advertising may also be deducted in full.

i) If a property is let **furnished** by an individual, on an habitual basis, the income is normally assessed under the rules for business income (*bénéfices industriels et commerciaux*). However, if the accommodation which is let is part of the principal residence of the landlord:

   i) the income is totally exempt if the accommodation constitutes the principal residence of the tenant; and

   ii) if it does not constitute the principal residence of the tenant, income of up to €760 is exempt (eg for the letting of guest rooms – *chambres d'hôtes*).

j) Individual taxpayers with income from furnished lettings not exceeding €76,300 per annum can be assessed under the *Micro-BIC* rules. The effect of this is that the taxpayer pays tax on 29% of his gross receipts. However he can elect to compute his income under the normal business income rules if he wishes. Companies are compulsorily subject to the normal business income rules. Individuals who hold property jointly and carry on furnished lettings, may be treated as a *société de fait* and thus excluded from the *Micro BIC* regime. However in the case of a married couple the *Micro BIC* is largely accepted.

k) Under the business income rules, the taxable income is calculated on one of the following bases:

   i) If the rental receipts are above €76,300 but below €763,000 (excluding VAT), the income will be calculated under the *réel simplifié* regime. The difference beween the 'simplified real' basis and the 'normal real' basis of calculating income lies primarily in the level of formality to be observed in the accounting. Businesses subject to the simplified real regime prepare accounts (for VAT purposes and eventually for income tax purposes) on a quarterly basis. For details of the expenses allowable when income is calculated on a 'real' basis, see (l) below. The taxpayer can elect to be taxed on the *réel normal* basis.

ii) If the rental receipts are over €763,000, the income must be calculated on the *réel normal* basis.

l) The basis period is the accounting year ended in the tax year and accounts are prepared on an accruals basis. Where the property is treated as a business asset the expenses relevant to property income that are deductible under the 'real' regimes, are:

i) The general expenses of the business. These do not include expenses which are required to be capitalised, for example the costs associated with acquiring a property or architects' fees. Such payments are added to the cost of the property and may be depreciated. However notarial fees, registration taxes and estate agents fees are treated as expenses. The general costs of the business include interest and bank charges paid or payable, the costs of insurance and the costs of repairs and maintenance;

ii) Depreciation, which on residential housing is 1 to 2% of the cost of the property per annum on a straight line basis;

iii) Provisions, for example for doubtful debts and land tax payable. Provisions for the expenses of construction or reconstruction or fitting out a property are not allowable.

m) However if the property is put at the disposal of directors or shareholders for less than a market rent, the expenses relating to the period when the directors or shareholders occupy the property are not deductible.

n) An individual whose rental income is less than €23,000 is normally classed as a 'non-professional' landlord. This means that he cannot deduct any losses on his rental activity from his other income (the losses can be carried forward for 5 years against future rental income), and any capital gain realised on a disposal of the property is taxed under the private capital gains tax rules. If the taxpayer is registered at the local *registre de commerce* and either the rental income constitutes more than 50% of his total income or his rental receipts exceed €23,000, he is classed as a professional landlord. This means that he can offset any losses on his rental activity against his total income, and any gain resulting from a sale of the property will be taxed as a business capital gain, with a possibility of exemption if the turnover is less than €250,000 (see chapter 8).

o) Furnished lettings in France are largely exempt from *TVA*. Nevertheless, if the turnover exceeds €76,300 and the property is a:

i) registered tourist hotel and bed and breakfast lodging; or

ii) registered tourist residence on a 9 year lease to a business which advertises abroad; or

iii) quasi-hotel business which provides, in addition to accommodation, at least three of the following hotel-like services: meals, regular cleaning, reception and linen; or

iv) property let (furnished or unfurnished) under a commercial lease to a business engaged in one of the activities described above.

Any type of letting that does not match one of these categories is exempt from *TVA*. If the turnover is below €76,300 but the activity qualifies for *TVA* under one of the above circumstances, it is possible to opt for the *TVA*.

When subject to *TVA*, the supply of furnished premises is charged at the reduced rate of 5.5%. However, the supply of food, telephone and other services is subject to *TVA* at the standard rate of 19.6%.

p) Furnished rentals can be liable to *Taxe Professionnelle* (see chapter 22) in certain circumstances. The tax on leases also known as *Contribution sur les Revenus Locatifs* or *CRL* was abolished with effect from 1 January 2006. However, companies liable to corporation tax and *SCIs* which have at least one corporation tax paying company amongst its shareholders remain liable to this extra tax on rentals. The charge is calculated at 2.5% of the gross rents received.

q) Profits realised by persons who trade in land (*marchands de biens*), profits of buying land with the intention of selling it after breaking it up into lots (*lotissement*) and profits of building (*profits de construction*) are calculated according to the business income rules (*bénéfices industriels et commerciaux*) and subject to income tax or corporation tax depending on the taxpayer. Building profits must be calculated under the normal real or simplified real regimes. The question of whether a taxpayer is trading is essentially one of fact. Habitual operations carried out with a speculative intention are trading. With companies, the objects of the company and the business activities of the shareholders are also taken into consideration.

r) Non-residents who engage in the activities described in (q) are subject to a withholding tax of 50% on their profits.

s) There are several forms of *société civile* which are employed for various types of property transaction, and the taxation of these is considered below under 18.5.

18.2.3 Local Taxes

French local taxes are the subject of a separate study in chapter 22.

18.2.4 Wealth Tax

a) The market value of real estate in France owned by an individual, whether used as a principal residence or not, is included in the computation of the taxable base for wealth tax purposes. Holiday homes must be included at their full market value, but the value of a principal residence can be reduced by up to 30% due to the fact that the home is occupied. Similarly the value of a house can be reduced if it is let to a third party and depending on the terms of the lease.

b) If the property is owned through the medium of a company more than 50% of the assets of which consist of French real estate, it is likely that the shares in the company will be subject to French wealth tax. However this will depend on the treaty protection available to the investor.

c) As with inheritance tax, loans acquired to finance the purchase of the property are deductible in computing taxable wealth, but the existence of the loan – and its connection with the French property – has to be proved. This means that the loan should be secured by a charge against the property.

d) A similar effect can be achieved by financing a company largely by loan capital.

18.2.5 3% Tax

a) A company which is predominantly a holding company for French property and which does not make a declaration (annually or on demand) of its French property interests and its shareholders, is liable to pay a tax of 3% each year on the market value of any French real estate which it owns in France (see chapter 12).

b) This tax is calculated on the gross value of the property, without regard to any loans that may have been taken out to finance the acquisition of the property.

18.3. Disposal of Real Estate

18.3.1 The Legal Process

The legal process is the same as for the purchase.

18.3.2 Costs

a) The vendor normally bears the estate agent's costs and the buyer pays the notarial fees.

b) The scale of estate agents charges varies from company to company and should be negotiated.

18.3.3 Taxes on Sale

The registration tax due on the sale of the property will normally be borne by the purchaser.

18.3.4 Capital Gains Tax

a) Non-resident individuals realising private (as opposed to business) capital gains are generally liable to tax of 16% or 33⅓%, depending on their residence, on capital gains arising on occasional disposals of French real estate. Certain non-residents may be exempt from tax on the gain on the first two sales of a residence in France if they have at any time previously been resident for tax purposes in France for at least two years (see 8.4.).

b) Where the gain is taxable, the amount of the gain is calculated in principle in the same way as if the taxpayer had been resident in France: thus

i) a gain on a property owned for more than 15 years will be exempt from tax;

ii) if taxable the gain will be computed as:

- the selling price less

- the purchase price increased by 7.5% or the actual expenses of purchase if greater, and the cost of improvements or 15% of the purchase price (provided the property has been owned for at least five years), whichever is the greater, and

qualifying loan interest not already deducted in computing income tax.

- the amount so computed is reduced by 10% per full year of ownership ('taper relief') beyond the fifth.

- less an abatement of €1,000 per owner.

iii) For an example, see 16.

c) Non-residents have to appoint a fiscal representative if the sale exceeds €150,000.

d) Where the non-resident owns French real estate through the medium of a company, a sale of the shares of the company can also give rise to a charge to French capital gains tax. If the company is unquoted and more than 50% of its assets consist of real estate, a sale of its shares is treated in the French tax system as equivalent to a sale of real estate (unless it is a *SICOMI*). This principle is overruled by some French double tax treaties. Two points to bear in mind here are:

   i) If the company is to avoid the 3% tax on the market value of its real estate in France, it will have to declare the identity of its shareholders each year. Therefore a change in the immediate ownership will be noticed by the tax administration;

   ii) If the company is partly financed by loans, from shareholders or third parties (which may be desirable to reduce the value of the French estate of the taxpayer for wealth tax and/or inheritance tax purposes) the base cost for capital gains tax purposes is limited to the share capital.

e) The taxpayer also needs to consider the capital gains tax rules of his country of residence, since the disposal may be taxable there as well as in France. There may well be provisions allowing him credit in his own country for the French tax paid on the same gain, either under the terms of a double tax treaty or under the law of his country of residence. Problems can arise however from the fact that the occasions of charge are not always the same: for example a lifetime gift does not attract capital gains tax in France, whereas it generally does in the UK (unless the transfer is subject to an immediate charge to inheritance tax or it is a transfer of business property and an election to hold over the gain is made).

18.3.5 *Gifts and Inheritance Tax*

a) The value of the real estate in France will normally be subject to gifts or inheritance tax if it is given away or if the owner dies in possession of the property, regardless of the residence or domicile status of the owner. If the property is of a very low value, this may not be important because the amount of value transferred may be covered by the exemptions accorded to the donees. However the potential French gifts or inheritance tax may be a serious problem if the property is valuable and particularly if the property passes to someone who is not a close blood relative of the owner.

b) Consideration of this matter is inextricably linked to French succession law, which prescribes the minimum interests of children and ascendants in the estates of individuals domiciled in France, and in the French real property holdings of individuals who are not domiciled in France. See 21.4 for a full discussion of this topic. Each donee/heir is entitled to an exemption in respect of the amount which he receives from the estate of a donor/deceased, so that the fragmentation of the estate imposed by French succession law operates to reduce the total tax payable. Furthermore the rates of inheritance tax are lowest for transfers within a family, and highest for transfers to unrelated persons, so that again the effect of French succession law is to reduce the tax paid.

c) Even where French property is held through the medium of a company, so that the assets belonging to the ultimate owner are shares and not land, it is likely that the value of the shares will be subject to French inheritance tax unless the owner is exempt from French inheritance tax on a transfer of shares under a double tax treaty.

d) In many cases involving individuals who are resident and domiciled outside France, the French tax payable will be creditable against any estate duty or inheritance tax payable in the donor's or deceased's country of residence.

e) However if the donor or deceased is resident or domiciled in a country which does not have an inheritance tax, the French tax payable will represent an increase in his total tax liabilities or those of his estate. Moreover, although double tax relief may be available when a transfer is subject to inheritance tax in both countries, it is entirely possible that a transfer will be subject to inheritance tax in one of the countries and not the other. The lifetime gift which escapes inheritance tax in the UK is likely to be assessable in France. French gifts tax paid on the transfer will not be creditable against the UK capital gains tax on the same transaction.

f) If a non-resident couple (marriage or *PACS*) own a French property *en tontine*, when one of them dies the transfer to the survivor is no longer subject to French inheritance tax (from 22 August 2007). However, a transfer between unrelated co-owners under a *tontine* attracts an inheritance tax charge of 60%.

g) *Tontine* clauses which are inserted in the articles of a company lead to the application of acquisition registration duties and not inheritance tax.

h) The value of the French estate of the owner can be reduced by financing the acquisition of the property with a loan. However in order that the loan should be deductible, the existence of the loan has to be proved in accordance with prescribed rules. It is advisable that a formal charge should be registered against the property in support of a mortgage or at the least that the loan should be noted at the *Bureau des Hypothèques*, if a non-resident wishes to rely on the deductibility of a loan from the value of his French estate. Where the property is financed by a mortage, the heirs inherit the mortgage along with the property (they can disclaim their inheritance if the net value is negative or if they just do not want it).

18.4. Offshore Companies and Trusts

18.4.1 Offshore Companies

a) Non-French resident individuals considering an investment in French real estate often ask whether they should form an 'offshore' (ie tax haven) company to own their new investment. The answer is generally negative for the following reasons:

    i) The French will assess the offshore company to 3% tax per annum on the market value of the property it owns in France;

    ii) In addition the company will pay French corporation tax on any rental income it obtains from the property. The rate of corporation tax will normally be 33⅓%, whereas an individual in receipt of rental income from France would be likely to suffer tax at the minimum rate for non-French residents which is 20%;

    iii) An individual is entitled to write off 10% of the gain for each year of ownership beyond the fifth. A company is entitled to neither of these reliefs;

    iv) The individuals who have the use of the French property would have a personal French income tax liability calculated either as a notional income of three times the rental value of the property (if they reside in countries which do not have double tax treaties with France) or in respect of the benefit in kind afforded to them in the form of the rent-free occupation of the property (if they live in treaty-partner countries).

b) A Cypriot or Maltese company would not itself be subject to the French 3% tax on market value, provided it is prepared to declare its French property interests and the identity of its shareholders, because of the French double tax treaties with those islands. However if that company was owned by a company or trust resident in a tax haven, the shareholder company or trust would suffer the tax. The French tax administration would look at each company in the chain (from the bottom up) to see if any of them could be assessed. If any company in the chain is liable for the tax, all of the companies in the chain are jointly liable for it.

c) Some advisers have been recommending the use of Irish non-resident companies, which are exempt from the 3% tax if they file the necessary declarations of ownership and French property interests. This only removes the problem one link further up the chain of ownership if the Irish company is itself owned by a company which is not protected by a double tax treaty. However Irish companies are now automatically resident in Ireland for Irish corporation tax purposes, unless they were incorporated before 11 February 1999 and either:

i) they carry on a trade in Ireland and are owned by EU residents or residents of another country with which Ireland has a double tax treaty; or

ii) they are owned by a quoted company or a company related to a quoted company; or

iii) they are regarded as resident outside Ireland under the terms of one of Ireland's double tax treaties.

18.4.2 Offshore Trusts

a) The concept of the trust is alien to the French legal system. The division of ownership, which a trust represents, is contrary to the principles of French property law. It is therefore not advisable for a trust to own real property in France. If trustees purport to acquire property in France, it is likely that they will be treated as the absolute beneficial owners of the property, with all the tax consequences that ensue. For example the property may constitute part of their estates for gifts, inheritance and wealth tax. Although the decision in the Zieseniss case (see 19.5.2) suggests that property in a trust would not be regarded as the property of the trustee, the existence of the trust might be denied where it could only exist in conflict with the French 'public order'. If the property was treated as that of the trustees, transfers from the trustees to a beneficiary could be treated as gifts outside the family of the donor (assuming that the trustees and the beneficiaries are not related) and therefore subject to gifts tax at the highest rate.

b) The 3% annual tax on the market value of property in France owned by foreign companies could also apply to a group of trustees. Bearing in mind the wide concept of 'company' in France, it is highly likely that trustees would be regarded as a *société de fait*. While there is French case law recognising the trust as a distinct legal creature of foreign law, it is likely that in applying French tax law all of the officials that would deal with the case in practice would seek to analyse the trust by comparison with the legal forms recognised by French law.

c) Nevertheless offshore trusts are treated as opaque structures for capital gains tax purposes and hence it is the detrimental regime described in 8.4. that applies to determine the taxable gains. All abatements, deductions and taper relief obtainable by individuals are therefore lost if a French property is acquired by a trust and later sold.

18.5. French Companies

18.5.1 General

a) In the French tax system, individuals owning real estate are generally more favourably treated than companies owning real estate, particularly in the case of capital gains tax. Nevertheless there may be many situations where a company would be desirable, for example where more than one investor is involved, or where foreign investors wish to avoid the consequences of French succession law by holding no immovable property in France in their own names.

b) A solution in some cases is to use a fiscally transparent or semi-transparent company (such as a *société civile immobilière*). This effectively allows advantage to be taken of the favourable tax treatment accorded to individuals, while using a corporate form. This is not however a universal panacea, and the prospective investor should consider the burden of complying with company law and tax reporting requirements when appraising this option. It may also be difficult to raise loan finance from a French bank if a company is used.

18.5.2 *"Sociétés Civiles"*

a) The basic distinction between companies made by French company law is not one that Anglo-Saxon countries make at all. French companies are not primarily divided into those which have limited liability and those which do not. Instead they are divided into those which have 'civil' objects and those which have commercial objects. The test of commerciality is essentially the intention to buy and sell goods. For all practical purposes those which have civil objects can be divided into two largely unrelated groups: property holding companies and partnerships formed by members of certain professions (generally the traditional professions such as medicine, the law, architecture and accountancy).

b) There are in fact numerous different forms of *sociétés civiles*. The following is a partial list of the various forms of *société civile* which may be found in the real estate context. It will be observed that all of these companies, with the exception of *société civile de construction-vente*, have non-commercial objects in the sense that they do not buy land with a view to developing it or selling it on at a profit. Such activities are generally treated as trading, and assessable to corporation tax (under the *bénéfices industriels et commerciaux* rules).

c) The *société civile immobilière de location* (or *de gestion*) is the most common form of the species, to the point where a reference to an *"SCI"* is normally a reference to this particular form. This is used by families to divide up the economic interest in a valuable investment property, by entrepreneurs who rent a commercial property to their own business, and by groups of investors combining to acquire a property jointly. Generally, if the property is let unfurnished, individual shareholders in these companies pay income tax under the property income rules (*revenus fonciers*), and pay capital gains tax on any gains under the private capital gains tax rules. However there are two forms of company which have rather similar purposes to the *société civile immobilière de location* but which have totally different juridical structures and tax regimes. These are:

i) *sociétés immobilières d'investissement*, which are *sociétés anonymes* which are formed exclusively for the purpose of renting properties in France, more than three-quarters of the surface area of which are used for habitation. The company is exempt from corporation tax on its income, and the French resident individual shareholder who made an investment in such a company between 1 January 1985 and 31 December 1997 qualifies for a tax reduction. Gains realised on properties held in the long term are taxed at 25% if the net gains are transferred to a special reserve (and a supplementary tax is paid if they are distributed to bring the total rate up to 33⅓%).

ii) *sociétés immobilières de gestion*, which are *SARLs*, but subject to a tax regime identical to the above.

d) The *société civile de construction-vente* is an unlimited company with a capital which is not divided into shares, formed for the construction of buildings with a view to their sale. It is exempt from corporation tax, and individual shareholders pay income tax on the income as business income.

e) The *société civile immobilière de placement immobilier (SCPI)* is a *société civile* under the general law, but which is allowed to invite the public to subscribe for shares, unlike the other companies listed above. Because of their public nature, their articles of association are more like those of a *société anonyme*. Indeed they are akin to *sociétés immobilières d'investissement*. Their objects are exclusively the acquisition and management of rental properties. The company is exempt from corporation tax, and individual shareholders pay income tax (under the property income rules) on their shares of the income, and capital gains tax under the rules for private capital gains on their shares of the companies gains. Moreover, if the funds raised by the company are used to construct or acquire new buildings more than three-quarters of the surface area of which are used for habitation, the investments of the French resident individual shareholders qualify for a tax reduction.

f) The *société immobilière de copropriété transparente* (which is normally a *société civile d'attribution*) is a company formed to build, acquire or manage a building or buildings for division into units destined to be used by the shareholders. The buildings can be commercial, industrial, professional or residential – the nature of the building does not matter. It is possible to create a *société d'attribution* under any legal form, but they are usually either *sociétés anonymes* or *sociétés civiles*. Such companies are completely fiscally transparent so far as direct taxes are concerned. That is to say that for all direct tax purposes the company is deemed to have no existence distinct from its members. For capital tax purposes, the shareholder is treated as an owner of the land. Income is assessed on the individual shareholders, usually under the property income rules (*bénéfices fonciers*), and gains realised on a sale of the shares by an individual are subject to the private capital gains tax rules. They file a simplified tax return (form 2071) each year.

g) The *société civile de lotissement* is a company formed by a group of individuals to acquire a parcel of land and break it up into lots, but without a speculative intention. It is sometimes used by the heirs and surviving spouse of an individual who has died co-owning property in common (*en indivision*). The profits realised on any sale of the lots are not subject to corporation tax, but the individual shareholders are taxed on the profits as private capital gains.

h) The *société de pluripropriété* or *multipropriété* are time-share companies. The shareholders do not own an interest in real property, but have the use of a property for part of the year. These companies are expressly excluded from the scope of the *société immobilière de copropriété transparente* regime described in (f) above. They can take any legal form, and in fact are usually *sociétés anonymes*. However one specific form is a *société civile*, the *société civile immobilière à temps partagé*. Provided that they have no income other than the recharging of their expenses to their shareholders, they are in effect exempt from tax. The benefit of the rent-free occupation of the property is ignored when calculating the income of the company, and is not treated as a distribution; the benefit in kind received by the shareholders is exempt from income tax.

18.5.3 *Treatment of the Shareholder*

a) In cases where the company makes available its property for the use of its shareholders on a rent-free basis, the question of whether or not the shareholders will suffer a charge to income tax in respect of the benefit-in-kind depends on the type of company concerned.

b) Generally no benefit-in-kind assessment will be raised against the shareholders of:

   i) a *société immobilière de copropriété transparente;*

   ii) a *société civile* or any other company taxed as a partnership;

   iii) a time-share company (*société de pluripropriété* or *multipropriété*).

c) Shareholders in companies subject to corporation tax, other than timeshare companies, can expect to be assessed. Further, the shareholders in the exempt companies listed above can be assessed to tax on the benefit-in-kind of the use of rural property which is not residential, for example fishing or hunting rights.

d) Whether or not the benefit-in-kind is exempt from tax in France, it may be assessable in the shareholder's country of residence or the country in which the company is resident. For example if an individual who is not protected from the notional income basis of assessment owns a home in France through a foreign company, not only is he assessable in France on the notional income of 3 times the rental value of the property (which will be greater than the benefit in kind of the rent-free use), but he could also be assessed to income tax on the benefit-in-kind, in the country of residence of the company (as a director of the company), without double tax relief.

18.6. Other Companies

a) For convenience many investors choose to use a company registered in their home country. They understand the company law applicable better and can carry on the administration themselves.

b) Provided the country of their residence has a double tax treaty with France, and they comply with the French reporting requirements, such a company will not suffer the 3% annual tax on the market value of French real estate.

c) However it is not possible to make a foreign 'capital company' fiscally transparent in France. The company will therefore be subject to French corporation tax, and any capital gain realised by the company on a sale of its French property will be subject to tax at 33⅓% without the benefit of any abatements or taper relief.

d) If it fails to file tax returns, the French tax administration are likely to raise estimated assessments for rental income calculated as a percentage of the market value of the property.

e) If the company invests in French residential property for the rent-free use of its directors or shareholders, the shareholders or directors will either be subject to French income tax on a notional income of three times the rental value of the property (if they are not resident in a country with an appropriate double tax treaty with France) or they will be subject to French income tax on the benefit-in-kind of the use of the property (if they are resident in a French treaty partner country). These individuals may also be assessable to tax on the benefit-in-kind in their country of residence, or the country in which the company is resident.

f) A danger with using any company is that tax charges are doubled by assessment once in the hands of the company and a second time in the hands of the shareholders. This is not generally a problem with respect to income in countries which have imputation systems of taxation (such as

France and Australia), but it does occur in countries with so-called classical systems of taxation such as the USA. Even in countries with imputation systems, the shareholder does not usually obtain a credit for any capital gains tax paid by the company, so that if a UK company is used to invest in French property, when the property is sold any gain will be subject to UK corporation tax. If a UK resident shareholder then sells his shares or the company is liquidated, the shareholder will pay UK capital gains tax on the increase in value in his shares, representing the same gain.

19. TAKING UP RESIDENCE IN FRANCE

19.1. Abandoning a Former Residence

19.1.1 General

a) It is possible for an individual to be resident in more than one country, or resident nowhere at all. By contrast, in countries which use domicile (ie 'permanent home') as a second 'connecting factor' (see Introduction), an individual can only have one domicile, but he must have a domicile. The country of residence and the country of domicile may differ – for example where an individual whose permanent home is in country A is resident for the time being in country B.

b) Residence is almost always the basic test for exposure to income tax on a worldwide income basis (although in the USA citizenship also has this effect). But domicile is also used as a connecting factor to establish exposure to taxation, for example in the case of UK inheritance tax.

c) It follows that an individual taking up residence in France may remain exposed to the taxation of other countries in several different ways:

   i)   he may remain resident in one or more other countries;

   ii) he may remain domiciled in another country;

   iii) he may remain a citizen (of the USA);

   iv) he may retain assets or sources of income in other countries.

d) Usually any risk of double taxation resulting from such a state of affairs is reduced or eliminated under a double tax treaty between the countries concerned. France has an extensive network of double tax treaties, covering most of the countries in the developed world. Moreover, these treaties usually provide 'tie-breaker' rules which determine the residence of individuals who would be regarded as resident under the domestic laws of both countries.

e) Nevertheless it may be wise for an individual moving to France to sever his taxable connections with his previous country of residence, either because the general level of taxation is higher in that country, so that continued exposure to its taxes may result in higher tax liabilities, or because the treaty protection available is inadequate in the context of his affairs.

f) Moreover, as we shall see, a change of residence often provides extraordinary opportunities for tax planning. Since people generally do not change their tax residence often, it is wasteful to let the opportunity slip when it does arise.

g) It is not possible to explain in detail the residence rules of all of the other countries from which a person may be migrating. Instead this chapter describes the rules for ceasing to be resident in the UK, which will hopefully raise several of the issues which need to be considered in abandoning a residence in other countries.

19.1.2 Ceasing to be Resident in the UK

a) An individual who goes abroad permanently is treated as remaining resident and ordinarily resident in the UK if his visits to the UK average 91 days or more per UK tax year. From 6 April 2008 HMRC will count days of arrival and departure as days in the UK, unless the individual is purely in transit.

b) An individual who claims that he is no longer resident and ordinarily resident in the UK will be asked to give some evidence that he has left the UK permanently, for example that he has taken steps to acquire accommodation abroad to live in as a permanent home, and if he continues to own property in the UK, the reason is consistent with his stated intention to reside permanently abroad. If he can provide this evidence, the individual may be treated as provisionally not resident or ordinarily resident in the UK from the day after the date of his departure. Normally this provisional ruling is confirmed after the individual has lived abroad for a whole tax year, provided that his visits to the UK since leaving have averaged less than 91 days a tax year.

c) If the individual does not have this evidence, a decision is postponed for up to 3 years. The decision will be based on what has actually happened since he left the UK. Until then he is provisionally treated as remaining resident in the UK.

d) However where the individual has become a resident of France, for French tax purposes, the double tax treaty between the UK and France will apply to determine the question of which country has the primary right to tax him, and this may well overrule any effect of a HMRC decision that the individual is provisionally treated as remaining resident in the UK.

e) In strict law the residence of an individual for UK tax purposes is determined by reference to whole tax years (ie 6 April to 5 April). However by virtue of an Inland Revenue concession, an individual who departs from the UK part-way through a tax year is normally regarded as non-resident for income tax purposes from the day following the day of his departure. For capital gains tax purposes he will be treated as remaining resident in the UK until the end of the UK tax year in which he departs, unless he was not resident and not ordinarily resident in the UK for at least 4 of the 7 immediately preceding years.

f) The individual who is planning to become non-resident should notify his tax office of his plans and arrange to submit form P85.

g) The effect of becoming non-UK resident is that the individual ceases to be liable to UK income tax on any income except UK source income (and may even be exempt from UK tax on that income under the France-UK double tax treaty). The position with regard to capital gains tax has been complicated by the 1998 Finance Act. In general an individual who is neither resident nor ordinarily resident in the UK is not liable to UK capital gains tax except in respect of gains on any assets which are used in connection with a business carried on in the UK through a branch or agency. However the 1998 Finance Act introduced a rule relating to 'temporary non-residents', who leave the UK for less than 5 complete UK tax years. Under this rule, gains realised during the period of non-residence on assets held while UK resident, are treated as having arisen to the taxpayer in the year in which he returns to the UK. Nevertheless the rule applies subject to the effect of any UK double tax treaty, and if under the France-UK double tax treaty a gain is taxable only in France the new rule cannot apply to it.

h) An individual who abandons a UK domicile is deemed to remain domiciled in the UK for inheritance tax purposes for three whole UK tax years following his change in domicile status under UK domestic law. However if the individual has in fact become domiciled in France his estate outside the UK will generally be protected from UK inheritance tax by virtue of the France – UK double inheritance tax treaty.

19.2. Taking up Residence in France

a) An individual who takes up residence in France becomes liable to French taxation on the basis of his worldwide income and assets on the day on which he arrives in France to take up permanent residence.

b) Before that date, he is only liable to French tax on his French source income (which may include a notional income from any home he has in France – see 6.6.2(b)) and his assets situated in France.

19.3. Creating a Tax Holiday

a) From the above it is obvious that an individual can easily create a tax holiday for himself by creating a gap in time between the date on which he ceases to be resident in the UK and the date on which he becomes resident in France. He could for example make a two week visit to Spain during which he would be resident nowhere.

b) The same general principle will apply to an emigrant from any country that does not impose some form of extended exposure to taxation – ie a rule that a person who ceases to have a taxable connection with that country remains exposed to its taxation for a period thereafter. Emigrants from the UK will need to bear in mind that they are deemed to be domiciled in the UK for three whole UK tax years after their departure. Until they become resident in

France, they will not be protected by the France – UK double inheritance tax treaty. They may also be affected by the UK's 'temporary non-residents' rule for capital gains tax if they return to the UK within 5 UK tax years (see 19.1.2(g) above).

c) A tax holiday can be used:

   i) to sell any assets held which are worth more than they cost, to shake out any capital gain that might become taxable if the asset is sold after the individual takes up residence in France;

   ii) to realise income that has been accumulated in a tax shelter; or

   iii) to organise the taxpayer's estate so that it will attract the least amount of capital taxation after he takes up residence in France, and so that income and capital gains from it are distributed to best advantage.

d) For example, suppose that a UK resident invests in an offshore 'roll-up' fund (that is a collective investment scheme in which the income from the investments held by the fund is added to the value of the fund and reinvested, instead of being distributed). Under UK tax rules he will suffer income tax on the increase in the value of his investment when it is realised. However if he has ceased to be resident or ordinarily resident in the UK before he sells his units in the fund, no UK tax will arise. An individual who knows that he is going to become non-resident at some time in the future can therefore avoid UK taxation on his investment income, to the extent that he does not need access to it while he remains resident in the UK. He would simply sell his units during a tax holiday.

e) As a second example, many well-advised UK residents have set up offshore trusts. These can have the effect of deferring income tax or capital gains tax, depending on the terms of the trust, the identity and tax status of the settlor and beneficiaries, and the date at which the trust was established. If such an arrangement is in existence, a tax holiday by the actual or potential beneficiaries could provide the trustees with an opportunity to convert the deferral into permanent exemption, by distributing the accumulated income or gains.

f) A third example concerns the distribution of wealth within a family. Once the individual becomes resident in France, gifts or legacies to other members of the family, including his or her spouse, may be taxable. Before the individual becomes a French resident, gifts of assets other than French situated assets to individuals not resident in France will not be taxable in France. If the family concerned wish to put, say, the shares in a family company outside France into the hands of a son or daughter who is taking an active role in the business, this could be a good time to do it.

19.4. Sale of a Former Home

a) An individual who retires to France may not have sold his former home before he arrives in France. If his country of origin has a double tax treaty with France this may not have any French tax consequences, because under many French double tax treaties the right to tax gains on real estate is granted exclusively to the other state.

b) For example Article 13(1) of the current France-UK double tax treaty gives the UK the right to tax gains arising on UK real estate. Under Article 24(b)(i) of the treaty, France exempts from tax income and gains which are taxable, under the terms of the treaty, in the UK. Therefore a gain realised by a French resident in respect of a sale of real estate in the UK is exempt from French tax. However, in the renegotiated France-UK double tax treaty this loophole will definitely be closed. Indeed France will effectively tax gains realised on the sale of UK real estate, since there will be no UK tax credit available to set against the French liability. The date from which the new treaty will be effective has not yet been confirmed.

c) Since an individual who is neither resident nor ordinarily resident in the UK is exempt from UK capital gains tax (other than on gains arising from disposals of assets connected to a UK branch or agency of a business conducted by the non-resident), gains realised by French residents on sales of UK real estate generally escape tax altogether. Such a gain could however be taxable in the UK if the French resident is a former UK resident who resumes UK residence within 5 UK tax years of his departure from the UK (see 19.1.2(g)).

19.5. Tax Planning Through Trusts

19.5.1 General

a) Both migrants and those who are already resident in France may wish to use trusts in their estate and tax planning. This is an area fraught with uncertainty in French law, because there is very little French jurisprudence on the subject of trusts.

b) The projet de loi "*fiducie*" was finally enacted in February 2007, after 15 years on the 'back-burner'. Nevertheless, it differs from its initial draft and is in fact quite restrictive as explained in 3.4.

c) France has signed the Convention on the Recognition of Trusts of 1985, but it has not ratified it. The Convention entered into force on 1 January 1992. Ratification by France would remove the last doubts over the validity in France of common law trusts, at least to the extent that they do not conflict with the principles of public order in French law.

19.5.2 *The Current Law*

a) At present there are very few articles of the *CGI* which refer to trusts. This principal reference is in Article 120(9), which says that French residents are subject to income tax on the 'products' of trusts. The term 'products' is not defined, so that it is not clear whether it means income (or income and capital gains), or whether it includes even a distribution of original capital from the trust. Moreover it is not clear whether trust income and gains retain their character when distributed to a beneficiary – eg whether a capital gain realised by the trust and distributed to a beneficiary is taxed in his hands as a capital gain.

b) For French resident beneficiaries of a US trust, the tax treatment of 'the products' of the trust was clarified by a 'bulletin' of 25 March 1981. The bulletin distinguishes between 'simple trusts' – trusts with fixed interests in the trust income – and 'complex trusts' – all other trusts, notably including discretionary trusts. A further distinction is made between trusts in which the settlor retains a beneficial interest or control, called 'grantor trusts' in the US, and other trusts.

   i) Simple trusts are treated as transparent, so that the income retains the same character at the beneficiary level as it has at the trustee level. The French resident beneficiary is taxed on his share of the income accordingly.

   ii) Complex trusts are also treated as transparent in determining the source of a payment to a beneficiary, but no credit is given in France for the tax paid by the trustees in the USA. Credit is only given for US tax suffered by the beneficiary at the time of distribution (ie withholding tax).

   iii) If the trust is a grantor trust, the income is treated as that of the settlor and is therefore not taxable in the hands of a beneficiary.

c) In view of the uncertainty surrounding the word 'products', it is to be hoped that these rules would be of influential value in the application of French tax law to the French resident beneficiaries of other foreign trusts.

d) The 1999 Finance Law introduced Article 123 bis (see 6.16.2), which makes any French resident liable to French income tax in respect of his pro-rata interest in the income of a foreign company, *fiducie,* trust etc if:

   i) the foreign entity is subject to a low tax regime; and

   ii) the principal activity of the entity is holding investments; and

   iii) the French resident directly or indirectly owns at least 10% of the shares, financial interests or voting rights in the entity. It is not at all clear how this condition can apply in the context of a discretionary trust.

iv) a minimum taxable income is applied by the authorities. This is calculated at a rate updated every year and based on the value of the underlying asset(s). It is apportioned to the interest held by the resident taxpayer, and from 2006 the taxable base is increased by 25%.

e) In terms of gifts tax, there is some uncertainty over the question of how a transfer into, or out of, a trust might be treated in France. There seems little doubt that a transfer into a revocable settlement would be regarded as a nullity. But if the trust is irrevocable, the questions have been whether a transfer to the trustees is a gift taking assets out of the settlor's estate, and if so whether it is taxable as a gift to the trustees (who may well be unrelated to the settlor and therefore exposed to French gifts tax at the highest possible rate) or whether it is taxed as an indirect gift, or a conditional gift, to the beneficiaries, and at what date the gift takes effect. Some light was shed on these issues by the decision in the Zieseniss case, rendered by the *Conseil d'État* on 20 February 1996. This case concerned a gift into a revocable trust created by an American under US law, under which the settlor reserved the right to receive the trust income during her life, and the trust capital was to be distributed to her grand-children on her death. She subsequently restricted the gift of the capital to the children of one of her sons, and eventually died domiciled in France. The terms of the trust were challenged by the children of her other son (deceased) under the French forced heirship rules. The *Cour d'Appel* in Paris had held that the trust was equivalent to a legacy, taking effect at the settlor's death, and upheld the plaintiffs' claim. The conditions for a gift to exist were not satisfied when the trust was created because the donee had not accepted the property, and because the trust was revocable the assets could be considered to have remained in the donor's estate until her death. The *Conseil d'État* overruled the appeal court and held that the gift was not a legacy but instead an indirect gift which took effect on the death of the settlor. The capital had left the donor's estate when the trust was established, and the conditions necessary for a gift were satisfied at the moment of the donor's death. One implication is that a gift to a trust cannot be considered to be a gift to the trustees, but will rather be taxed at the rates applicable to gifts from the settlor to the beneficiaries.

f) In terms of wealth tax, it seems unlikely that a purely discretionary beneficiary of a trust established by someone else could be considered to own the trust fund. However where a beneficiary has a right to receive the income, the position is unclear. If the right to receive income was treated as equivalent to an usufruct in French tax law, the owner of the right would be treated as the owner of the capital which produced the income for wealth tax purposes. There are however substantial differences between the position of a life tenant under a trust and that of an *usufruitier* in French civil law. The view of most commentators, and of the French *Direction de la Législation Fiscale,* is that a life interest cannot be treated as an usufruct. The life interest certainly has a value, but it should be valued as a stream of income. There is no set method of valuing such an interest, but one solution would be to apply the French scale for valuing annuities.

g) This is the position of the *Nanterre Tribunal de Grande Instance* which held on 4 May 2004, that a French resident beneficiary of a US trust should be exempt from wealth tax in France on the value of the trust assets. The decision was reached in the context of two irrevocable US Will Trusts. The French tax resident beneficiary, together with other beneficiaries, received regular income distributions from the trustees. The French tax authorities considered that the individuals should be deemed to own a proportion of the income-producing assets and thus be subject to wealth tax on these. The Court rejected the above arguments. This is a useful decision as it provides an insight into the French tax treatment applicable in the context of trusts and with regards to wealth tax. Nevertheless such decisions may not be easily transposed to other cases and could later be overturned.

19.5.3 The General Terms of the Fiducie

a) Previous editions of this book referred to the *Fiducie* draft of 1992 which was enacted in February 2007, but after numerous amendments. The terms of the French *fiducie* and its use are very restrictive and remain too distant from common law trust to serve as any "benchmark" when dealing with foreign trusts. The main rules of the French *fiducie* are explained in 3.4.

b) In particular, the *fiducie* can only be set up by corporate entities. In addition the text clearly states that the use of the French *fiducie* in the context of estate planning is strictly forbidden. Such *fiducies* would simply be treated as null and void.

19.5.4 Planning Considerations

a) The scope for making use of trusts is clearly greater for the individual who is about to take up residence in France than it is for existing French residents, because the former do not need to concern themselves with French gifts tax in respect of non-French assets.

b) If a taxpayer has fully divested himself of an asset before he arrives in France (and it is not available to any member of his household), he will clearly not be subject to wealth tax in respect of it and nor would it be easy for the administration to assess him to income tax in respect of the income which it produces. There may well be advantages to beneficiaries resident in other jurisdictions to being the beneficiaries of a trust set up by a person who is not domiciled in their jurisdiction, so this kind of planning can confer substantial tax privileges on the beneficiaries of the trust.

19.6. French Anti-Avoidance Legislation

a) There is a growing list of specific anti-avoidance measures in French tax law. For example it should be noted that:

   i) since 1 January 1999, there has been a general rule applying to controlled foreign corporations (see 6.16.2). Before that date only French corporate investors were subject to such a rule; and

   ii) there is a provision to counter avoidance of tax on earned income through the use of offshore companies; and

b) However there is no rule which treats as income a gain realised on the disposal of units in an offshore roll-up fund (ie equivalent to the passive foreign investment company rules in the USA, or the offshore income gain rules in the UK).

c) Moreover an important general principle of French tax law is the concept of 'abuse of law' (*abus de droit*). This relates to fiscal fraud involving the use of legal documents. For example a taxpayer who creates a fictitious rental agreement to claim expenses on a property would be caught under this principle. There has to be an element of dissimulation, using a contract or deed – the documents will therefore not reflect the true substance of the arrangement. The principle does not prevent a taxpayer who has a choice of means to effect a transaction from choosing the option which costs the least tax. Because of this principle, if a taxpayer wishes to use a legal structure, such as a trust, it is very important that the structure is so designed and operated that it cannot be said to be a sham.

19.7 Foreign Tax Legislation

a) Having abandoned a former tax residence, the individual will usually be free of the anti-avoidance rules of that country. However several countries operate rules extending the exposure to taxation of individuals who become non-resident or who abandon their citizenship to avoid taxation. Care must be taken that the emigrant does not fall foul of one of these rules.

b) Just as importantly, many countries operate tax systems that confer privileges on 'foreigners', and the emigrant may be able to take advantage of these to benefit himself or other members of his family.

   i) For example many countries do not assess non-residents to tax on certain kinds of capital gains. In general the UK does not assess non-residents to tax on any kind of capital gain, so an individual with a valuable company or farm in the UK is free to sell it without suffering UK capital gains tax once he has become non-resident.

ii) As a second example, an individual who is not domiciled in the UK can confer immensely valuable tax benefits on individuals who are resident in the UK by creating a trust for them. Properly structured, the assets in the trust will be exempt from UK inheritance tax throughout the life of the trust (perhaps 100 years). It is also possible to defer UK tax on the trust income. It is at least theoretically possible to acquire a domicile in France for UK tax purposes at a point in time before the moment at which the French would regard the individual as having become resident in France.

19.8. Summary

a) A well-planned change of residence can secure the financial future of a family for generations. The important precondition is the advance planning, because individuals who simply pack their bags and move will almost certainly miss opportunities which may be extremely valuable.

b) This is an area in which sophisticated advice is needed, however, because the taxpayer has to plan his or her way around at least two tax systems, and the optimum planning may involve other jurisdictions.

20.   INVESTMENTS FOR FRENCH RESIDENTS

20.1.   Economic Background

a) Like many developed countries, France faces a crisis due to the combined effects of demographic changes in the structure of the French population. The French state pension scheme is not 'funded', which means that the contributions of the working population today are used directly to pay the pensions of the retired population. As birth rates have fallen and life expectancy has increased, the proportion of the population in work relative to the retired population is declining. It is therefore easily demonstrable that within the foreseeable future it will become impossible for the working population to sustain the current level of benefits for the population drawing state pensions. Either the retirement age will have to increase or the level of benefits will have to be reduced.

b) It has therefore long been an object of French public policy to encourage individuals and businesses to save to finance a larger share of their own retirements. The result was a wide range of generous savings schemes and tax credits for investment to the point where for those living on investment income, France was truly a tax haven.

c) However, against this trend of public policy, the French government has also been under intense pressure to reduce their budget deficit to meet the Maastricht convergence criteria, and to maintain it at those levels. There is now therefore a significant retreat from the original high-water mark of these savings incentives.

d) In this chapter we examine the current savings and investment incentives, and the themes which should inform the investment planning of a French resident.

20.2.   Capital Gains Compared with Income

20.2.1 Exemptions and Reliefs

a) All long-term capital gains (generally gains on assets held for more than 2 years) and all gains on securities are taxed under rules which are markedly more favourable to the taxpayer than the rules for the taxation of ordinary income.

b) Of particular relevance here are the rules relating to the taxation of capital gains on securities. A gain on a sale of shares is generally only taxable if the vendor has sold more than €20,000 (2007) increased to €25,000 for 2008 of such securities during the year. There is no minimum holding period for securities, so the gains can be exempt even if the shares have been held for only a few weeks or months, provided that the taxpayer is not dealing in shares.

c) However the threshold is an all-or-nothing limit: if the total proceeds of sales made by the taxpayer is €25,000 (2008), all of the gains on the sales are taxable.

d) Shares in unit funds qualify for this treatment, even if the funds accumulate their income rather than distributing it as dividends (ie they are 'roll-up funds'). This allows investors to convert income into capital gains which are potentially tax-free.

e) No relief for inflation is given when calculating the gains. However, from 1 January 2006 and strictly available for EU or EEA company shares, there is a taper relief per year of ownership which is set as one-third from the fifth complete year. In effect the gain is exempt after eight years of ownership. As this taper relief came into effect on 1 January 2006, the total exemption will not apply before 2014 and the application of the first one-third reduction will only be in 2012.

f) Losses realised up to and including 2001 can be carried forward for 5 years. Losses realised from 2002 onwards can be carried forward for a period of 10 years.

20.2.2 Tax Rates

a) Not only are the rules relating to the computation of gains generous to the taxpayer, but the rates of tax on gains are also much lower than the rates of tax on ordinary income.

b) A French resident pays capital gains tax at the rate of 29% on chargeable gains arising on sales of securities (including all of the current social contributions). In comparison, the income tax rates rise to 40%, before the social contributions (of 11% for investment income) are taken into consideration.

20.3. Savings Plans, Life Assurance and Special Accounts

20.3.1 The Plan d'Epargne en Actions

a) French residents can invest up to €132,000 each In a *plan d'épargne en actions ('PEA')*. Since both husband and wife can have a *PEA*, the total amount that a couple can invest is €264,000. The *PEA* is a personal equity scheme invested mainly in French company shares, and managed by a bank, fund manager, the post office or an insurance company. The contributions to the scheme are not deductible from the taxpayer's income and nor do they give rise to any tax credit. However the gains and income accruing within the scheme can be exempt from income tax (but not the social contributions).

b) Provided that the investor does not withdraw from the scheme for 8 years, he may make subsequent withdrawals without automatically closing the scheme. However he cannot make further contributions to the scheme after the first withdrawal. If he does make a withdrawal from the scheme within the first 8 years, the scheme is automatically closed and does not thereafter benefit from tax exemption.

c) All of the income and capital gains accruing within the *PEA* up to the date of the first withdrawal are exempt from tax provided that the investor does not withdraw from the scheme during the first 5 years. If he withdraws any amount from the scheme before 5 years have expired, the scheme is closed. If the value of the assets in the scheme, together with the taxpayers other disposals of equities during the year, is less than €25,000, the gain is exempt. However if the disposal proceeds exceed the threshold, the increase in value of the *PEA* is taxable as a gain on the following scale:

Elapsed Time	%
Less than 2 years	22.5
2 to 5 years	18

To these rates must be added 11% in social surcharges on capital gains. A taxpayer who redeems a *PEA* before 5 years and invests the proceeds into a newly created company or business within 3 months, may benefit from an exemption. However, the increase in value will remain subject to the social surcharges.

20.3.2 The Plan d'Epargne Populaire

a) Up to 25 September 2003, French residents (and non-French residents) were able to invest up to €92,000 each (ie €184,000 for a married couple) in a *plan d'épargne populaire ('PEP')*. Although it is no longer possible to open a new *PEP* since 25 September 2003, the tax advantages described below continue to apply to the schemes existing before that date. The *PEP* is either a savings account at a bank or a life assurance policy. As with the *PEA*, the taxpayer cannot deduct the amount invested from his taxable income and he receives no tax credits for making the investment. However the income and gains accruing within the scheme can be tax free.

b) Any withdrawal from the scheme during the first 10 years automatically closes the scheme. Withdrawals after 10 years do not close the scheme unless the taxpayer subsequently pays funds into the scheme. The scheme is closed on the death of the investor.

c) The income and gains accruing within the scheme are exempt from tax provided that the investor does not withdraw from the scheme during the first 8 years. If the taxpayer makes a withdrawal from the scheme during this period, the difference between the value of the fund at the date of closure and the premiums contributed by the taxpayer is subject to income tax at normal rates except as follows:

i) If the withdrawal takes the form of an annuity (a *rente viagère*), the annuity is taxed under the annuity income regime (see 6.6.6(h)(i)).

ii) The taxpayer can opt to pay a *libératoire* withholding tax at the following rates:

Elapsed Time	%
Less than 4 years	35
4 to 8 years	18

To these rates must be added social surcharges of 11%.

d) French residents who do not pay income tax can qualify for a premium subsidy.

20.3.3 Life Assurance Contracts

a) The proceeds of contracts issued before 1 January 1983 are entirely exempt from income tax, (however, see (i) below). The increase in value of any life assurance contract issued after 1 January 1983 is potentially subject to French income tax but if the proceeds are used to buy an annuity, they are exempt from tax and the beneficiary pays tax on the annuity income. The proceeds can also be exempt if the withdrawal relates to the retirement of the policyholder or his redundancy.

b) Where the increase in value on a policy issued after 1 January 1983 is subject to income tax, the increase is potentially subject to income tax at normal scale rates. However, there is an optional withholding tax regime for policies issued by French insurance companies or foreign insurance companies with permanent establishments in France ('French life assurance contracts'). For French life assurance contracts with a duration of less than 8 years, the optional withholding tax rates depend on when the encashment takes place:

Withdrawal in first 4 years	35%
Withdrawal in next 4 years	15%

To the above withholding taxes must be added the social contributions of 11%. A taxpayer will obviously elect to suffer these withholding taxes if his marginal rate of income tax, on the normal tax scale, is higher than the withholding tax rates.

c) In the event of a partial encashment of a policy, the taxable amount is calculated on a pro-rata basis.

d) For French life assurance contracts with a duration of more than 8 years, the regime was substantially modified by the 1998 Finance Law. Encashments during the first 8 years are subject (at the option of the taxpayer) to the withholding tax rates above. In terms of encashments after 8 years, it is now necessary to distinguish between:

   i) insurance contracts valued in units of account which are mainly invested in defined classes of shares ('qualifying contracts'), including existing contracts which are converted into qualifying contracts before 31 December 1998; and

   ii) other life assurance contracts ('non-qualifying contracts').

e) Non-qualifying contracts which were in existence at 25 September 1997 need to be partitioned into two separate funds. One fund (the 'exempt fund') consists of the premiums paid up to 25 September 1997 and the income accumulated on those premiums (even if the income arose after 1 January 1998). It also includes the following premiums and the income accruing thereon:

   i) regular premiums paid after 25 September 1997 in accordance with the terms of the original contract; and

   ii) additional premiums up to €30,500 per person contributed during the period 26 September 1997 to 31 December 1997.

f) The other fund consists of any other premiums contributed after 25 September 1997, and the income which accrued on those premiums after 1 January 1998.

g) New non-qualifying contracts entered into after 25 September 1997 but before 1 January 1998 must also be divided into two funds, one containing the premiums paid, and the income accruing thereon, up to 31 December 1997 (the 'exempt fund'), and the other containing the rest of the fund, including all premiums paid and income accruing after 31 December 1997.

h) Non-qualifying contracts issued on or after 1 January 1998 fall entirely within the new rules and are not divided into two funds.

i) Exemption from income tax (but not the social contributions of 11%) continues to be available in respect of encashments occurring more than 8 years after the policy was taken out for:

   i) qualifying contracts (see (d)(i));

   ii) the exempt funds of pre-26 September 1997 contracts (see (e)); and

   iii) the exempt funds of contracts taken out in the period 26 September 1997 to 31 December 1997, inclusive (see (g)).

j) In respect of all other encashments after 8 years, there is an annual abatement per household of €4,600 for a single person and €9,200 for a married couple. Withdrawals from taxable funds of non-qualifying policies, within these limits, are exempt from income tax if the withdrawals take place more than 8 years after the policy was taken out.

k) Above these amounts, the increase in value of a policy reflected in encashments after 8 years is subject upon option to withholding tax at the rate of 7.5%, plus the social contibutions of 11%. If the option is not exercised the *barème* rates apply.

l) These rules do not affect the tax treatment of a life assurance contract taken out in the form of a *PEP* or *PEA*, which is taxable as explained above.

m) The option for taxation at source is available in respect of the increase in value realised on policies offered by establishments resident:

   i) in EU member countries

   ii) in EEA countries (excluding Liechtenstein) which have signed a double tax treaty containing a clause providing mutual assistance against tax fraud (see 5.7.7).

n) French residents who enter into, contribute to or withdraw from foreign life assurance contracts must declare the details of their transactions when they file their income tax returns. They must also provide a complete list of all foreign policies they hold.

20.3.4 Savings Accounts

a) Interest accruing on a *Livret A* account at the post office (*la poste*) or a savings bank *(caisse d'épargne)* is free of income tax. Every person can have one, including children (who make up about 40% of the account holders). About 80% of all French households have at least one of these and the total amount invested in them exceeds €107 billion. The maximum amount that can be invested in the *Livret A* is €15,300 per person.

b) The rate of interest is revised regularly and is only credited at the end of the year. There are also rules relating to the calculation of the interest in the month when the deposit is made or withdrawn which work against the investor. The *Livret Jeunes*, offers tax-free savings for minors but the total investment is limited to €1,600.

c) Interest received on a *Livret Bleu* account managed by *Le Crédit Mutuel*, is partially exempt and the limit of deposits is €15,300 per person. However the taxpayer may not have both a *Livret A* and a *Livret Bleu* account.

d) The tax-free account known as *CODEVI* is now renamed as *Livret de Développement Durable (LDD)*. The maximum investment in this type of account is currently €6,000.

e) There is a savings account for those saving to buy a property, called a *plan d'épargne logement*. The maximum amount that can be invested in such an account is €61,200 (with a minimum of €250) and the minimum period for which the account can be held is 4 years. To benefit from a tax free interest (revised regularly) the investor must take out a mortgage at the term of his investment. The maximum amount that can be borrowed at a reduced rate is set at €92,000. The 11% social surcharges apply to interest earned on a *PEL*.

f) The *compte d'épargne logement* is a savings account which allows the investor to take out a mortgage at a reduced rate of 3% provided the funds are kept on the account for at least 18 months. The total amount borrowed, however, is limited to €23,000. The interest paid on a *CEL* is tax-free but it still suffers social contributions of 11%. Taxpayers who do not wish to apply for the mortgage facility may use the account for savings with a minimum balance of €300 and a maximum of €15,300.

g) The *livret d'épargne populaire* is an account for those of modest means saving for their retirement. The maximum amount that can be invested is €7,700 per person and the interest is tax free.

h) Employees are effectively obliged to invest through their company profit sharing scheme. Further details of this are given at 7.3.7(b).

20.4. French and Foreign Dividends

a) Dividends and distributions from French, EU or EEA companies benefit from a 40% abatement.

b) A single taxpayer can also deduct €1,525 and a married taxpayer can deduct €3,050 from his French dividends. There is in addition a credit calculated as 50% of the distribution (before the 40% abatement mentioned above) but limited to €115 for a single person and €230 for a couple.

c) Double tax relief may be available by exemption or in the form of a credit under a treaty to ensure that no additional tax is suffered by virtue of the dividend withholding tax in the source country.

d) For example, under the France-UK double tax treaty the maximum rate of UK tax payable by a French resident in respect of a UK source dividend is 15%. In practice, since 5 April 1999 the tax credit on a UK dividend has been reduced to one-ninth of the net dividend received, which is 11% of the gross dividend and therefore within the 15% limit. France gives a French resident individual a credit for the 11% UK tax "suffered".

e) As indicated above, French taxpayers apply a 40% abatement on dividends they receive from qualifying foreign companies. Nevertheless, from 1 January 2009, the benefit of the 40% abatement will be restricted to distributions from companies resident in a country which has signed a treaty containing a clause providing for mutual assistance against tax fraud (see 5.7.7(a)). The deduction of €1,525 for a single person and €3,050 for a couple is granted for distributions from qualifying foreign companies.

f) The most extreme forms of double tax relief are found in the France-USA double tax treaty. Where a French resident who is not a US citizen receives dividends, interest, royalties, capital gains, directors fees or income for his services as an artist or athlete from the USA, France gives the French resident a tax credit for all of the US tax suffered on the income (but limited to the French tax on the same source). US source rental income does not suffer French tax in the hands of such a person, although the amount of the income is taken into account in determining his French tax liabilities on his other income.

g) If the French resident is also a US citizen, France also grants a tax credit to him of the full amount of the French tax due on US source dividends, interest and royalties paid by:

    i)   the USA or any political subdivision thereof;

    ii) any US entity quoted on a recognised stock exchange;

    iii) a US corporation in which the recipient of the income does not own more than 10% of the stock and in which French residents collectively do not own more than 50% of the stock; or

    iv) a resident of the USA which did not derive more than 25% of its income for the previous taxable period from sources outside the USA.

h) Where the beneficial owner of the income is both a resident of France and a US citizen, France grants a credit of the full amount of the French tax due in respect of capital gains realised on any assets which produce income described in (d)(i) to (iv) above, profits or gains derived from any transactions on a public US options or futures market, private sector pensions relating to services performed in the USA, income paid to teachers, researchers, students and trainees and, subject to proof that the taxpayer has discharged his US tax obligations, alimony and annuities from US sources.

20.5. Rental Income

a) The taxation of French source rental income is explained at 6.6.2.

b) Rental income from property situated outside France is very often exempted from French tax by a double tax treaty. For example under the terms of

Articles 5(1) and 24(b) of the France-UK double tax treaty rent received by a French resident from property situated in the UK is exempt from French tax. It remains, of course, taxable in the UK at basic and higher rates. It is also taken into account when computing the French liability, so it must be reported on a French resident taxpayer's return if he receives this source of income.

20.6. Final Withholding Taxes

20.6.1 Bank Interest

a) Generally speaking, tax of 18% (from 1 January 2008, 16% before) plus the social surcharges of 11% is deducted at source from French bank interest arising on accounts held by French residents. The tax deducted discharges the tax liability of the depositor in respect of the interest, so for the well-advised taxpayer the maximum rate of tax on bank interest is 29%. There is no limit to the amount of interest which qualifies for this treatment.

b) This treatment is optional and the taxpayer elects for the withholding tax (normally when he opens the account, but at latest before the interest is credited). If the taxpayer does not elect to pay the withholding tax, the interest is taxed as part of his general income – which will be beneficial to him if his marginal rate of tax is below 29%. It is important to note however that there is no deductible *CSG* in respect of income taxed at source. This has to be taken into account to determine whether the taxation at source option is favourable or not.

20.6.2 Bond Interest

a) The 18% withholding tax (plus 11% in social surcharges) is also applied, at the taxpayer's option, to French bond interest paid to French residents who declare their identity to the payer. Again there is no limit to the amount of interest which qualifies for this treatment.

b) Non-residents who declare their identity are exempt from French tax on interest on bonds and certificates of deposit.

c) There are penalty withholding taxes levied compulsorily on interest paid to bond holders who do not declare their identity, being 60% of the interest and 2% of the capital value of the bond.

20.7. Tax Credits

There are a wide range of investments which qualify for tax credits, including investment in small companies, the film industry and investment in the French overseas departments.

20.8. Foreign Tax-Privileged Investments

a) It should come as no surprise that an investment which carries tax benefits under the law of some other country may attract no such advantages in France. For example a former resident of the UK who holds investments in UK ISAs, PEPs or TESSAs cannot expect the income, gains or bonuses accruing within these to be exempt from French tax.

b) Similarly the UK exempts from tax the interest on UK government savings certificates and the prizes on premium savings bonds. Any such income will be taxable in France. In the latter case it should be noted that France does not tax lottery winnings, but correctly regards the prizes on premium bonds as interest, because the bond is a negotiable instrument (and therefore the 'gambler' can recover his 'stake').

20.9. Investing to Mitigate Inheritance Tax

20.9.1 Life Insurance

a) The principal avenue open to the French resident who wishes to mitigate French inheritance tax is the use of life insurance policies written on his own life in favour of his heirs. The proceeds of such a policy are exempt from French inheritance tax unless either:

   i) they relate to premiums in excess of €30,500 paid after the life insured reached the age of 70; or

   ii) the proceeds of the policy paid to any one individual exceed €152,500 and these proceeds relate to policies entered into and premiums paid after 13 October 1998.

b) If the proceeds are taxable for the first reason listed above, the rate of tax applied to the taxable proceeds is the rate applicable to a gift from the deceased life insured to the beneficiary of the policy.

c) If the proceeds are taxable for the second reason, the excess over €152,500 is taxed at 20%, except if the beneficiary is a surviving spouse or *PACS* partner in which case it is exempt.

20.9.2 Listed Buildings

Buildings classed as historic monuments and their related furniture can be exempt from gifts or inheritance tax if they are open to the public. The same is true for shares in an *SCI* which owns a listed building (eg an apartment block).

20.9.3 Business Assets

Assets used in an industrial, commercial, artisanal, agricultural or professional activity, and large shareholdings in companies which carry on such activities, can be exempt to the extent of 50% of their value (see 10.3.3(g)).

20.9.4 Forestry

Under certain conditions, up to 75% of the value of a forestry investment is exempt from inheritance tax.

20.9.5 Agricultural Property

Agricultural property let on a long term agricultural lease can benefit from a partial exemption from inheritance tax.

20.9.6 Foreign Assets

a) Under French double inheritance tax treaties, the treaty partner country is sometimes given an exclusive right of taxation in respect of certain assets.

b) This is very commonly the case in respect of real estate situated in the foreign country. For example the following countries are given an unambiguous and exclusive right to tax real estate situated in their territory:

Algeria	Gabon	Niger	Sweden
Austria	Ivory Coast	Oman	Switzerland
Benin	Kuwait	Qatar	Togo
Burkina Faso	Lebanon	Saudi Arabia	Tunisia
Cameroon	Mali	Senegal	United Arab
Cent. African	Mauritania	Spain	Emirates
Republic	Monaco	St Pierre &	
Finland	New Caledonia	Miquelon	

c) For example it might be the case that the Spanish inheritance tax on real estate situated in Spain is lower than the equivalent French inheritance tax, so that the total tax on an estate can be reduced by investment in Spanish real estate.

20.10. Investing to Mitigate Wealth Tax

20.10.1 Industrial and Commercial Companies

a) Shares in fiscally transparent companies held by working shareholders and shares in corporation tax paying companies held by working directors are exempt from wealth tax if the company has an industrial, commercial, artisanal, agricultural or professional activity. In general, the shareholders in a corporation tax paying company must hold, together with their families, at least 25% of the shares to benefit from the exemption.

b) Shares in foreign companies which suffer a tax equivalent to French corporation tax can also be exempt.

20.10.2 Forestry Investments

Forestry investments can be exempt from wealth tax up to 75% of their value.

20.10.3 Agricultural Assets

Agricultural land let on long leases (for at least 18 years) to members of the landlord's family for use in the tenant's principal activity is exempt. Up to 75% of the value of the land can be exempt if it is let to persons who are not related to the landlord.

20.10.4 Business Assets

Business assets may be exempt from wealth tax. For this, the asset must be essential to the exercise of the profession or activity which represents the taxpayers' main source of income. Properties rented out furnished may be considered as exempt business assets but only if the owner is registered as a *loueur en meublé professionel* (see 18.2.2(p)) and the annual rental income exceeds €23,000 <u>and</u> represents more than 50% of the taxpayer's income.

20.10.5 Works of Art

Works of art are exempt from wealth tax. This includes tapestries, paintings, engravings, lithographs, statues, stamps, collections (of coins, books etc) and objects which are more than 100 years old.

20.10.6 Pension Funds

Approved pension funds created in respect of a past employment may be exempt. The savings period should last at least 15 years and the pension terms must provide for the payment of an annuity upon the cessation of the professional activity. The capitalised value of the corresponding annuities should also be exempt provided the funds meet the above requirements. Nevertheless, there remain a number of grey areas regarding the treatment of foreign pension funds, especially if the above criteria cannot be met, so it is advisable to obtain professional advice on this issue.

20.10.7 Foreign Assets

As with inheritance tax, some of France's double tax treaties prevent France from taxing wealth situated in the treaty partner country.

20.10.8 *Assets Exempt for Non-Residents*

a) Non-residents are exempt from French wealth tax on financial investments.

b) This exemption can also be used to protect investments in French real estate. If the investor acquires a valuable property in France through the medium of a *société civile immobilière* or any other form of company, financing the major part of the investment by a shareholders loan account, the loan account is, in the opinion of most tax practitioners in France, a financial investment which benefits from the exemption mentioned above.

21. RETIREMENT IN FRANCE

21.1. Taxation of Pensions

21.1.1 General

a) French double tax treaties will often grant exclusive rights to tax occupational pensions received by French residents from foreign countries to either the country of source or to France. For example:

   i) Under Article 18 of the France – UK double income tax treaty, the right to tax pensions (other than pensions paid in respect of government service) is given to the country of residence of the taxpayer. Therefore a former UK resident who has retired to France will generally pay tax on any UK source occupational pension (other than a government service pension) only in France. He can reclaim any UK withholding tax suffered on the pension from the UK (by applying to the Paris tax centre for non-residents for the appropriate form. By contrast a pension in respect of government service is taxable only in the country of source, and therefore a former resident of the UK who retires to France will continue to pay UK tax on his pension for UK government service. He is exempt from French tax on such a pension, but must nevertheless report it on his annual French income tax return.

   ii) Certain disability pensions paid to members of the UK armed forces are exempt from tax in both the UK and France. The France-UK double tax treaty does not refer to other pensions paid out of UK public funds, such as the DSS old-age pension, which means that in accordance with Article 22(1) they are taxable only in France when received by a French resident.

   iii) Under Articles 18, 19, 24 and 29 of the France – USA double tax treaty, US source pensions paid out of private sector funds, received by residents of France who are not nationals of the USA, are taxable only in France. Pensions paid to French residents out of US public funds are taxable only in the USA. Pensions paid from US sources to US citizens resident in France remain taxable in the USA, and the taxpayer receives a credit against his French tax liability in respect of the income of the whole amount of that liability.

b) The French have separate tax regimes for pensions and annuities. In France occupational pension schemes are unfunded and it would not necessarily occur to a French tax inspector that an annuity paid by, for example, an insurance company might be related to a past employment. It seems likely that if this fact was taken fully into consideration, the annuity would be taxed as a pension. However as a practical matter the French tax administration has in some cases been content to tax annuities paid out of pension funds, or purchased using funds from a pension fund, as annuities.

c) That having been said, in most French double tax treaties pensions and annuities are treated in the same way.

21.1.2 Purchased Annuities

a) When the annuity was purchased by the taxpayer in exchange for money, a property or movable goods, only part of the annuity is taxable, the percentage depending on the age of the taxpayer:

Age	%
under 50	70
between 50 and 59	50
between 60 and 69	40
over 69	30

b) This percentage of the annuity is added to the taxable income of the taxpayer and taxed in the normal way. It is liable to the 11% social contributions (CSG, CRDS and PS).

21.1.3 Pensions

a) A pension is taxed like earned income and the whole of the pension is included in taxable income for French purposes after deductions similar to those available to salaried employees.

b) The taxpayer can deduct from his pension income an amount of 10% of the income, subject to a minimum of €357 and a maximum of €3,491.

21.1.4 Lump Sums

a) Quite commonly under the pension scheme regulations of a common law country, a person who reaches retirement age is permitted to commute part of his pension fund into a lump sum, which is often tax-free in that country. In principle, and subject to the terms of double tax treaties, the French authorities may allow a taxpayer to repatriate his lump sum to France free from any French tax. Nevertheless, as the French pensions system does not normally allow tax-free lump sums, this remains a grey area and it is thus advisable to seek prior advice on the matter. Plans for adequate legislation to render these lump sums unequivocably taxable in France are high on the French tax administration's agenda. However, at the time of going to print no law was published to that effect.

b) If taxable, and if the amount received exceeds the average of the taxpayer's net taxable income for the previous 3 years, it will be taxed under the system for 'exceptional items of income'. (see 6.6.9).

c) To avoid any difficulty, the taxpayer would be well-advised to take the commuted amount before he becomes resident in France.

21.2. Other Income

There are many forms of investment which are efficient for French tax purposes, and these are explored in chapter 22.

21.3. French Succession Law

21.3.1 General

a) Under French law, individuals are not free to dispose of their estates entirely as they see fit. Descendants, and in some cases ascendants, have rights in the estate of the deceased which cannot be overturned by will. These rules are sometimes unattractive to migrants and investors from common law countries, who are reluctant to lose their freedom to dispose of their estates as they see fit. It should be observed however that although the law confers rights to a minimum share of an individual's estate on his or her children etc, the reserved heirs do not have to enforce these rights. If they renounce their rights the succession proceeds as if they had never been heirs.

b) French succession law applies to:

i) the worldwide personal property and the real estate situated in France of an individual who dies domiciled in France;

ii) the real estate situated in France of an individual domiciled elsewhere; and

iii) any assets situated in France of someone who dies domiciled outside France when there is a French national individual who would have received more from the deceased individual if the succession had been governed by French law (see (e)). This rule derives from a law of 1819 and it offends against the normal principles relating to conflict of laws, but it nevertheless remains in the Civil Code.

c) The concept of domicile for succession law purposes is explained at 4.2.

d) The rights of forced heirship constitute part of the 'public order' (the vital principles of French law), and cannot easily be defeated.

e) A French national reserved heir has a preemption right (*droit de prélèvement*) over assets situated in France to the extent that his inheritance would have been greater if French law had applied to the succession. This right extends to tangible movable property which is situated in France (even if it was outside France at the time of the death), at least so long as the property has not been attributed to anyone else by a foreign court, and to intangible property if there is a possibility of realising the property in France. For example, suppose a French national child of a father domiciled in the UK would have had a right to one-third of his father's estate under French succession law, and movable assets representing at least one third of the estate are situated in France. The French child can seize assets situated in France sufficient to satisfy his 'entitlement', even though under the law governing the succession he was entitled to nothing.

21.3.2 'La Réserve Héréditaire'

a) If the deceased is survived by any children, they all have rights to a minimum share of the estate. All the children of the deceased have a right to an equal share in the estate. The reserved heirs include adulterine, illegitimate or adopted children as well as children of previous marriages. The minimum share of the estate in which they share is as follows:

If there is one child	one half of the estate;
If there are two children	two thirds of the estate;
If there are three or more children	three quarters of the estate.

b) Ascendants may renounce their rights, usually in favour of the surviving spouse when there are no children. The part of the estate not covered by these rights may be disposed of as the testator pleases (this part is called the *quotité disponible*).

c) If any of the children have died before the deceased, but have themselves left children (the grandchildren of the deceased), the grandchildren are entitled to share equally the part of the estate to which their father or mother would have been entitled, and so on through successive generations.

d) If the deceased is not survived by any descendants, but leaves parents, grandparents or remoter ancestors, the ascendants have a right to the estate, which may nevertheless as a result of recent legal changes, be overturned through a will. The part of the estate which the ascendant share is as follows:

If there are ascendants from both the maternal and paternal line	one half of the estate;
If there are ascendants from only one line	one quarter of the estate.

e) It will be observed that the spouse of the deceased is not a reserved heir. Part of the explanation for this is that most French couples are married under community property rules, which means that a part of the family's wealth belongs to the 'community' of the marriage. On the death of one of the spouses, the community is liquidated and that property may pass under the terms of the marriage contract to the survivor provided it contains a clause to that effect usually called a '*clause d'attribution intégrale au conjoint survivant*'. Therefore the above rules apply only to assets which are owned by the deceased spouse in his or her own right, which means that:

i) the rights of the reserved heirs only 'bite' on the assets owned by the deceased spouse personally; and

ii) even if the testator leaves the part of his or her estate which is freely disposable to other people, the surviving spouse will still get the community property.

f) When a couple are married under the separation of estates regime, each of the spouses owns the property registered in his or her own name. Assets held in joint bank accounts or registered in joint names are deemed to be owned by the parties in the proportion in which they contributed to the account or to the cost of the asset. There is no 'property of the marriage', and so:

i) the rights of the reserved heirs may 'bite' on a much larger slice of the cake; and

ii) by leaving the freely disposable part of his or her estate to other people, the deceased spouse can disinherit the surviving spouse absolutely. In this respect the situation is little different from that pertaining in most common law countries.

g) Since most couples from common law countries are married under the separation of estates regime, the application of these rules concerns many people moving to France. However it should be stressed here that a husband or wife can do a great deal to protect the interests of his or her spouse if he or she wants to. There is no reason why the couple should not enter into a community property marriage contract. In French law a couple are free to change their matrimonial regime at any time during their marriage. This will not however be effective against children from a previous marriage. If the idea of executing a marriage contract does not appeal, each party can by will give his or her spouse the freely disposable part of his or her estate absolutely. The options containing a transfer of life interest are not available in the presence of children from a previous relationship.

h) In an intestate succession (where the deceased has not left a will) the law does afford the surviving spouse the following rights:

i) If the deceased leaves no ascendants or descendants, the estate passes entirely to the surviving spouse (provided that the couple were not legally separated); however half of any assets inherited or received through lifetime gifts by the deceased from his pre-deceased parents would pass to the brothers or sisters of the deceased, or their descendants.

ii) If the deceased leaves descendants all issued from the marriage, the surviving spouse may choose between a usufruct in the whole of the estate or a quarter of the estate absolutely;

iii) If the deceased leaves one or more illegitimate or adulterine children the surviving spouse has a right to a quarter of the estate absolutely.

iv) If the deceased leaves ascendants in both lines, but no descendants, the surviving spouse inherits half of the estate absolutely. The father and the mother of the deceased inherit each a quarter share in the estate. If only one parent survives the deceased, the surviving spouse inherits the quarter share that would have passed to the pre-deceased parent in addition to the half share absolutely. The parents of the deceased may now renounce their share and in doing so, allow the surviving spouse to inherit the whole estate (in the absence of any descendants).

i) The law also provides a right for the surviving spouse to occupy the matrimonial main home and use of the contents gratuitously for a whole year following the demise. If the couple were renting their main accommodation the rent is paid from the estate for the whole year. The surviving spouse has to have occupied the home as a main residence at the time of the demise. If the home is no longer adapted to the surviving spouse's needs at the time the above right is exercised, the property may be rented out to generate sufficient funds to finance alternative accommodation.

j) The testator who does leave a will can of course give the surviving spouse the disposable part of the estate absolutely. Alternatively he or she can give the surviving spouse:

i) a usufruct over the whole of the estate; or

ii) one quarter of the estate absolutely and the remainder in usufruct.

And the testator can direct that the surviving spouse should choose between these options.

k) If the interests given to the surviving spouse, whether in full ownership or in usufruct, encompass more than half of the assets left by the deceased, the children or remoter descendants of the deceased can each convert their share of the surviving spouse's interest into an annuity. (This right is not extended to children conceived during the marriage by the deceased and someone other than the surviving spouse). However they cannot convert the interest of the surviving spouse in the matrimonial home or its furnishings into an annuity.

l) If the deceased only leaves ascendants, he can convert the shares of the ascendants into a usufruct, leaving the capital interest to the surviving spouse.

21.3.3 The PACS (Pacte Civil de Solidarité)

a) The *PACS* was set up with effect from 13 October 1999, to improve the position of unmarried couples with regards to French inheritance tax and other taxes. The *PACS* confers civil, social, fiscal rights and status to same sex or heterosexual couples.

b) To be valid, the *PACS* needs to be registered with the *Tribunal de Grande Instance*.This necessitates a certificate confirming that each partner is single. As matters stand, it would appear that a UK civil partnership entered into prior to a *PACS* application may compromise the latter. Indeed the certificate cannot be produced in these circumstances. Any couple who have entered into a UK civil partnership prior to their arrival in France should take legal advice on these issues. In legal terms the individuals party to the *PACS* are treated as if they had entered an *indivision* arrangement. Unless otherwise specified in the contract each individual owns half of all the assets.

c) The *PACS* couple's income has to be declared on one tax return. The situation is unchanged in terms of wealth tax, as couples living in *concubinage notoire* (cohabiting) had to file a joint wealth tax return before the existence of the *PACS*.

d) The main benefit of the *PACS* is for inheritance tax purposes. Instead of the 60% inheritance tax rate applicable to transfers between non-blood related individuals, the transfers between *PACS* registered individuals are now exempt. Lifetime gifts however follow the same rules as for married couples (see chapter 9).

e) The *PACS* has no incidence on normal French succession rules, and thus *PACS* registered individuals must prepare a will to protect the survivor.

21.3.4 The Effect of Trusts

a) A trust created before the settlor became resident in France may be effective to defeat the French succession laws. Courts in France accept the trust as a valid creation of foreign law, which cannot be assimilated to any creature of French law (eg as in Courtois v De Ganay, Court of Appeal of Paris, 10 January 1970), and they have on several occasions expressly recognised the effects of a trust (see for example the commentary on the Zieseniss case at 19.5.2(f) above).

b) However a trust is unlikely to be effective if the settlor has retained control over the assets in the trust, particularly if the plaintiff is a French national reserved heir and there are assets in France (see 21.3.1(e)).

c) Besides the Zieseniss case, the French courts have decided on two other cases in which attempts were made to defeat the *réserve héréditaire* by the use of structures involving trusts. In one case land in France was sold to an offshore company in which two-thirds of the shares were owned by the vendor, a resident of the Virgin Islands. He then settled the shares which he owned in an offshore trust. In the second case investments were transferred to a Liechtenstein foundation by an Italian national resident in New York. In both cases it was the intent that French national children of the settlor/founder should be excluded from benefit. In the second case the assets had ended up in France because they had been transferred to the French bank accounts of the three sisters of the founder in accordance with the terms of the foundation. In both cases the scheme failed:

i)   In the first case the series of transactions were held to constitute a fraud. However it has been argued that the fact that the trust remained effectively under the control of the settlor was sufficent grounds for treating the trust assets as forming part of his estate at death (Caron v Odell, 20 March 1985).

ii) In the second case the court took into account the fact that the investments had remained at the disposal of the founder during her lifetime as an argument for reintegrating them into her estate at death for the purpose of operating the *réserve* (Holzborg v Holzberf, 4 February 1986).

d)   Moreover the French tax administration has stated, in a ministerial reply to a parliamentary question that they intend to apply the theory of apparent ownership (laid down in article 2279 of the *Code Civil*) to irrevocable trusts (ministerial reply Mourot, 8 October 1970). This theory states, with respect to movable property, that possession is equivalent to ownership.

21.3.5 Conversion of Realty into Personalty

a)   It is possible for a non-resident to convert realty into personalty by holding the real estate through a company.

b)   The transfer of land in France to a company, with the sole object of converting the asset into personalty which will devolve according to the law of the ultimate owner's nationality or domicile, is regarded as a fraud (*fraude à la loi*) against those whose rights of inheritance would be defeated. However there is a distinction between such an artificial arrangement and a modification of the nature of assets comprised in an estate for bona fide reasons.   The transfer is only fraudulent if it is motivated solely by consideration of the succession law effects.

21.3.6 Assets Situated Outside France

a)   UK courts and the courts of most other countries will apply French succession law to the estate of an individual who dies domiciled in France, except where immovable property situated outside France is concerned.

In the latter case, the UK and many other legal systems apply the succession law of the country in which the land or buildings are situated. However a court in New York has held that, in the circumstances of one case, the common law policy of freedom from forced heirship claims prevailed over the *réserve héréditaire* in respect of all assets situated in New York, even though the deceased was domiciled in France at death (Estate of Jane M Reynard, 16 March 1981). This is probably not good law, and a court in Florida has reached the opposite conclusion (Estate of Mario Sanchez, 30 December 1987). It may be noted in passing that the New York Court cited the existence of the French *droit de prélèvement* (see 21.3.1(e)) as a reason for declining to enforce the French rules.

b) There is an interesting problem when a French domiciliary owns assets in a common law country like the UK, jointly with someone else. Take for example the case of a French domiciled man and his wife who have a joint bank account in London. As a matter of UK property law, the interest of a joint owner is extinguished on his death, and the property passes automatically to the surviving joint owner. The interest of the deceased joint owner does not form part of his estate (having disappeared). This situation must have arisen in practice countless times, but there appears to be no reported UK case in which it has been decided whether the effects of UK property law override the effects of French succession law. It is simply assumed in the UK that since the interest of the deceased in the jointly held property does not fall into his estate, the application of succession laws does not arise. The French, of course, might take a different view, but it seems that the correct interpretation of the situation is that if the result of the events is a gift from one joint owner to the other, the gift took place when the asset was acquired in joint names, and not on the death of the first owner to die. This does not necessarily avoid any French succession law problem, since if a person gives away during his or her life more than the freely-disposable part of his or her estate, this may be challenged by the reserved heirs at the time of probate. Moreover, where the joint owners are a married couple, there could be a further legal problem, because the French Civil Code forbids spouses to give each other by indirect means more than they could legally give each other directly. All such gifts, whether disguised or made via an intermediary, are null and void.

c) If the deceased was not domiciled in France at his death, the assets comprised in his estate which are not situated in France (and the movable assets which are situated in France) will not normally be affected by French succession law.

d) However if any French national would have had a claim against the estate if the devolution of the estate had been governed by French succession law, and there are assets situated in France, the claimant can take his 'share' out of the French assets. This may indirectly allow him to obtain a share of the foreign assets.

21.4 Inheritance Tax

21.4.1 General

a) It has been noted in chapter 20 that certain investments are exempt from inheritance tax, and that the proceeds of life insurance contracts are sometimes exempt (eg if the person insured was under 70 when the policy was taken out, and if the proceeds of the policy are less than €152,500).

b) There are also some planning techniques based on forms of ownership under French law, which are examined below.

21.4.2 Usufructs

a) When an individual reserves to himself the life interest in an asset (a *usufruit*) and gives away the right to receive the asset after his death (the *nue-propriété*), the value of the gift is determined on a scale related to the age of the donor. The scale is as follows:

Age of the life tenant	Value of the Life Interest % of market value	Value of Remainder % of market value
Less than 21	90	10
21 to 30	80	20
31 to 40	70	30
41 to 50	60	40
51 to 60	50	50
61 to 70	40	60
71 to 80	30	70
81 to 90	20	80
91 or over	10	90

b) For example if a man and his wife, each aged between 41 and 50 give the remainder interest in a house worth €375,000 to their 3 children in equal shares, the value of the gift is €150,000 (40% of €375,000). This is well within the amount of the abatements which the children can set against gifts from their parents. There is no inheritance tax charge on the reunification of the *usufruit* and the *nue-propriété* that results from the death of the *usufruitiers* provided that the gift was made formally and the donors/*usufruitiers* survive at least 3 months after making the gift. The children will simply have to pay a registration tax of €75 to record the extinction of the *usufruit*.

c) If the value of the *nue-propriété* had been higher in the example above, so that a tax charge arose on the gift to the children, the tax on the gift would have qualified for the reduction accorded in respect of *donations-partages* – see 9.6.2.

21.4.3 Companies

a) Holding assets in companies can facilitate the transfer of the asset in stages, to take advantage of the fact that the abatements of the beneficiaries can be reused every 6 years. Part of the share capital can be given away every 6 years.

b) Equally a company can be used to facilitate a transfer of wealth in other ways. For example if a father aged under 70 wants to transfer a commercial property worth €400,000 to his son who already has some wealth of his own, the son could form an *SCI* with a capital of, say €76,000, and the *SCI* could obtain finance from a bank to enable it to purchase the property from the father. The father could subscribe the €400,000 he receives as a single premium on a life insurance contract in favour of his son. Even though the excess of the proceeds of the policy over €152,500 would be subject to French inheritance tax, it would be taxed at only 20%.

22. LOCAL TAXES

22.1. General

a) There are 3 main taxes collected for the benefit of French local authorities (the *régions*, *départements* and *communes*) and certain public agencies such as the local *chambres de commerce*. These are:

   i)   the *taxe d'habitation* (residential tax);

   ii) the *taxes foncières* (landowner's tax) which is levied on built and unbuilt land; and

   iii) the *taxe professionnelle* (business tax).

b) The *cadastre* (land registry) is responsible for the taxation of interests in land. The concept of a cadastral value was introduced with the first land tax (called *contribution foncière*) during the French revolution in 1790. However proper land records were not available before 1850. Nowadays land and buildings are systematically registered with the cadastre, which keeps a record of the theoretical rental value of every property in France. These values are the basis of assessment for the two local property taxes and form part of the basis of assessment for the business tax. Any modifications of a property must be declared by the owner within 90 days of the completion of the work, and will result in a revaluation. However the last general revaluation took place in 1974, and despite adjustments for inflation since, the cadastral values are now significantly below true market rental values. A general revision of cadastral valuations has been under way since 1990, and the new values are currently being used to calculate the local taxes.

c) The local taxes are direct taxes, and the taxpayer is notified of his liability by an assessment called an *avis d'imposition*. The assessment shows the breakdown of the total tax bill between the parts assessed for the benefit of the *région*, *département* and *commune*, and the date by which the tax must be paid.

d) There are also a range of less important local taxes which are either annexed to one of the three main taxes or which stand alone. These include taxes for the development of certain regions (including the Ile-de-France), taxes to finance the local chambers of commerce etc. and charges for refuse collection.

22.2 Taxe D'Habitation

22.2.1 Taxable Buildings

a) The *taxe d'habitation* is levied on the occupiers of any furnished habitable buildings used as a dwelling, whether as a main home or a holiday home.

b) The assessable buildings include any outbuildings (such as garages or accommodation for domestic staff) which are located within 1 kilometre of the main building, and business premises if they form part of the main building and could be used for habitation. Mobile homes if used as a main home will become liable from 1 January 2010.

c) The following buildings are exempt

   i) buildings used exclusively for business purposes and subject to the *taxe professionnelle*;

   ii) farm buildings;

   iii) student lodgings; and

   iv) government buildings.

22.2.2 Taxable Persons

a) The tax is paid by the occupier of the building, whether that person is the owner or a tenant. If the building is unoccupied the tax is paid by the owner.

b) It is equally payable by non-resident owners (if the property is not let).

c) However the following persons are exempt

   i) persons on very low incomes;

   ii) diplomatic personal who have foreign nationality and some international civil servants (in respect of their official residences only).

22.2.3 Calculation of the Tax

a) The tax is assessed for a calendar year on the basis of the cadastral value as at 1 January in the year.

b) The rates of tax are determined by the local authorities themselves. If the property has a cadastral value in excess of €4,573, a part of the charge is also levied for the national government.

c) A household is entitled to a *taxe d'habitation* reduction in respect of its principal home, if its taxable income for the previous year (2007) did not exceed the limits set out below:

   €22,481 for the 1st family *part*, increased by

   €5,253 for the 1st family half *part*, and

   €4,133 for each subsequent half *part*

d) Where the *taxe d'habitation* is established in the name of several cohabiting taxpayers who submit separate income tax returns, it is the sum of their respective taxable income that is considered to determine whether they would qualify for a reduction.

e) The reduction is calculated as the portion of *taxe d'habitation* which exceeds 3.44% of the 2007 net taxable income reduced by a total amount depending on the size of the fiscal household and set as follows:

€4,877 for the 1st family *part*

€1,409 for the 1st family half *part* up to the 4th

€2,493 for subsequent family half *parts*

22.3. Taxes Foncières

22.3.1 Taxable Land and Buildings

a) The *taxes foncières* are sub-divided into taxes on buildings and taxes on land.

b) The following are taxable as built-up land:

   i)   all permanent buildings;

   ii) installations such as hangars and warehouses (but not pylons);

   iii) private access roads;

   iv) boats on permanent moorings;

   v) cellars and parking lots;

   vi) uncultivated land used for industrial or commercial purposes;

   vii) land on which industrial buildings are constructed (although the buildings themselves are exempt); and

   viii) land used for publicity hoardings.

c) Some buildings benefit from a permanent exemption. These include:

   i)   buildings that are public property and produce no income;

   ii) waterworks;

   iii) religious buildings;

iv) foreign embassies;

v) agricultural buidings (which are in agricultural use); and

vi) buildings belonging to industrial businesses.

d) In addition there are temporary exemptions for certain newly constructed buildings, reconstructed buildings and building extensions, including:

    i) housing for needy persons, which can be exempt for long periods (the length of the exemption depending generally on when the housing was built); and

    ii) all other new buildings, which are generally exempt for 2 years commencing on 1 January following the date of their completion. It is a condition of exemption that a declaration is made in respect of the completion of the building within 90 days of completion (Form H1 for a house and Form H2 for a flat). In some cases the exemption applies only to the elements of the tax paid for the benefit of the *région* and *département*.

e) Unbuilt land is also subject to the tax. However the following classes of land are permanently exempt:

    i) public property;

    ii) public roads;

    iii) navigable rivers; and

    iv) agricultural property, but this is only exempt from the parts of the tax paid to the *région* and *département*.

    v) at the discretion of the local authorities, land planted with walnut trees (8 years) or oak trees planted to produce truffles (15 years), and/or olive trees.

f) Temporary exemptions are available in respect of forestry land (30 years).

22.3.2 Taxable Persons

a) The tax is paid by the owner of the property.

b) Certain aged and handicapped persons who are not liable to income tax are exempt from the *taxes foncières* in respect of their principal residence.

22.3.3 Calculation of the Tax

a) For built-up land, the tax is based on 50% of the cadastral rental value, the principle being that an allowance of 50% is made for maintenance, administration, insurance and depreciation.

b) For unbuilt land the tax is based on 80% of the cadastral rental value.

c) The rates of tax are set by the *région*, *département* and *commune*.

d) Under very restrictive conditions the taxpayer can obtain full relief from the tax charge for up to 3 months in respect of a building owned for rental purposes which is vacant or a building owned for industrial or commercial purposes which is disused.

e) Relief from the tax is also available when land is subjected to an extraordinary event such as a flood or avalanche, and partial relief is available when crops are destroyed by freezing weather, fire etc.

f) Households with a taxable income for the previous year, below €9,560 for the first family *part* plus €2,553 per additional half family *part*, are exempt from the *taxes foncières*.

22.4. Taxe Professionnelle

22.4.1 General

a) The business tax is the most significant of the local taxes. It raises 45% of the income of the *communes* and *départements* and 57% of the income of the *régions*.

b) The rates of tax are the highest in some of the poorest areas of France but this is partly due to the low rental values in those areas. The wealthier areas have been able to set very low rates of tax.

22.4.2 Taxable Persons

a) Subject to numerous exceptions, the business tax is paid by all persons carrying on a non-salaried business in France. Companies subject to corporation tax are assessed in their own names. Sole traders and the members of fiscally transparent companies and partnerships are assessed in their individual names.

b) Certain businesses are permanently exempted from paying the tax. These include:

   i) artisans who work by themselves or with help from their family, an apprentice or a necessary assistant;

ii) taxi drivers;

iii) fishermen;

iv) agricultural businesses and *collectivités*;

v) private colleges;

vi) painters, sculptors, engravers and designers who only sell their art;

vii) authors, composers and lyricists;

viii) teachers;

ix) sportsmen;

x) editors of periodicals;

xi) press agencies and correspondents;

xii) certain travelling salesmen;

xiii) operators of mining concessions;

xiv) certain mutual societies; and

xv) public bodies.

c) There are also numerous temporary exemptions, which are generally available only at the discretion of the local authorities, including:

i) industrial or commercial businesses established in specified areas (which currently are the zones eligible for *la prime d'aménagement du territoire* and the *territoires ruraux de développement prioritaire*) (maximum period of 5 years);

ii) decentralised businesses (in respect of any increased in the tax basis caused by their move);

iii) new businesses or businesses formed to rescue businesses in trouble (exempt for 2 years);

iv) businesses established in run down areas (exempt for 5 years);

v) for theatrical, cinematic, etc businesses (partial exemption); and

vi) for doctors moving to small villages (exempt for 2 years).

d) Lettings of holiday accommodation which is part of the lessor's principal residence to someone who occupies it as their main residence is exempt. Lettings of holiday accommodation which is part of the lessor's principal residence, lettings of *gîtes ruraux* or lettings of second homes can be granted permanent or temporary exemption at the discretion of the local authorities. However, in practice local authorities tend to apply the charge to seasonal lettings of a second home especially in touristy areas.

22.4.3 Calculation of the Tax

a) The taxable basis consists of the total of the following:

   i) The first is the sum of the cadastral rental value of the premises occupied by the business plus

   ii) 16% of the market value of the other fixed assets owned by the business plus

   iii) the rentals paid for equipment leased by the business, less

   an abatement against (ii) and (iii).

b) For certain intermediaries and members of professions with smaller businesses, only the cadastral rental value of the properties that they occupy is taken into account.

c) The taxable basis computed as the sum of the above elements is reduced by specific allowances granted to businesses which employ extra people or which make investments.

d) The taxable basis is then reduced by an abatement of 16%.

e) The tax is calculated by applying the tax rates determined locally to the adjusted figure. However there are numerous adjustments to the tax figure so calculated, the most important of which is that the liability is subject to a ceiling related to the value added by the business. The value added by the business is the excess of its turnover over the sums it pays to third parties for goods and services.

f) Companies with a turnover in excess of €7,600,000 are subject to a minimum *taxe professionnelle* which is fixed at 1.5% of the valued added of the business. When the *taxe professionnelle* liability is under the minimum calculated as above, the company pays the difference, as an additional contribution.

INDEX